CELEBRATION DAY

LED ZEPPELIN

Wise Publications
part of The Music Sales Group
London / New York / Paris / Sydney / Copenhagen /
Berlin / Madrid / Hong Kong / Tokyo

Published by
Wise Publications
14-15 Berners Street, London W1T 3LJ, UK.

Exclusive Distributors:
Music Sales Limited
Distribution Centre, Newmarket Road,
Bury St Edmunds, Suffolk IP33 3YB, UK.

Order No. AM1005906
ISBN: 978-1-78038-845-8
This book © Copyright 2012 Wise Publications,
a division of Music Sales Limited.

Unauthorised reproduction of any part of this
publication by any means including photocopying
is an infringement of copyright.

Supervisory editors: Brad Tolinski and Jimmy Brown.

Project manager and music editor: Adrian Hopkins.
Music arranged by Arthur Dick.
Additional transcription and editing:
Tom Farncombe, Jimmy Brown, Dan Begelman and Jack Allen.

Music processed by Paul Ewers Music Design.

Printed in the EU.

This book presents new transcriptions of
the songs from the set as originally recorded
on the classic Led Zeppelin studio albums.

Your Guarantee of Quality:

As publishers, we strive to produce every book
to the highest commercial standards.

This book has been carefully designed
to minimise awkward page turns and to
make playing from it a real pleasure.

Particular care has been given to specifying
acid-free, neutral-sized paper made from pulps
which have not been elemental chlorine bleached.
This pulp is from farmed sustainable forests and
was produced with special regard for the environment.

Throughout, the printing and binding have been
planned to ensure a sturdy, attractive publication
which should give years of enjoyment.

If your copy fails to meet our high standards,
please inform us and we will gladly replace it.

www.musicsales.com

GOOD TIMES BAD TIMES 10
RAMBLE ON 17
BLACK DOG 24
IN MY TIME OF DYING 33
FOR YOUR LIFE 50
TRAMPLED UNDER FOOT 70
NOBODY'S FAULT BUT MINE 80
NO QUARTER 91
SINCE I'VE BEEN LOVING YOU 98
DAZED AND CONFUSED 109
STAIRWAY TO HEAVEN 120
THE SONG REMAINS THE SAME 132
MISTY MOUNTAIN HOP 146
KASHMIR 153
WHOLE LOTTA LOVE 160
ROCK AND ROLL 167

GUITAR TABLATURE EXPLAINED 9

JIMMY PAGE

ROBERT PLANT

LED·ZEPPELIN · CELEBRATION DAY

JOHN PAUL JONES · JIMMY PAGE
ROBERT PLANT AND JASON BONHAM

RECORDED LIVE DECEMBER 10TH, 2007
O2 ARENA, LONDON

GUITAR TABLATURE EXPLAINED

Guitar music can be notated in three different ways: on a musical stave, in tablature, and in rhythm slashes

RHYTHM SLASHES: are written above the stave. Strum chords in the rhythm indicated. Round noteheads indicate single notes.

THE MUSICAL STAVE: shows pitches and rhythms and is divided by lines into bars. Pitches are named after the first seven letters of the alphabet.

TABLATURE: graphically represents the guitar fingerboard. Each horizontal line represents a string, and each number represents a fret.

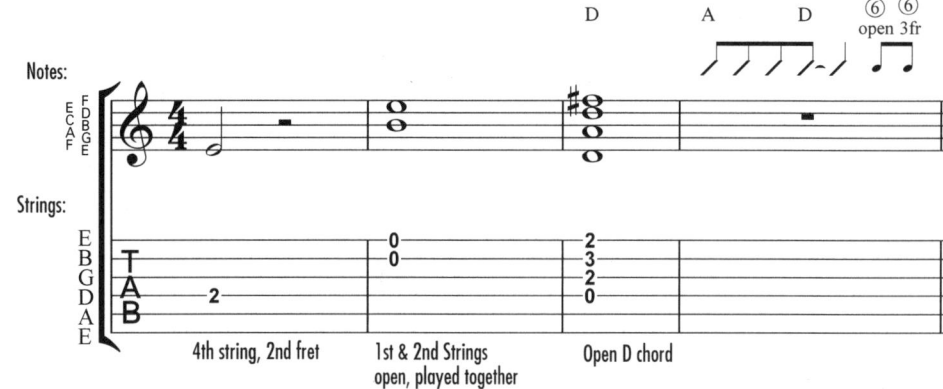

DEFINITIONS FOR SPECIAL GUITAR NOTATION

SEMI-TONE BEND: Strike the note and bend up a semi-tone (½ step).

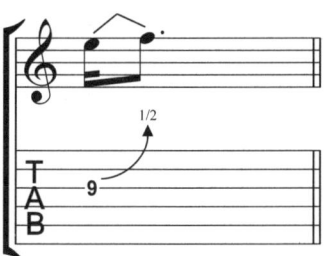

BEND & RELEASE: Strike the note and bend up as indicated, then release back to the original note.

HAMMER-ON: Strike the first note with one finger, then sound the second note (on the same string) with another finger by fretting it without picking.

NATURAL HARMONIC: Strike the note while the fret-hand lightly touches the string directly over the fret indicated.

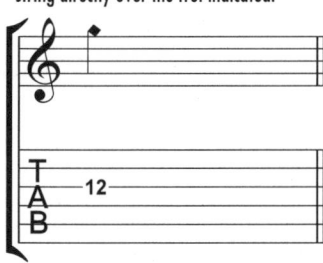

WHOLE-TONE BEND: Strike the note and bend up a whole-tone (full step).

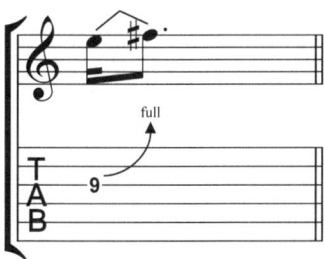

COMPOUND BEND & RELEASE: Strike the note and bend up and down in the rhythm indicated.

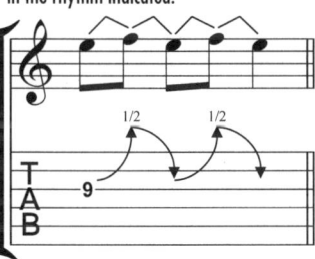

PULL-OFF: Place both fingers on the note to be sounded, strike the first note and without picking, pull the finger off to sound the second note.

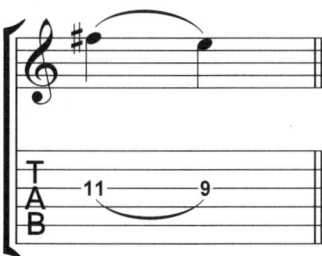

PICK SCRAPE: The edge of the pick is rubbed down (or up) the string, producing a scratchy sound.

GRACE NOTE BEND: Strike the note and bend as indicated. Play the first note as quickly as possible.

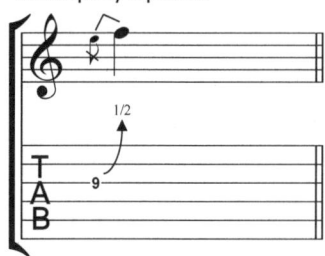

PRE-BEND: Bend the note as indicated, then strike it.

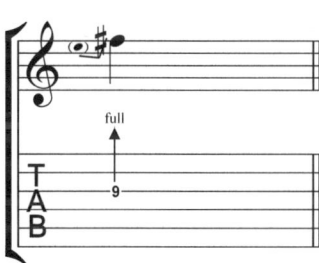

LEGATO SLIDE (GLISS): Strike the first note and then slide the same fret-hand finger up or down to the second note. The second note is not struck.

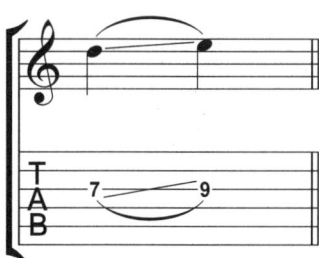

PALM MUTING: The note is partially muted by the pick hand lightly touching the string(s) just before the bridge.

QUARTER-TONE BEND: Strike the note and bend up a ¼ step

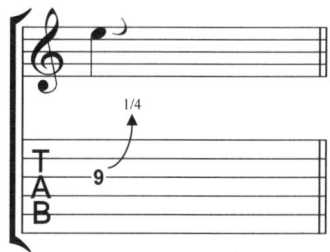

PRE-BEND & RELEASE: Bend the note as indicated. Strike it and release the note back to the original pitch.

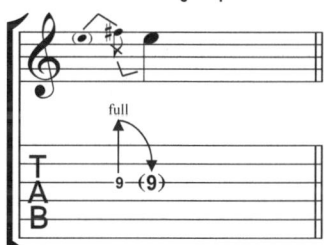

MUFFLED STRINGS: A percussive sound is produced by laying the first hand across the string(s) without depressing, and striking them with the pick hand.

SHIFT SLIDE (GLISS & RESTRIKE): Same as legato slide, except the second note is struck.

9

GOOD TIMES BAD TIMES

Words & Music by Jimmy Page, John Paul Jones & John Bonham

© Copyright 1969 Succubus Music Limited/Cap Three Limited/Estate of J. Bonham.
Print Rights Administered by Music Sales Limited.
All Rights Reserved. International Copyright Secured.

E5 A D5 A E5 A D5 A
Solo
open
cont. sim.
Gtr. 3 (elec.)
ff w/dist.+ rotary speaker fx
hold...
Fig. 3
Gtr. 1 plays Fig. 3
8va
(8)

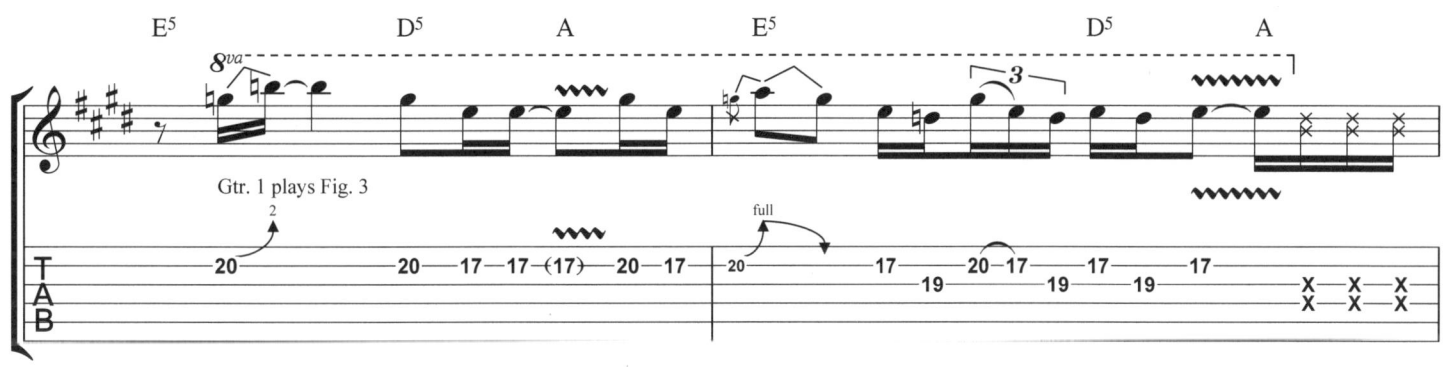

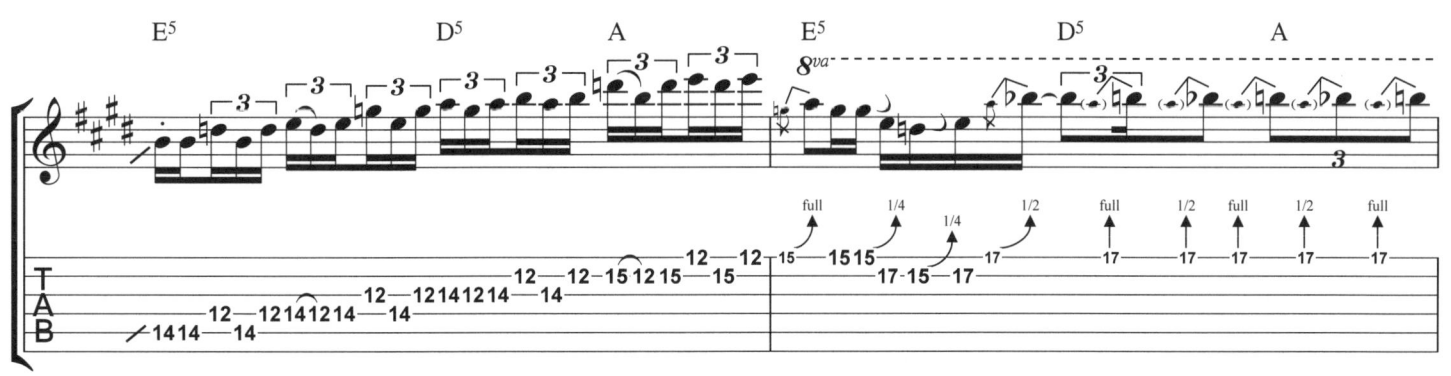

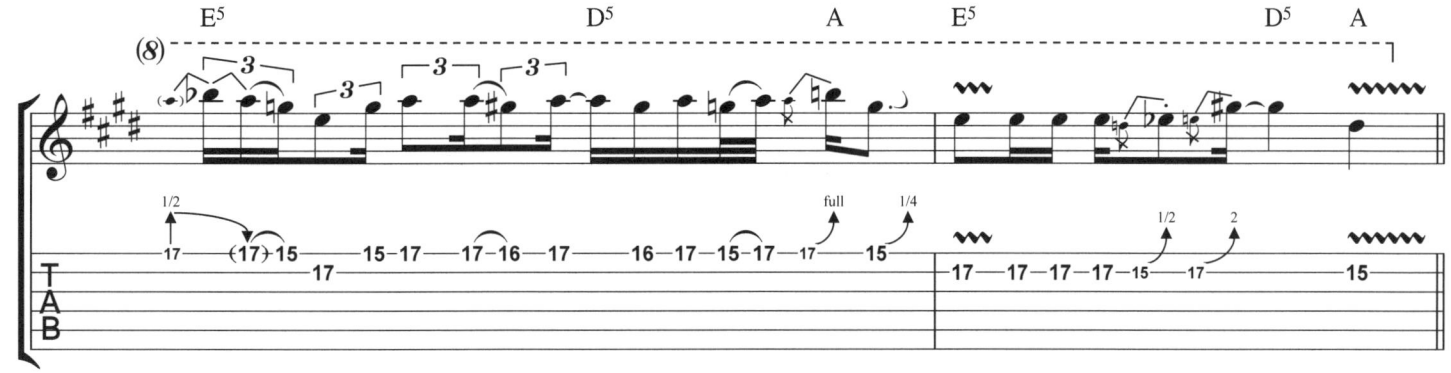

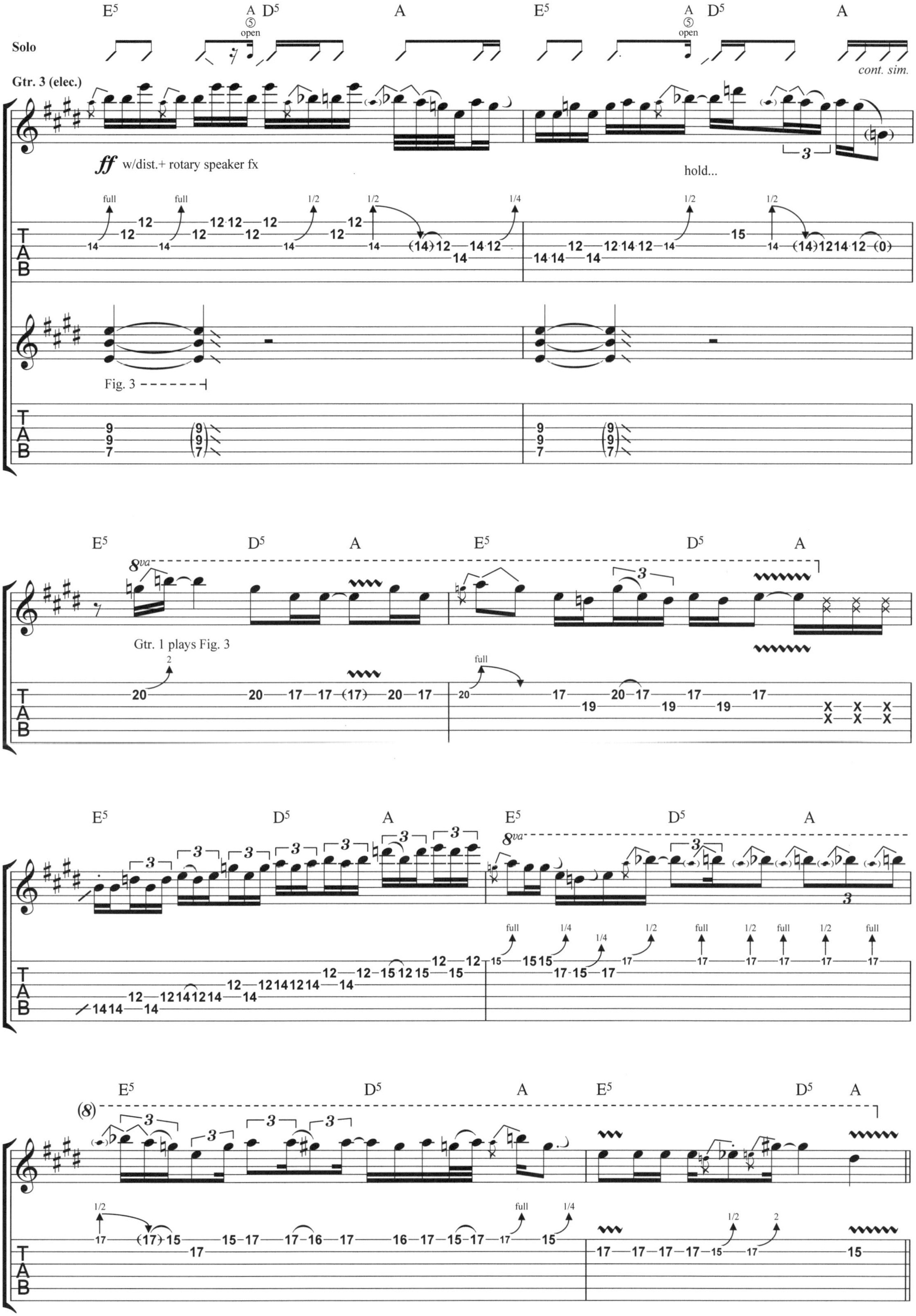

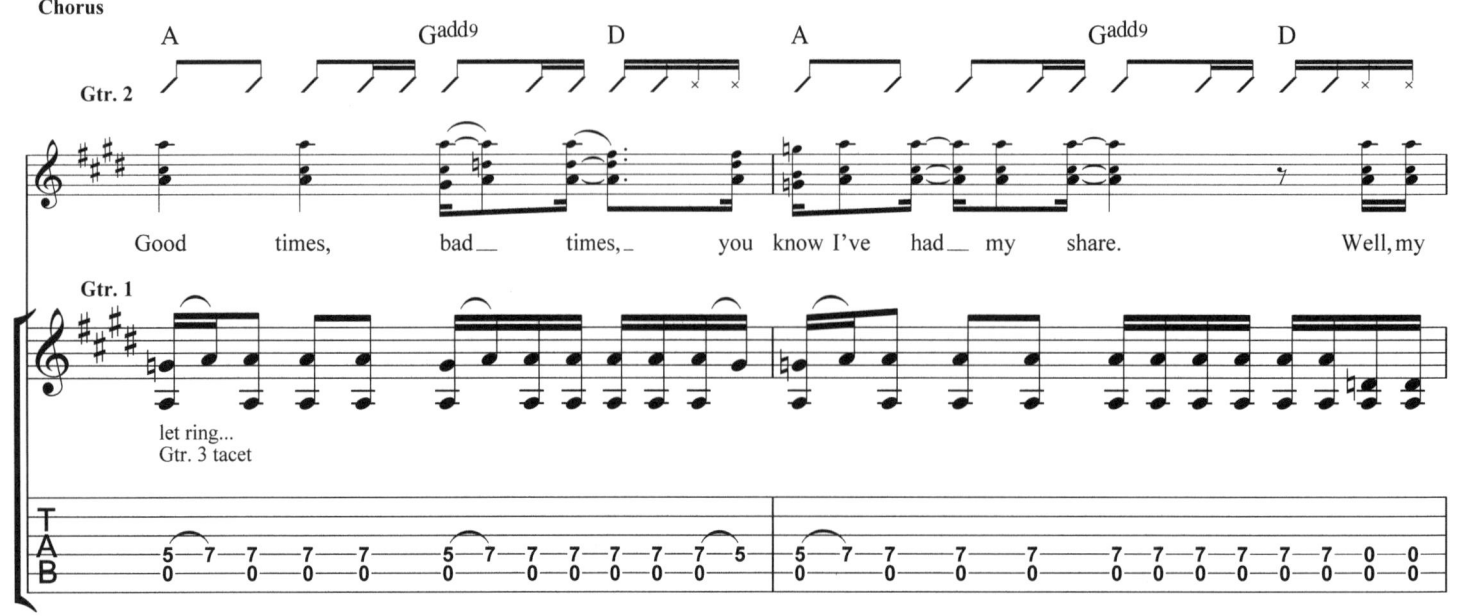
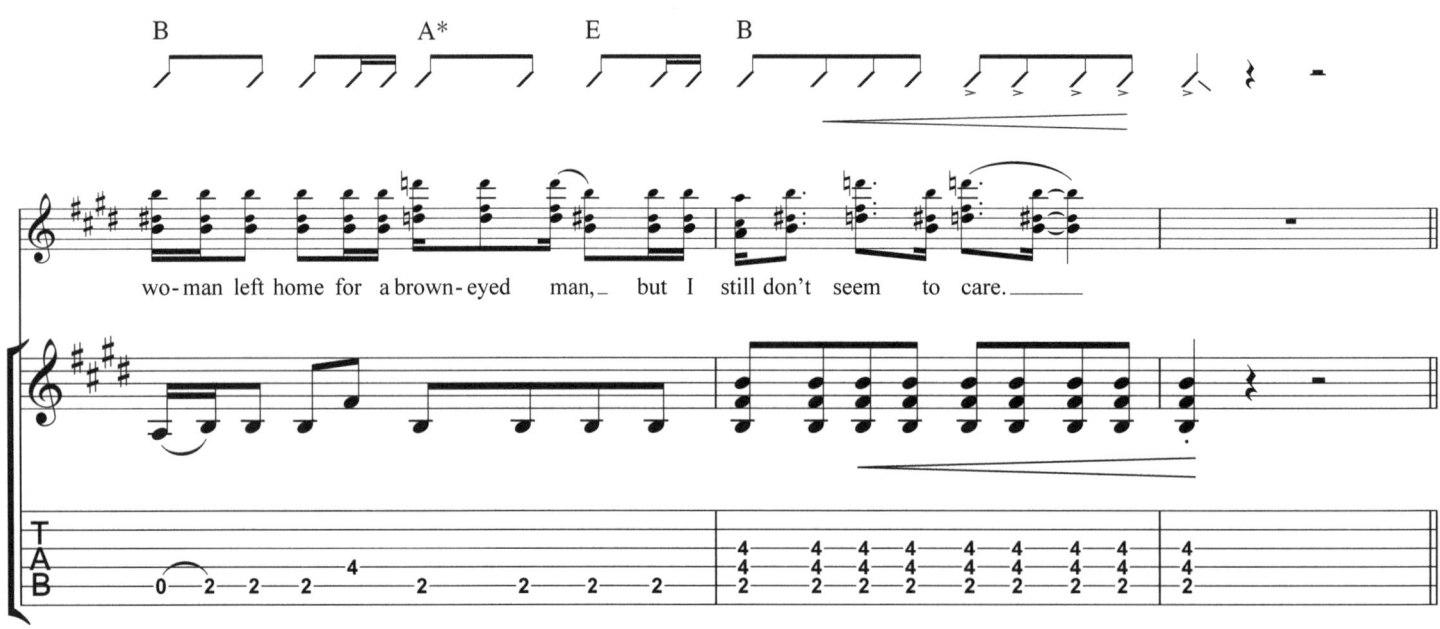
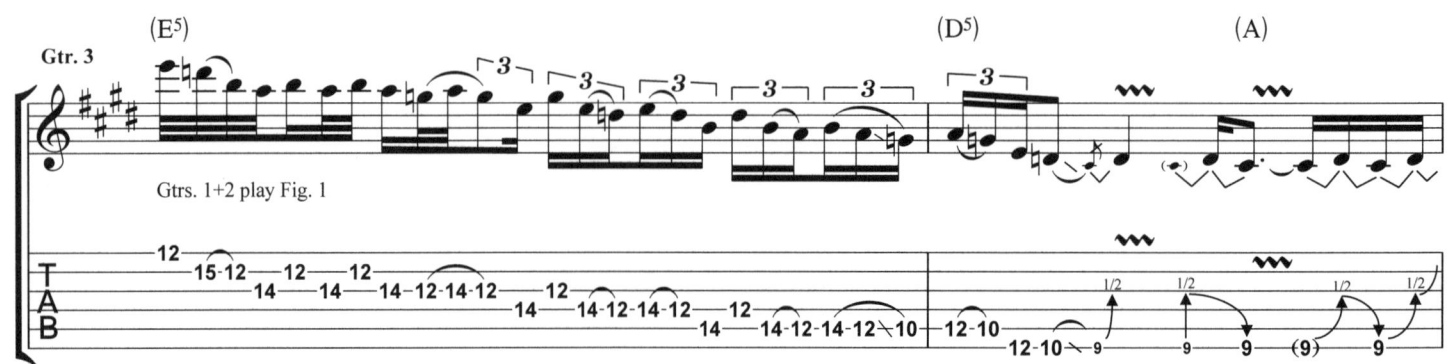

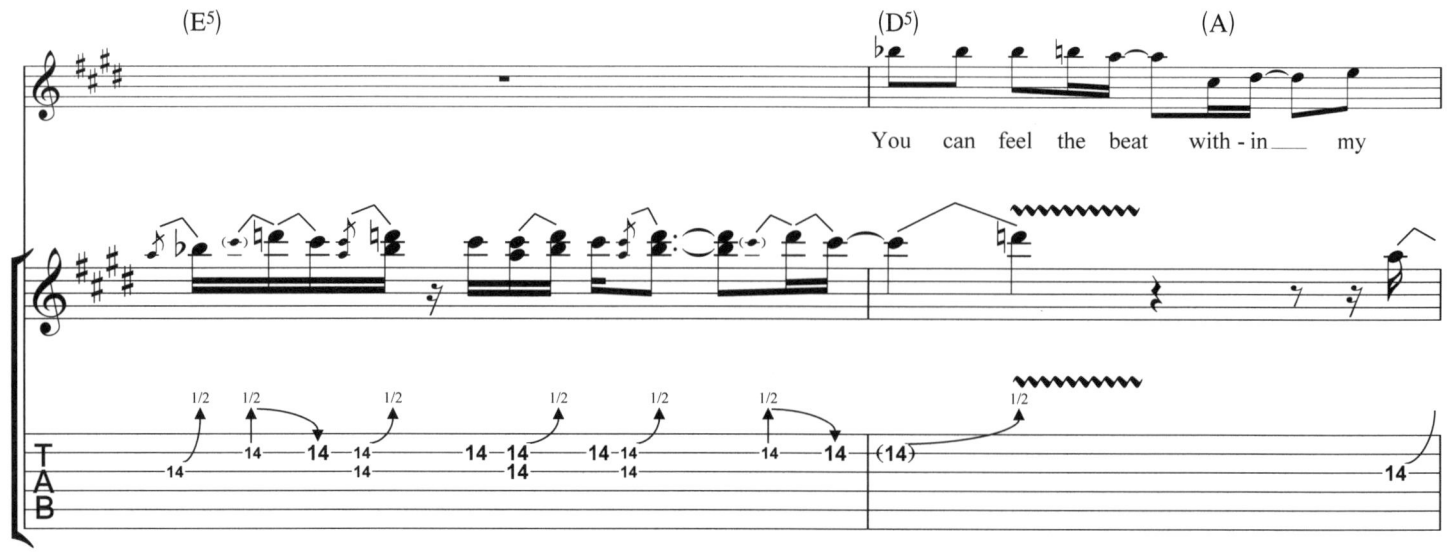
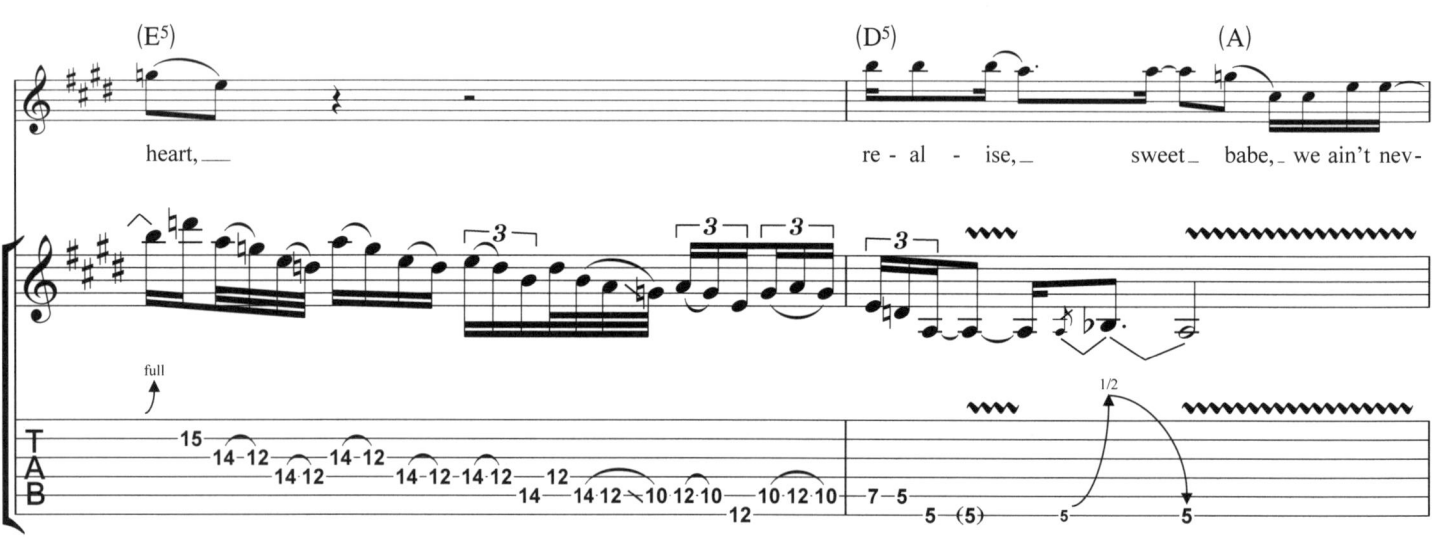
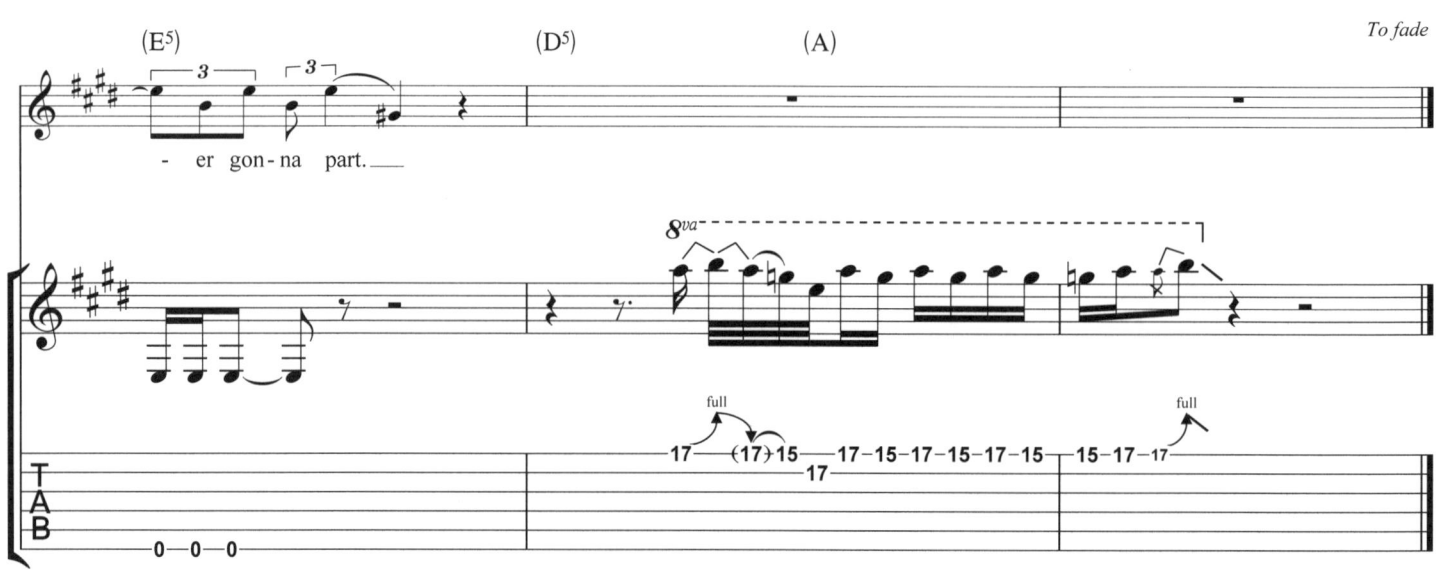

RAMBLE ON

Words & Music by Jimmy Page & Robert Plant

NOTE: Due to a manipulation of the tape speed in the mastering process, the pitch of the recording sounds 25 cents (an eighth tone) sharp of standard concert pitch. To match recording, tune all strings accordingly.

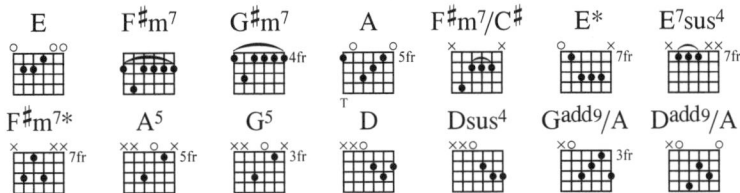

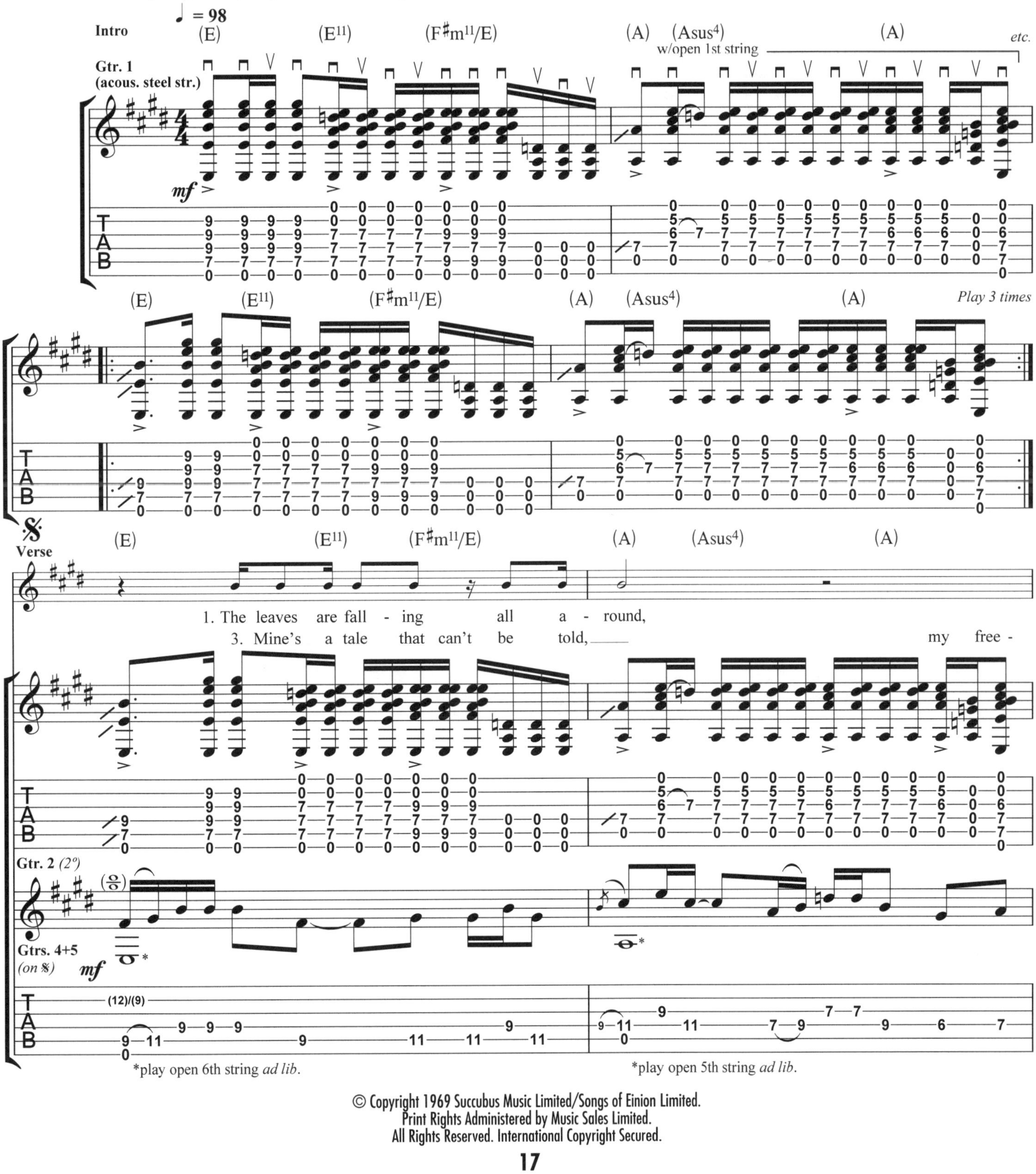

(E) (E11) (F#m11/E) (A) (Asus4) (A)
time I was on my way.
-dom I hold dear.
sim.

(E) (E11) (F#m11/E) (A) (Asus4) (A)
Thanks to you, I'm much ob-liged,
How years a-go, in days of old, when ma-gic filled the
Fig. 1
Fig. 3

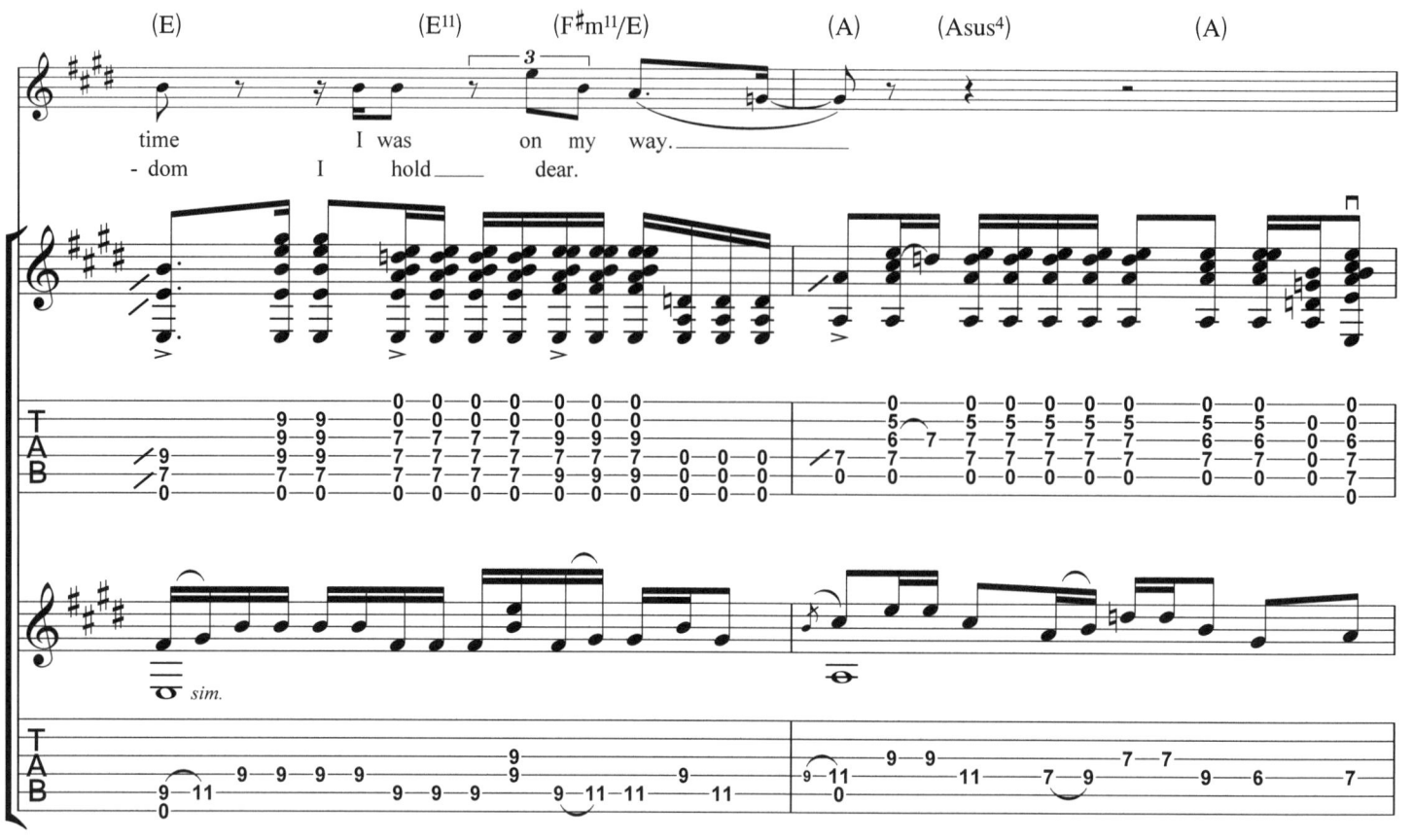

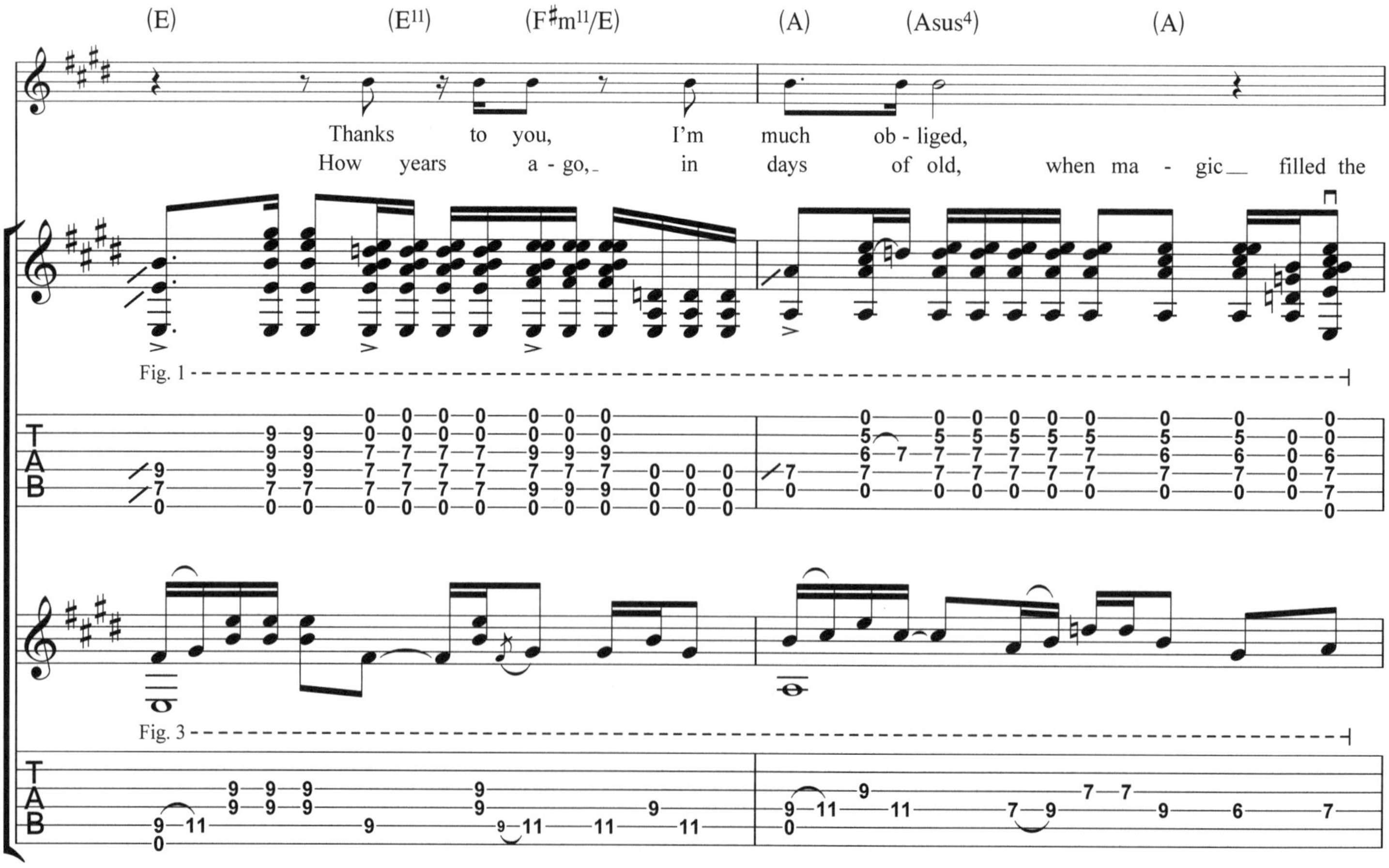

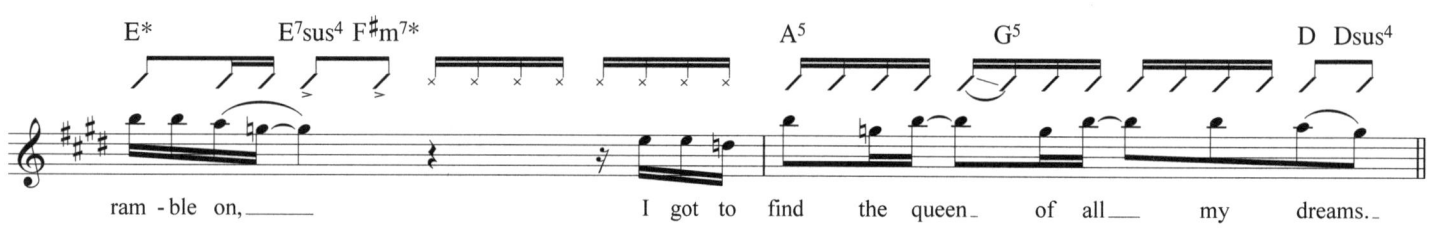
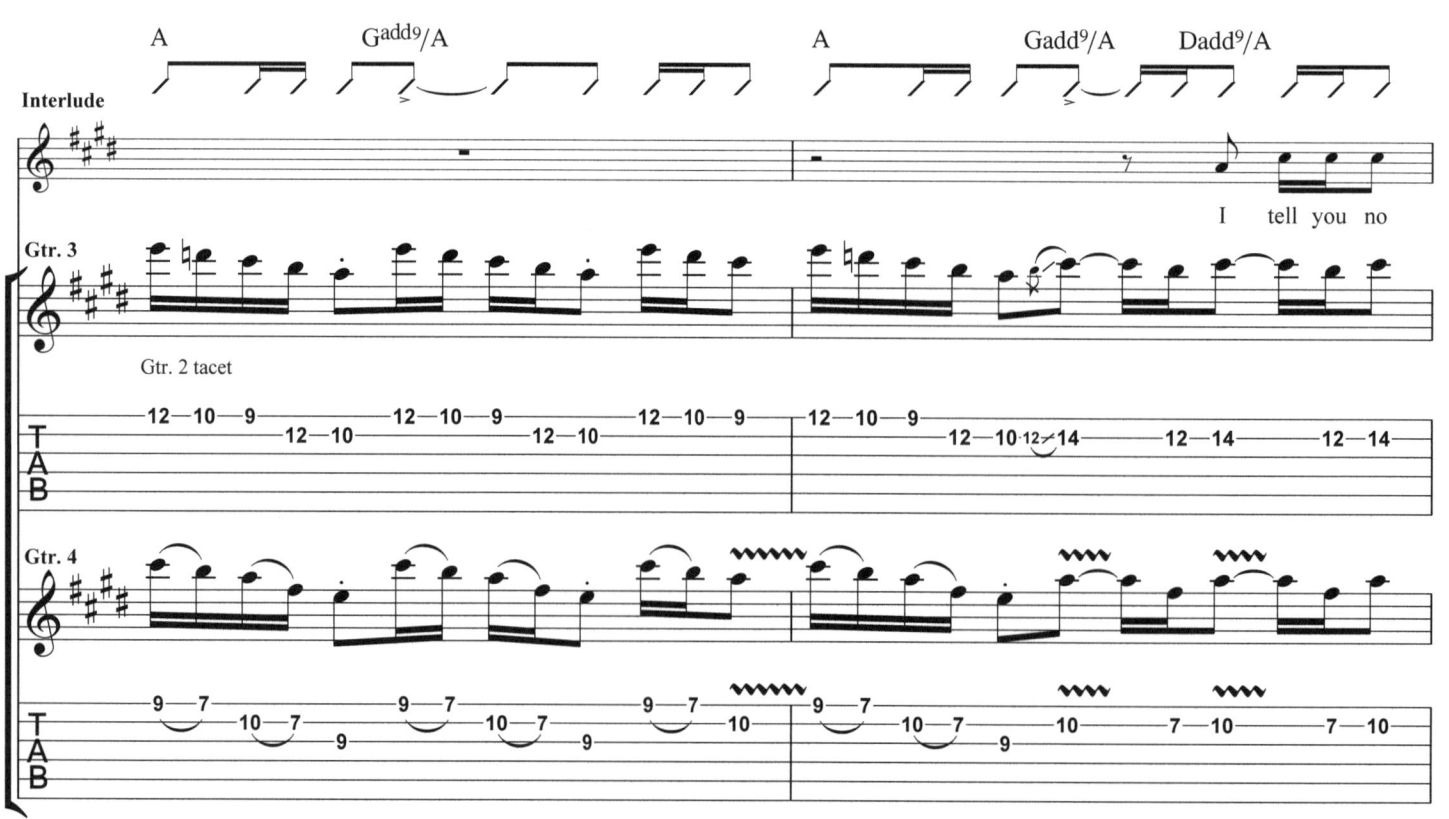

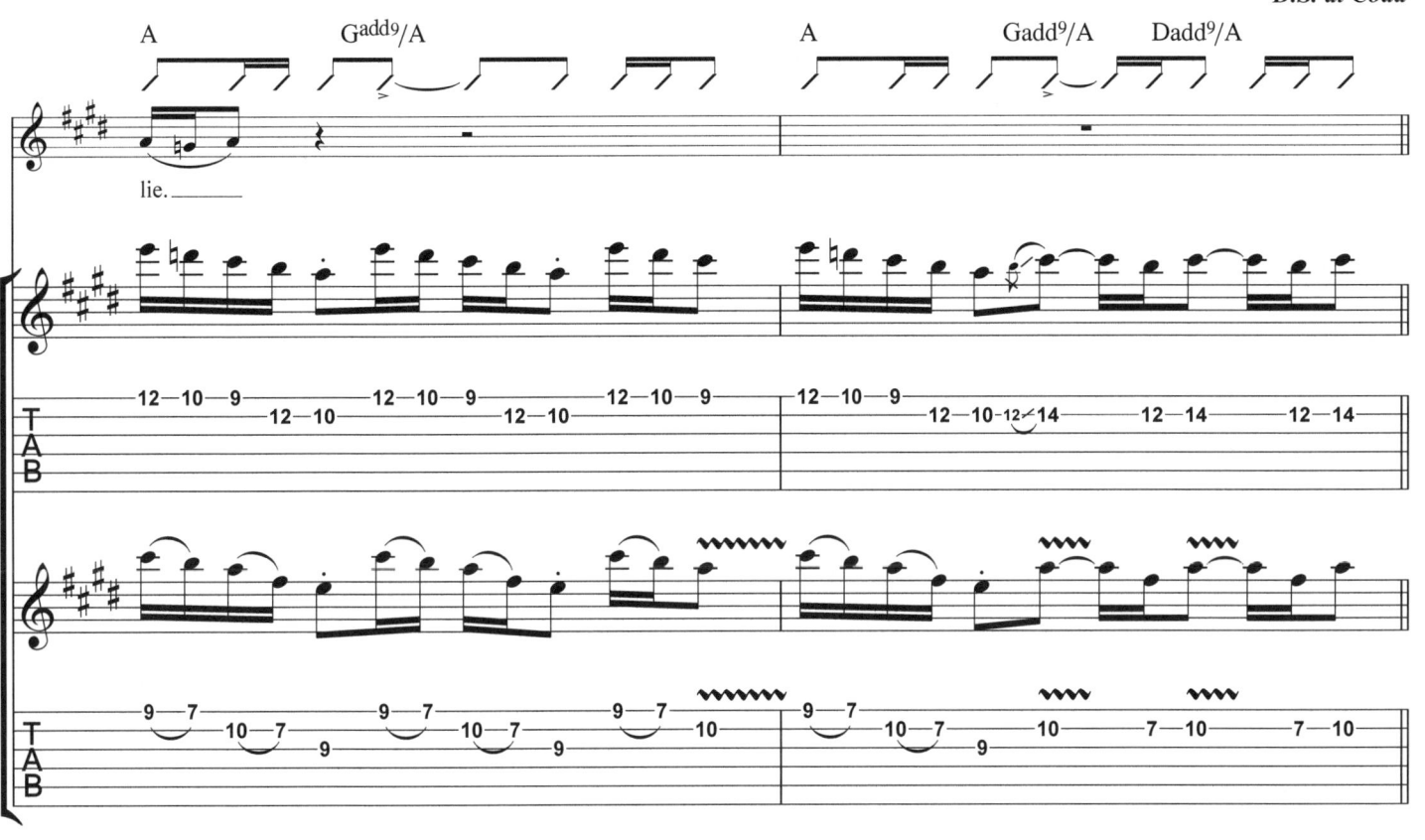
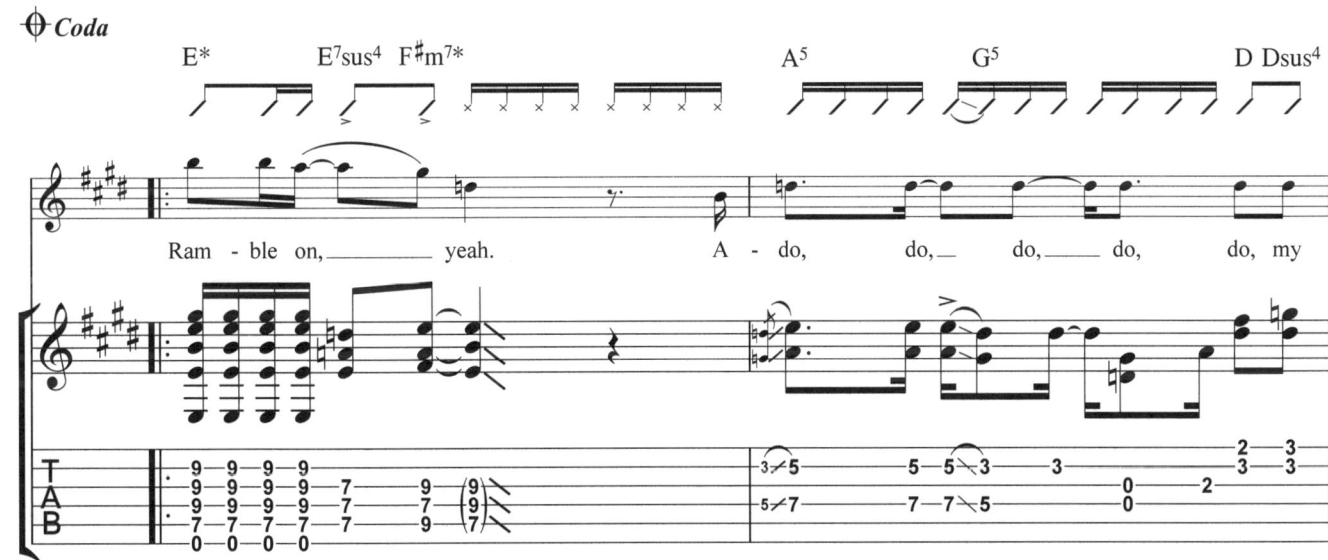
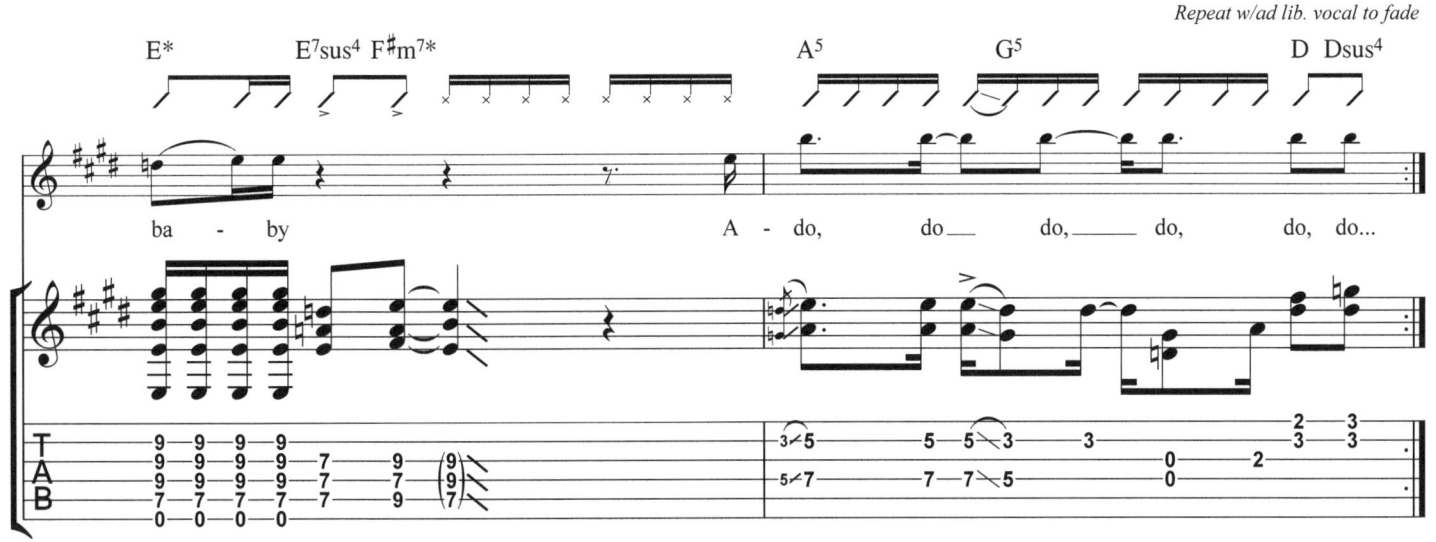

BLACK DOG

Words & Music by Jimmy Page, Robert Plant & John Paul Jones

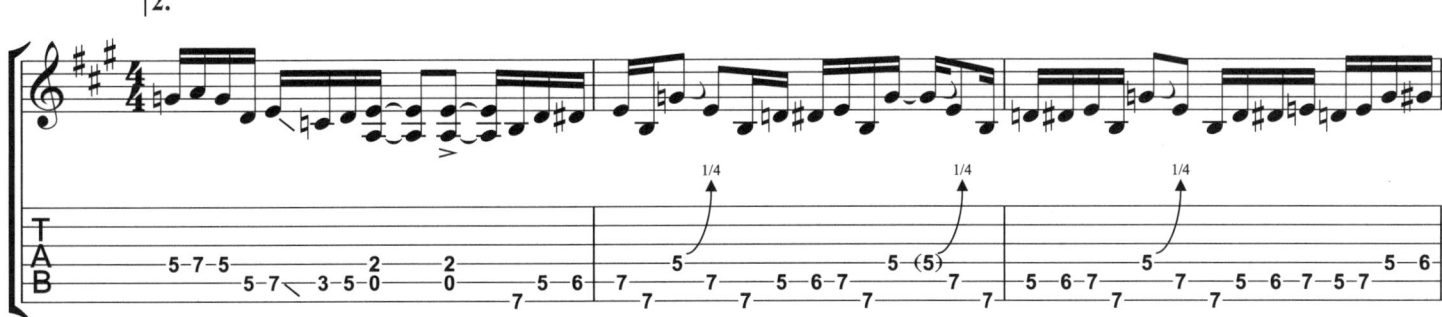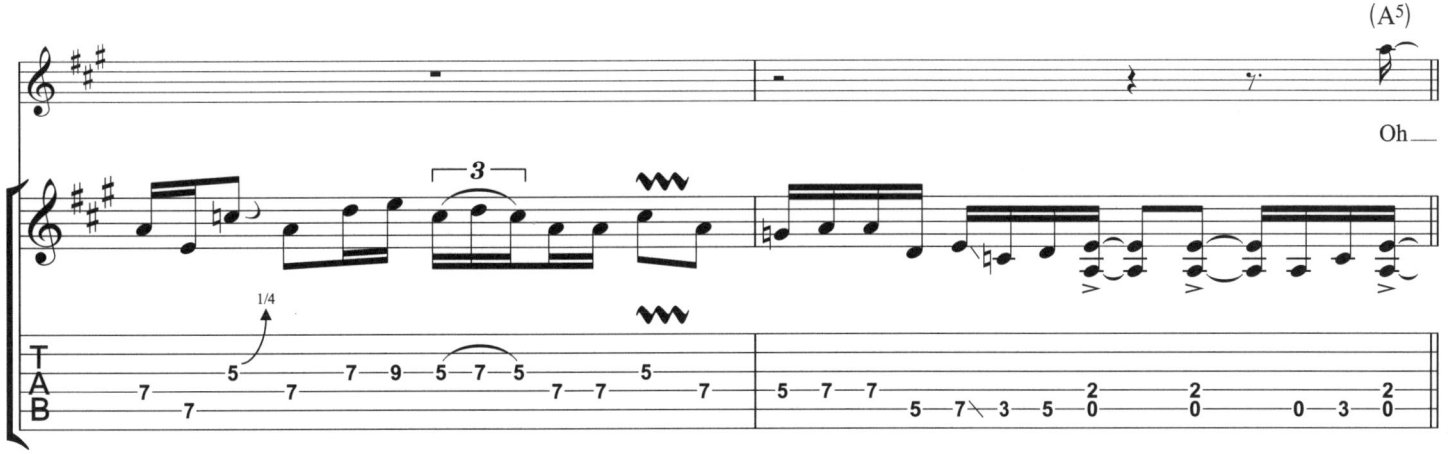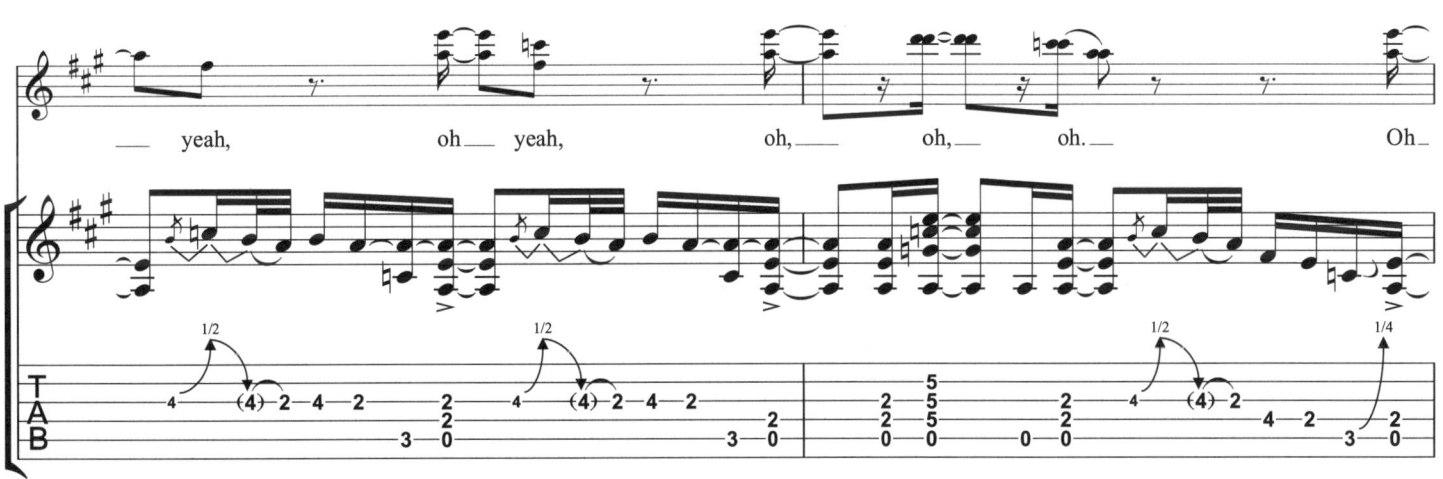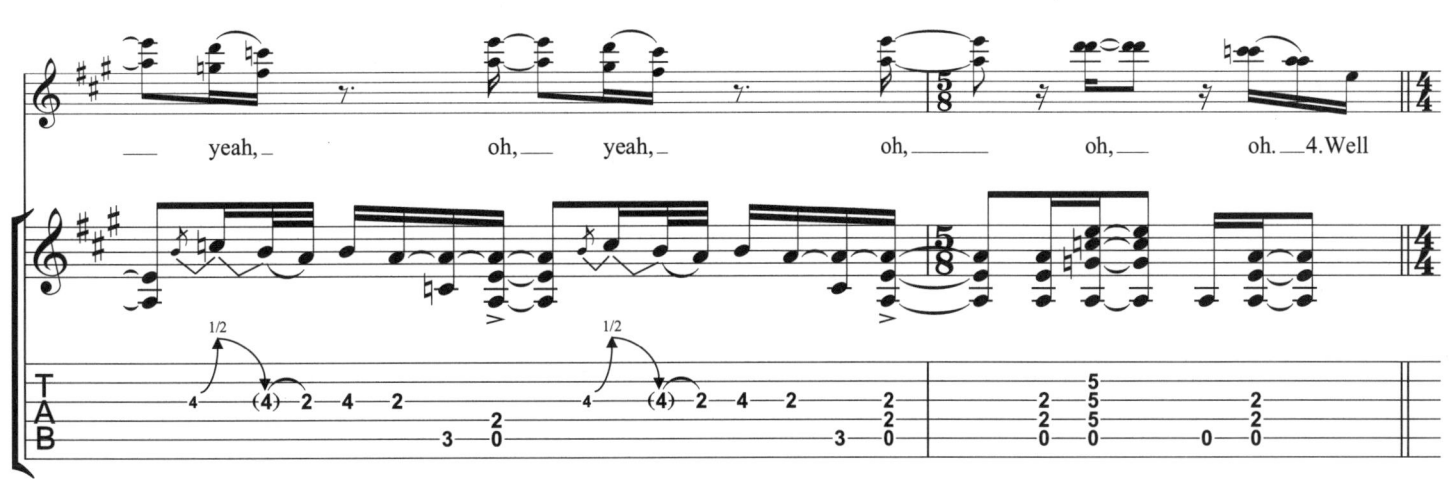

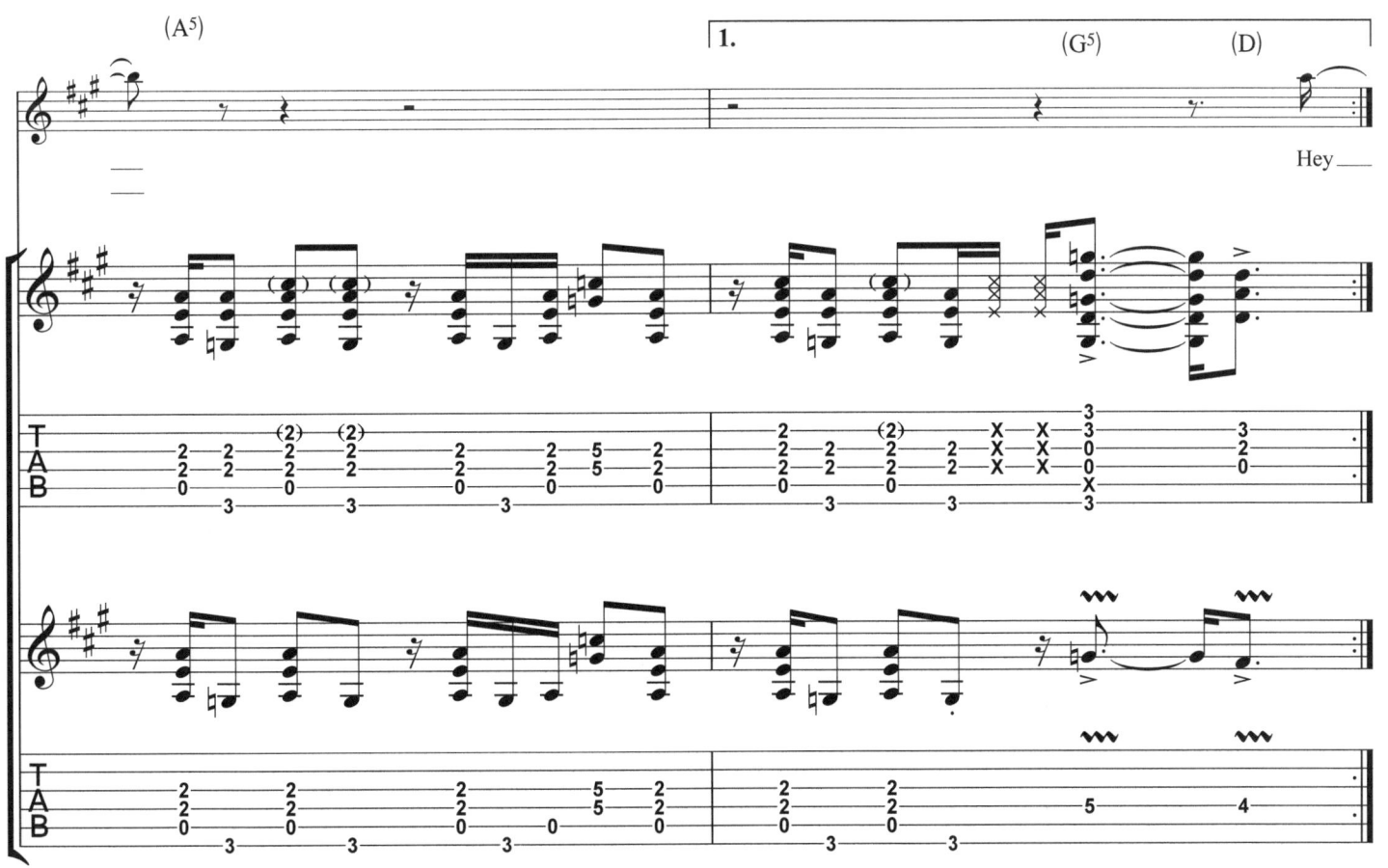

*The metre of this song is somewhat controversial, especially in the **Chorus** and **Solo** sections.
Previous editions suggest that the kick drum indicates the downbeat, meaning irregular bars at certain points.
However, the drum clicks and cues before these sections would make it seem that the metre actually remains constant, in 4/4;
therefore the snare drum remains on the backbeat throughout. This is reflected in this arrangement.

IN MY TIME OF DYING

Words & Music by Jimmy Page, Robert Plant, John Paul Jones & John Bonham

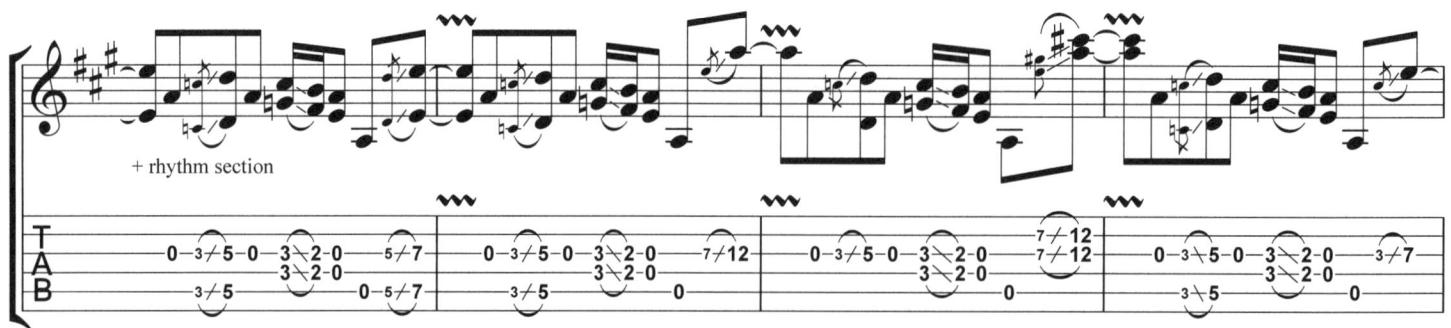
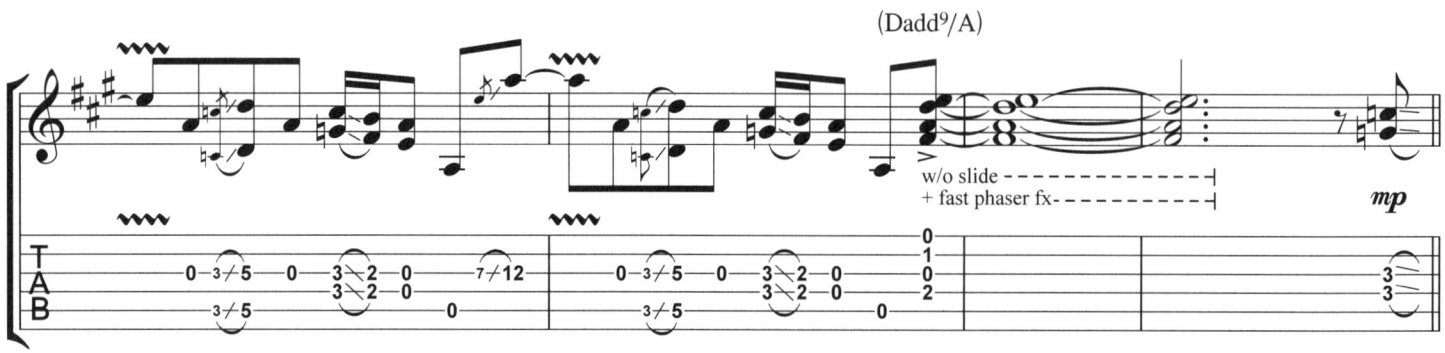

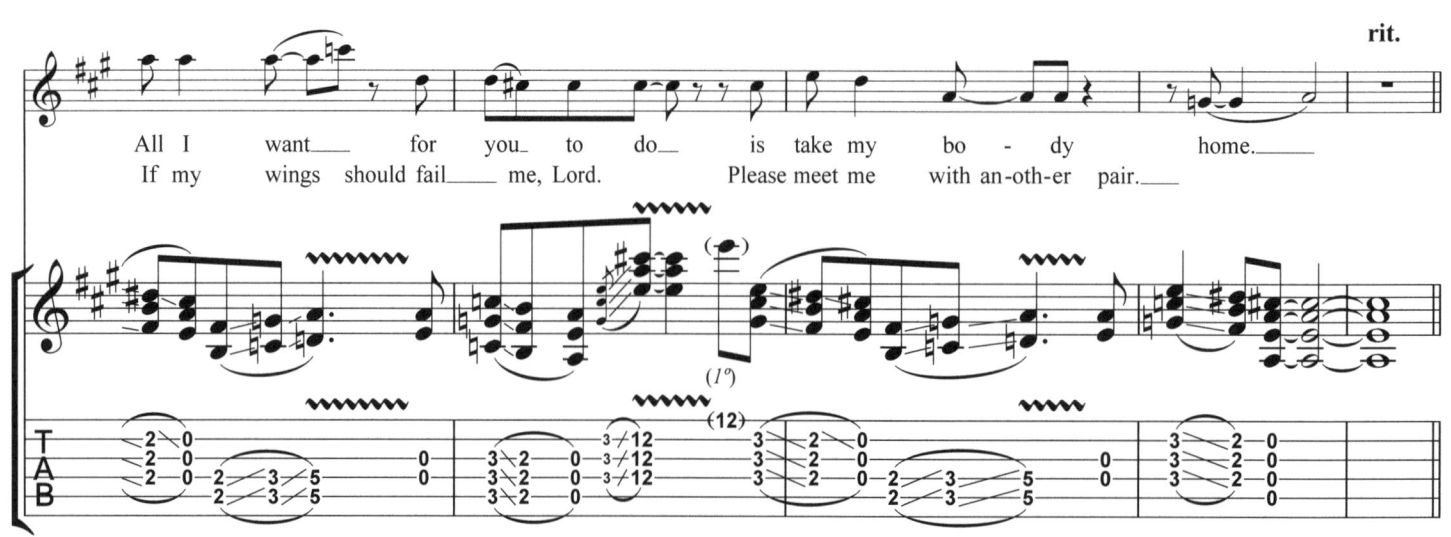

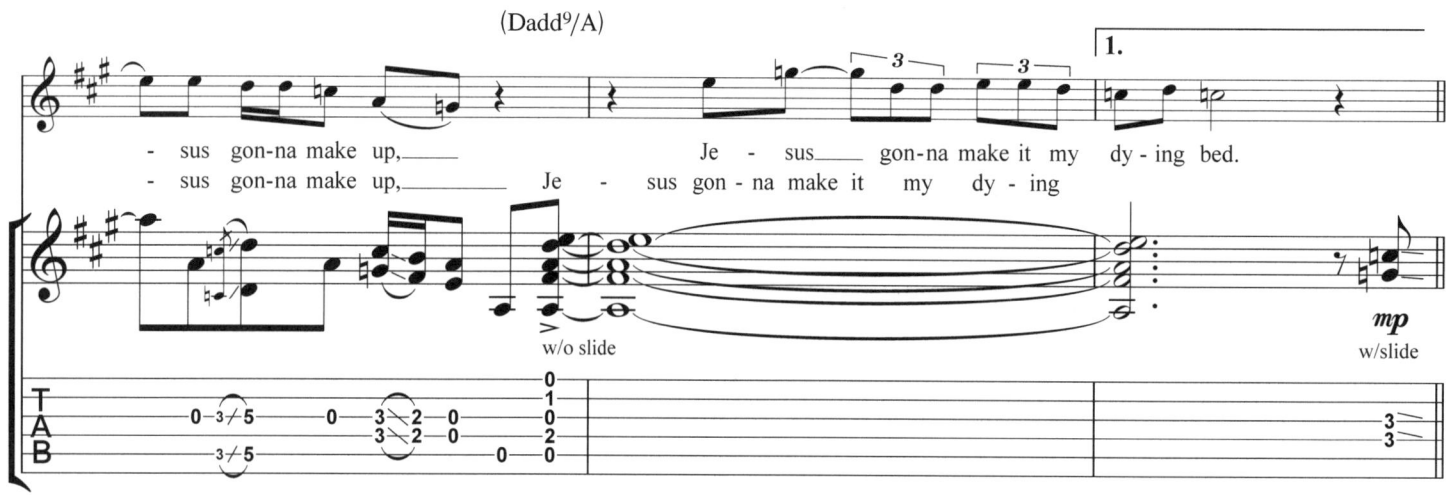
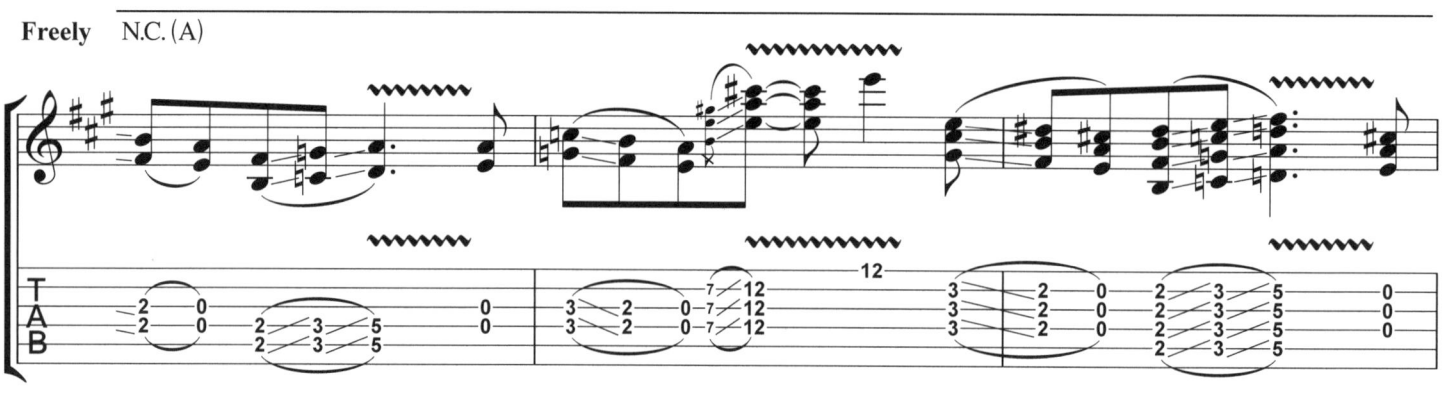
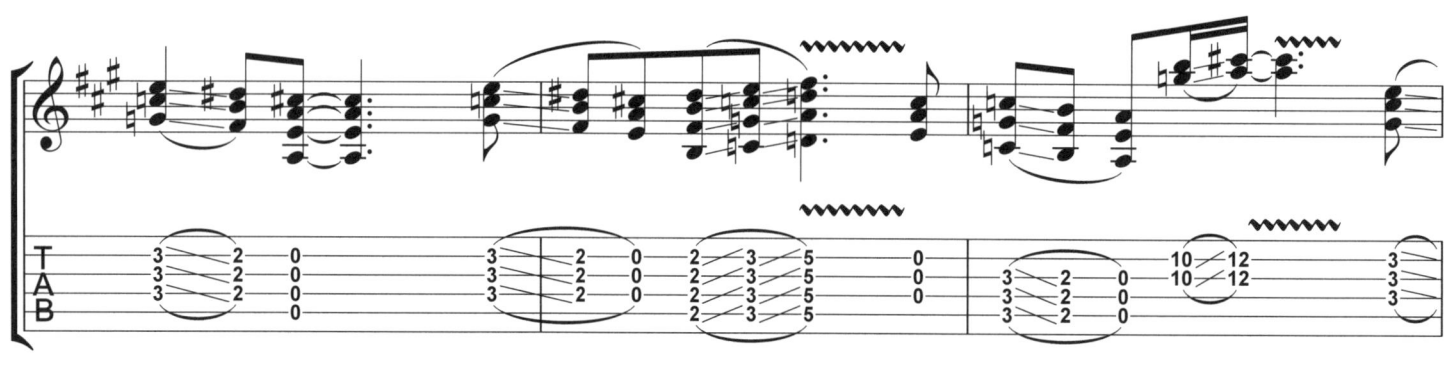
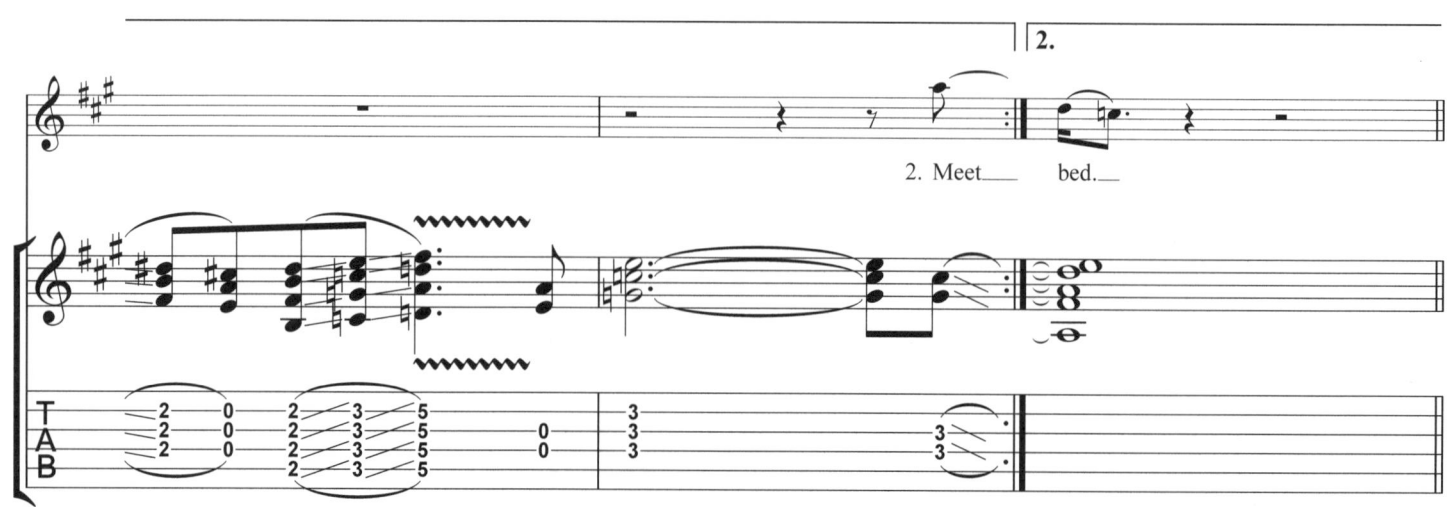

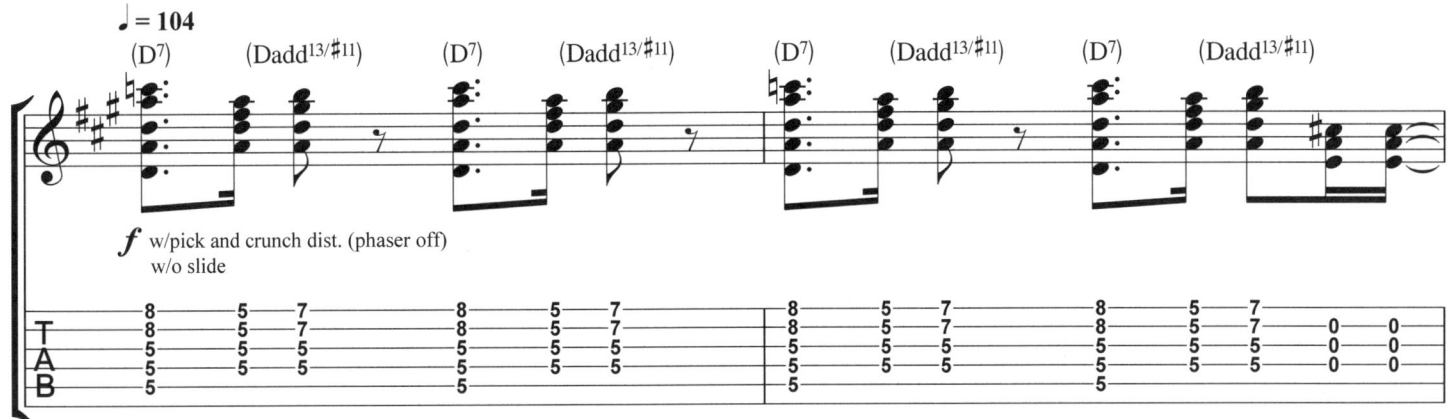
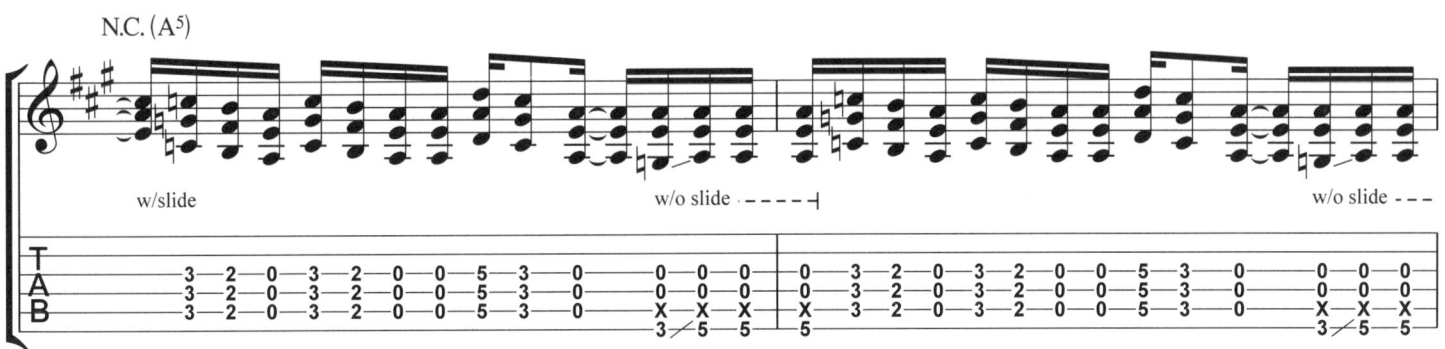
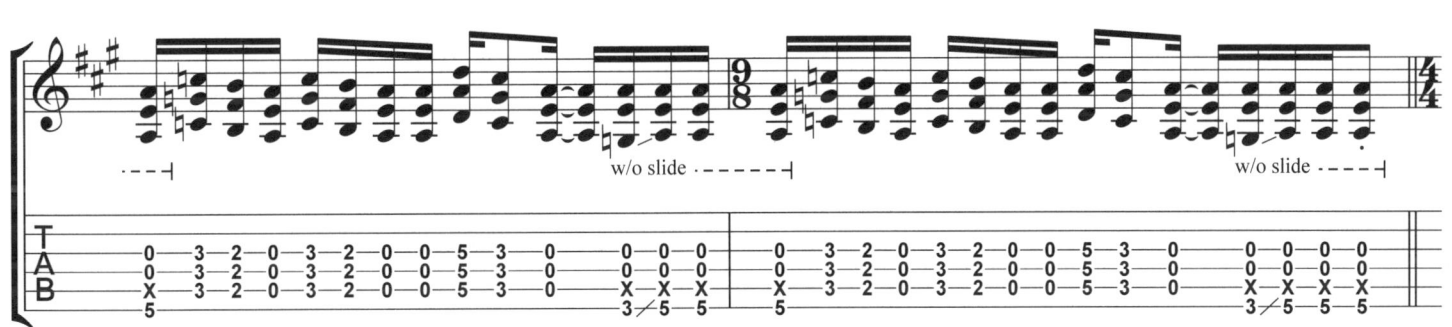
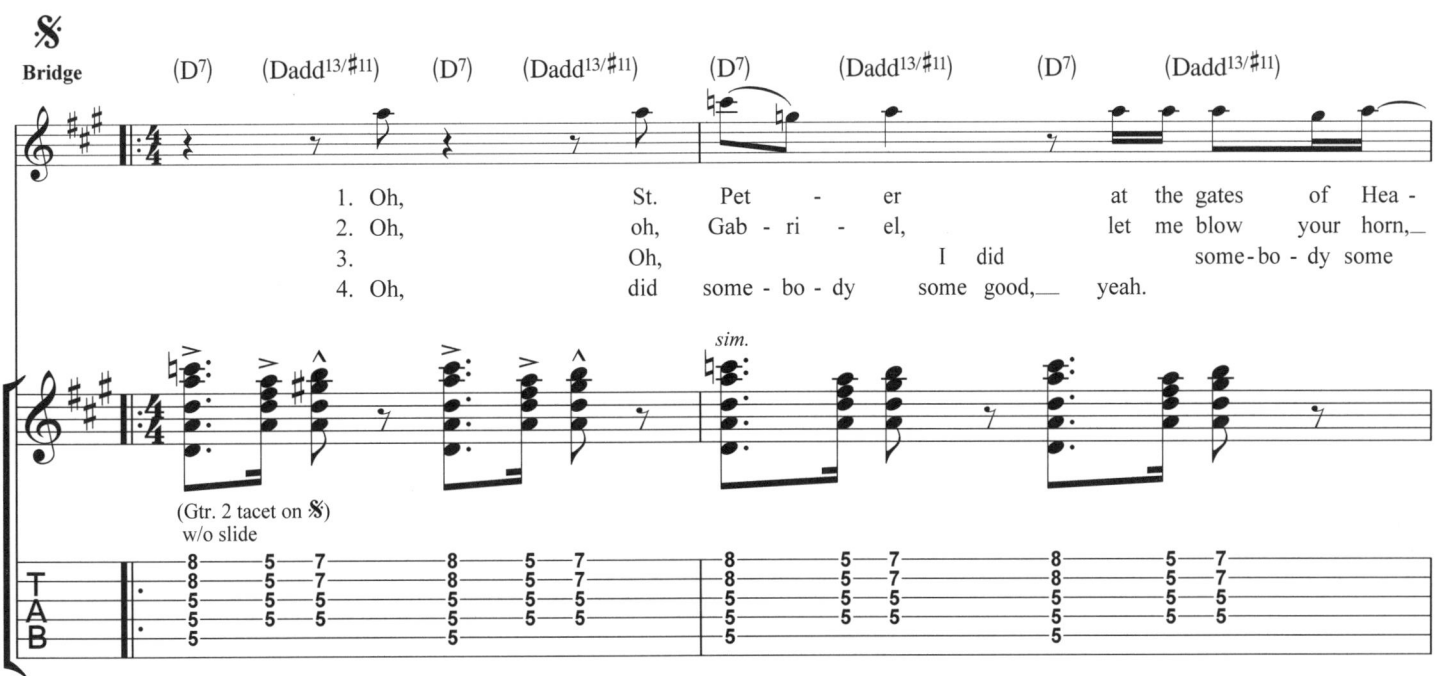

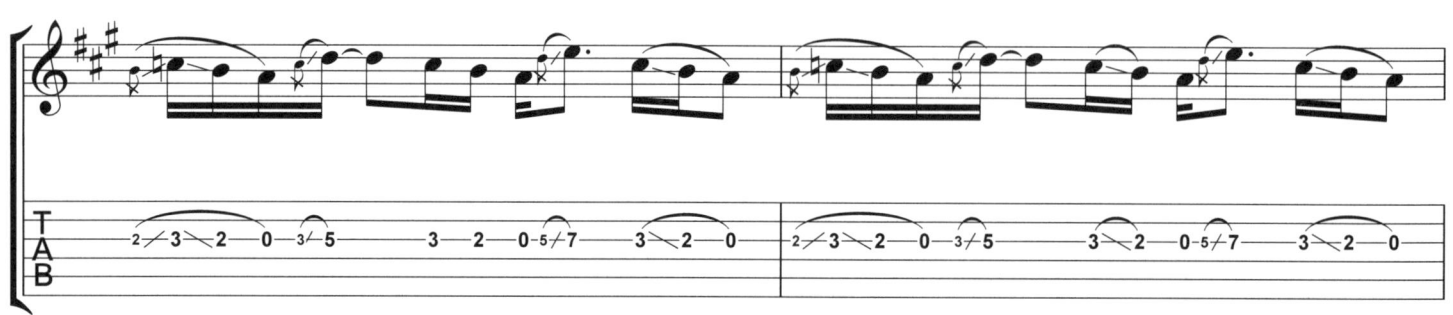
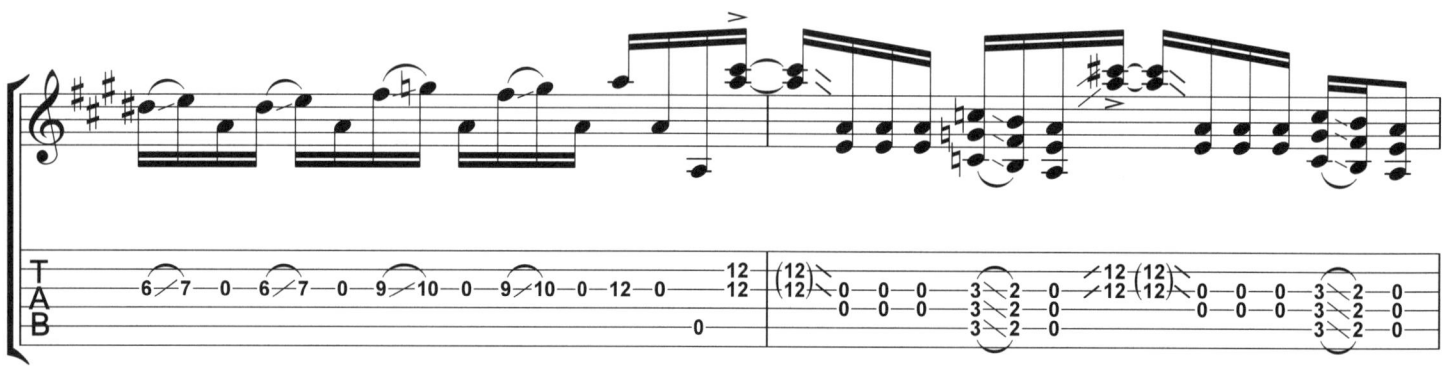
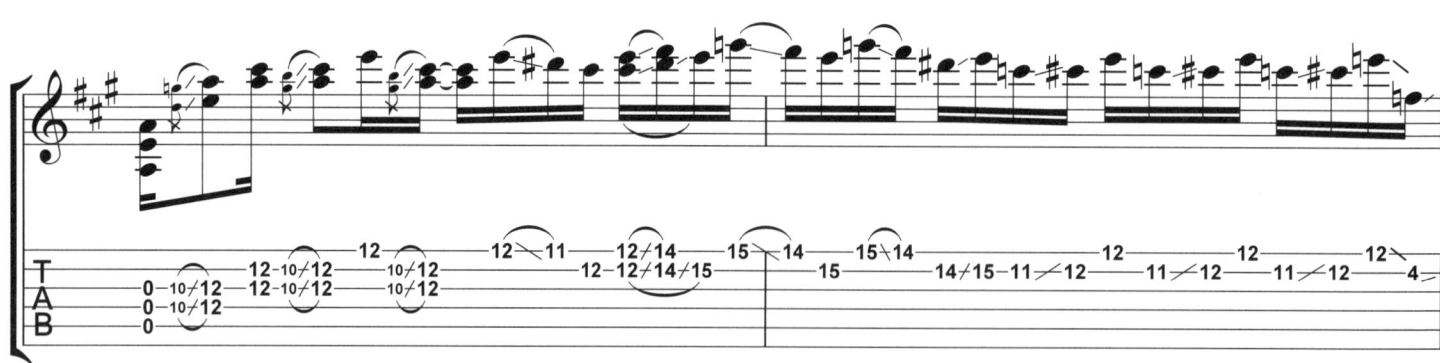
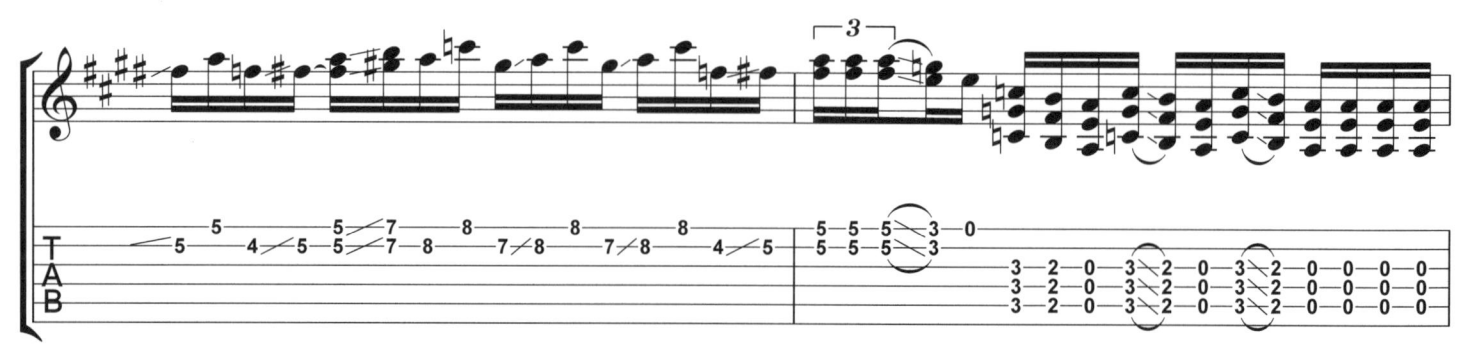

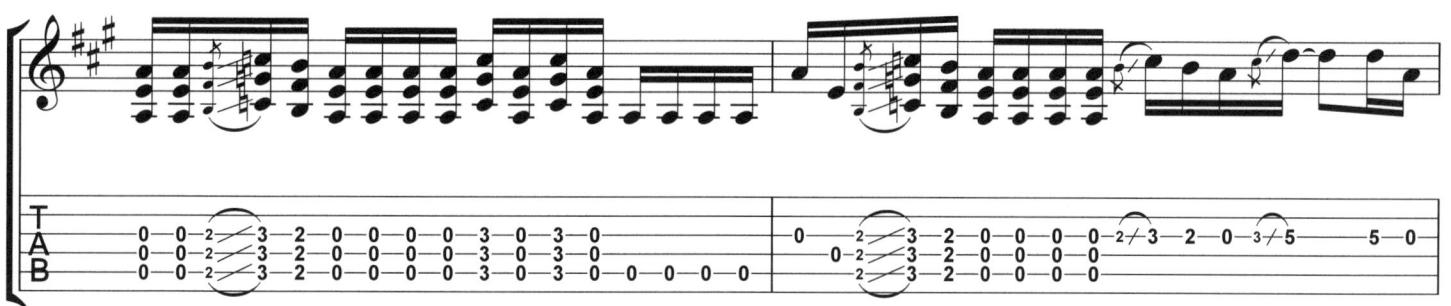

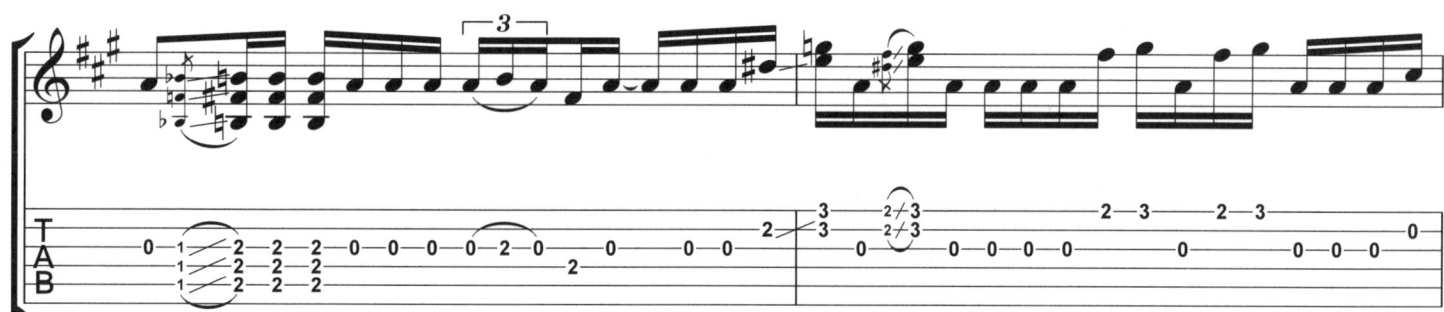

D.S. al Coda
(with repeat)

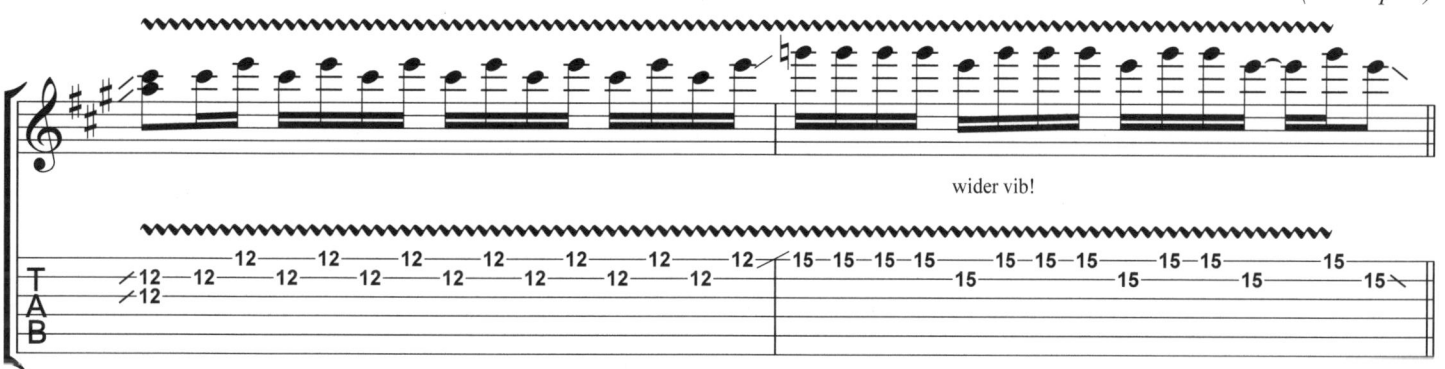

wider vib!

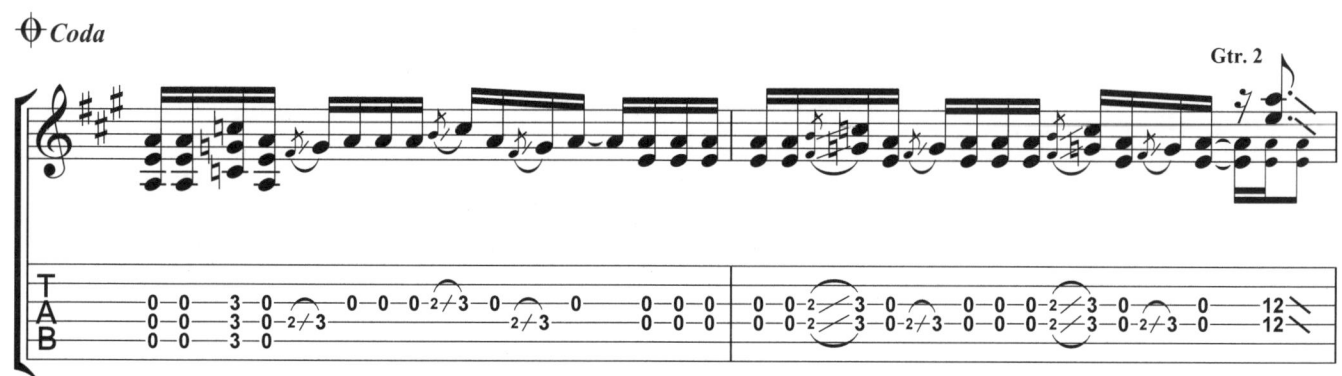

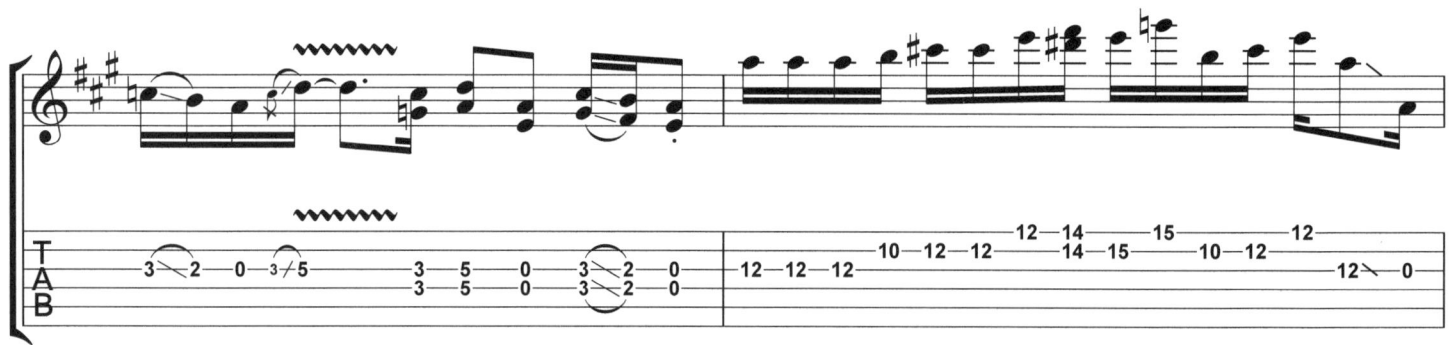

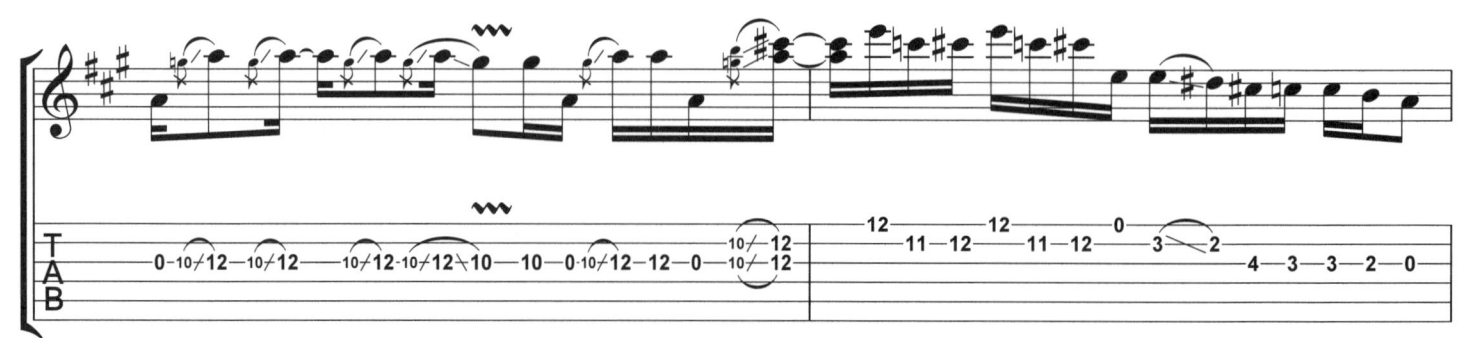

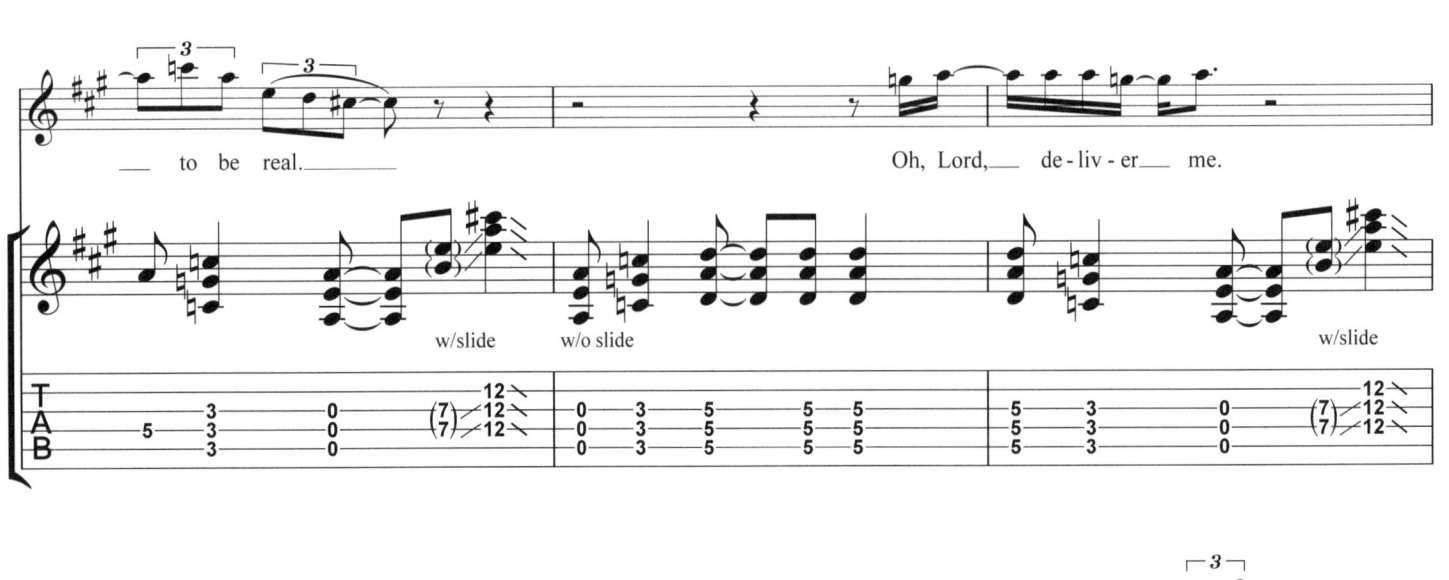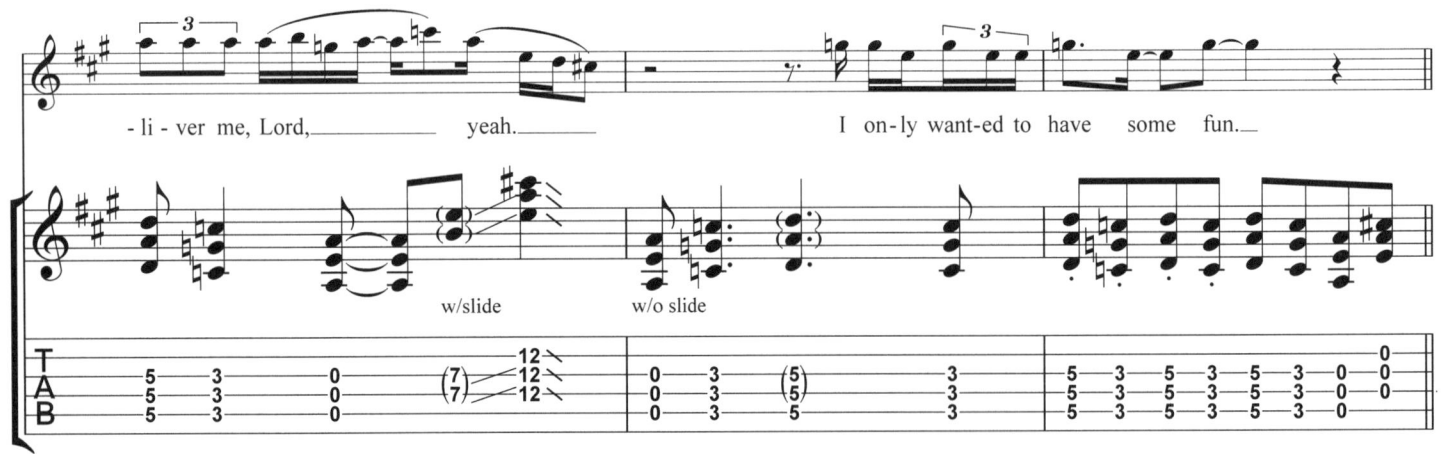

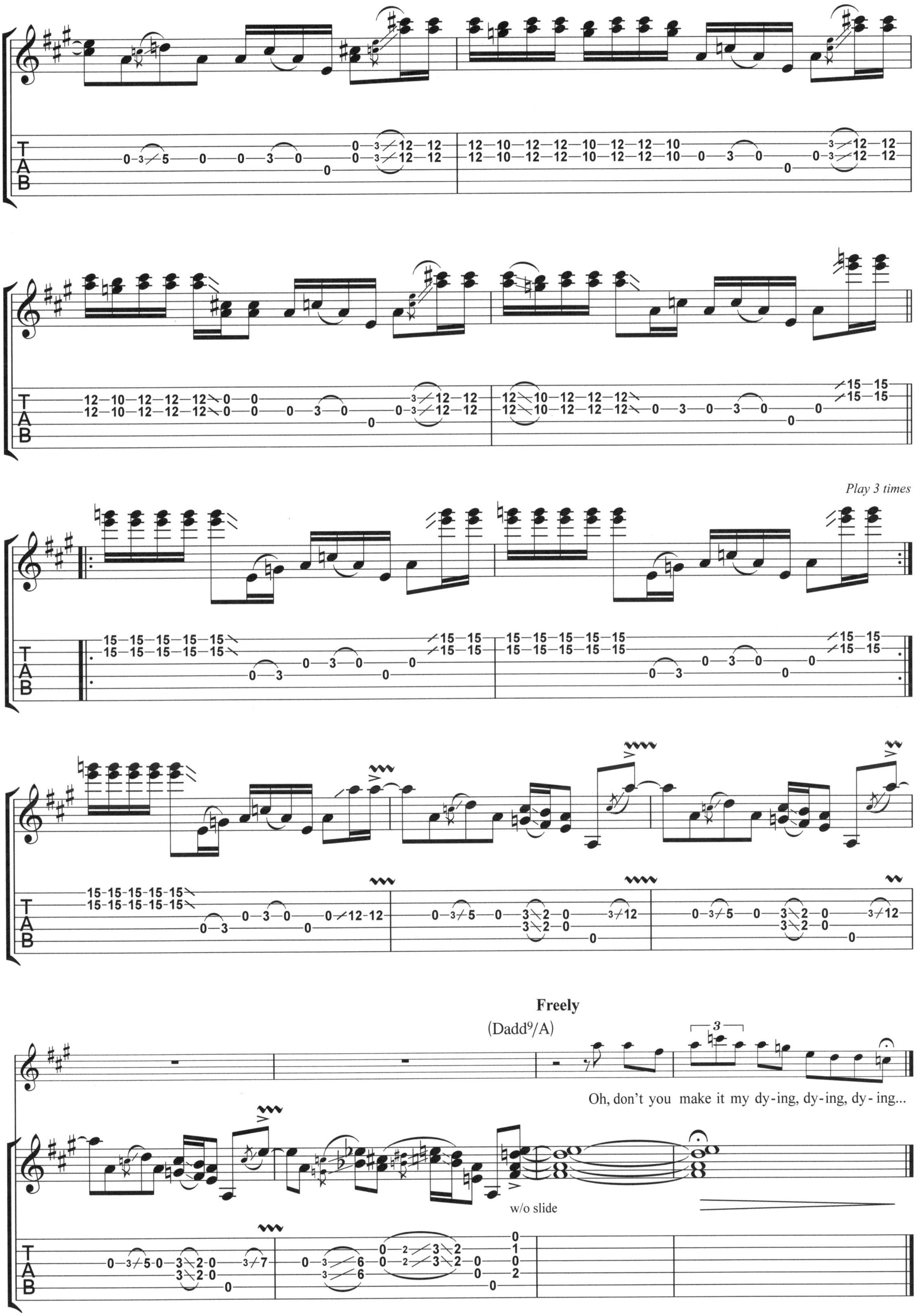
Play 3 times
Freely
(Dadd9/A)
Oh, don't you make it my dy-ing, dy-ing, dy-ing...
w/o slide

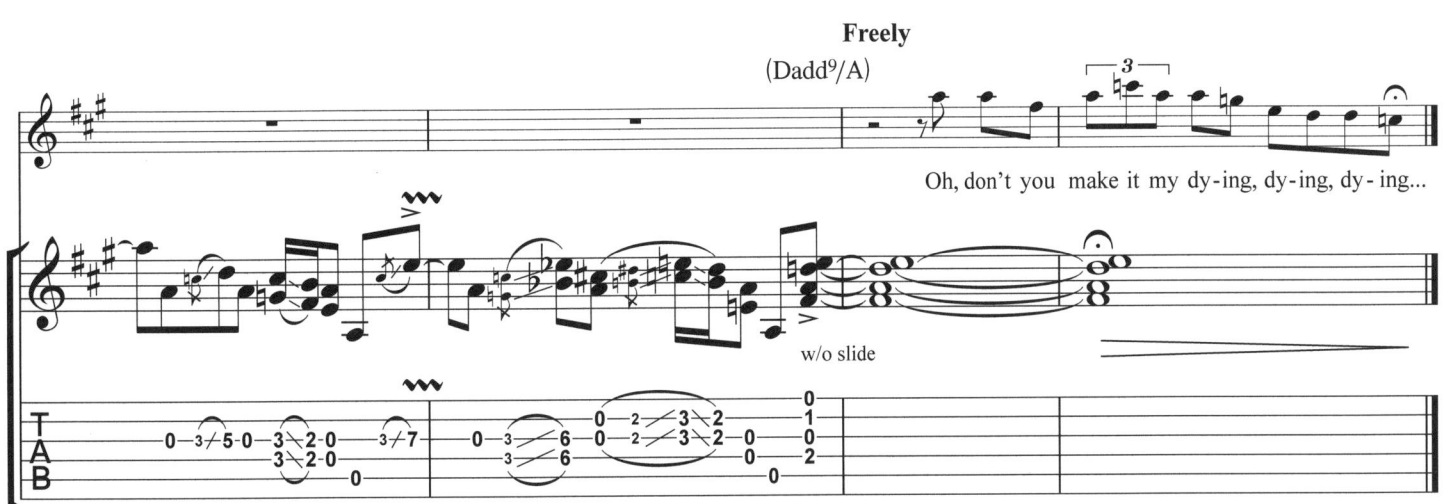

FOR YOUR LIFE

Words & Music by Jimmy Page & Robert Plant

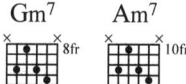

Chorus
(E♭5) (F5) (B♭5) (C5) (G)
"Don't you want to, don't you want to cook it, cook it, cook it."
w/bar + pan fx
-1 approx pitch +1
(E♭5) (F5) (B♭5) (C5) (G) (G5)
Hadn't planned to, could not stand to try it, fry it,
w/bar…
-1 approx pitch +1
na, na, na, na, yeah.
w/bar + pan fx...
-1.5 +1.5
(approx pitch)
(C5)
Whooh.

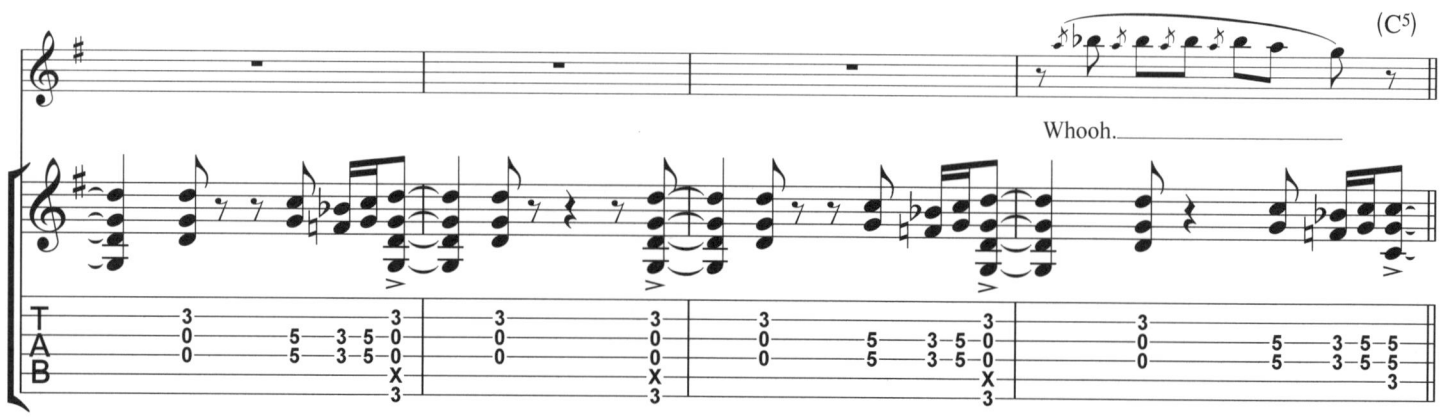

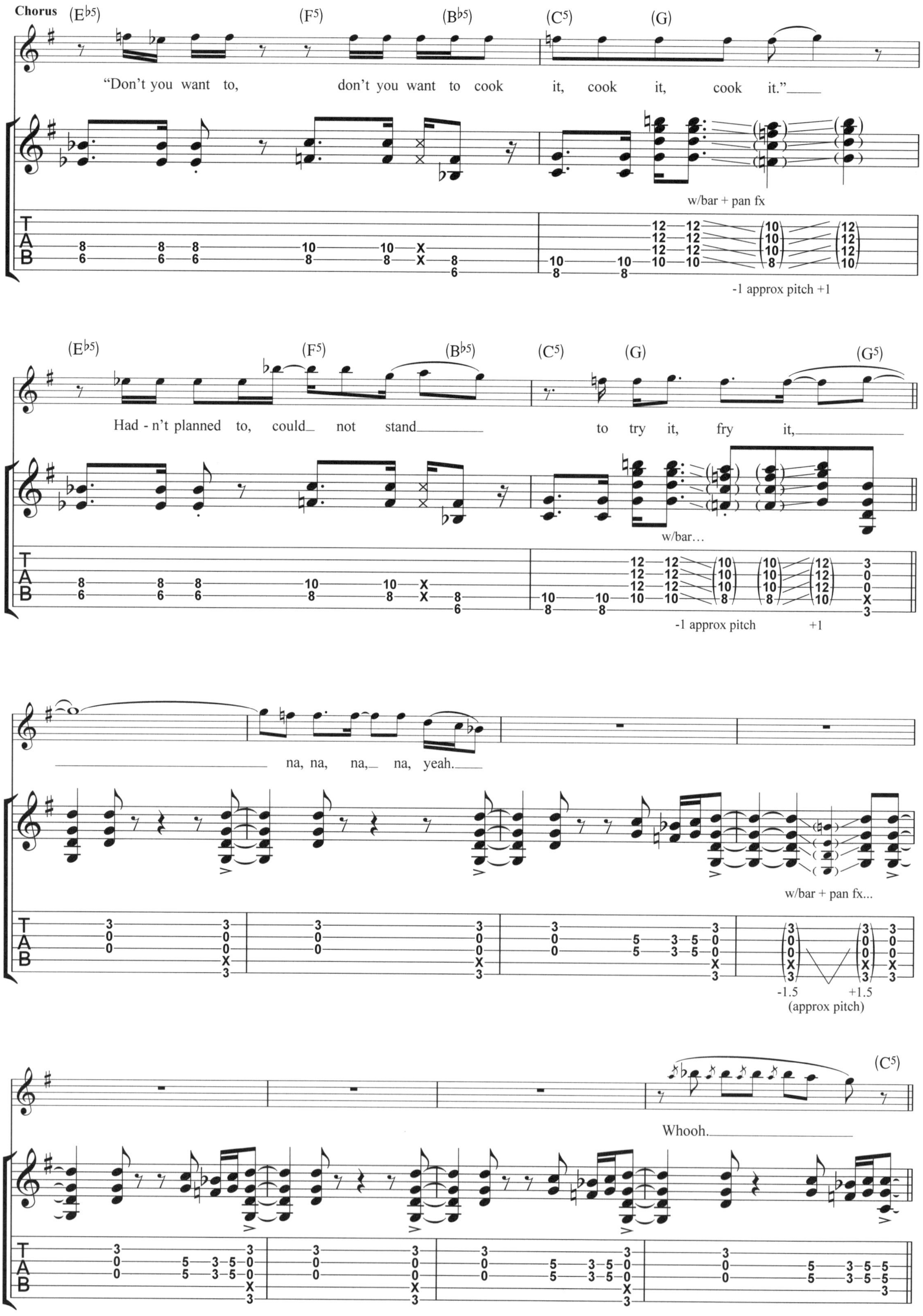

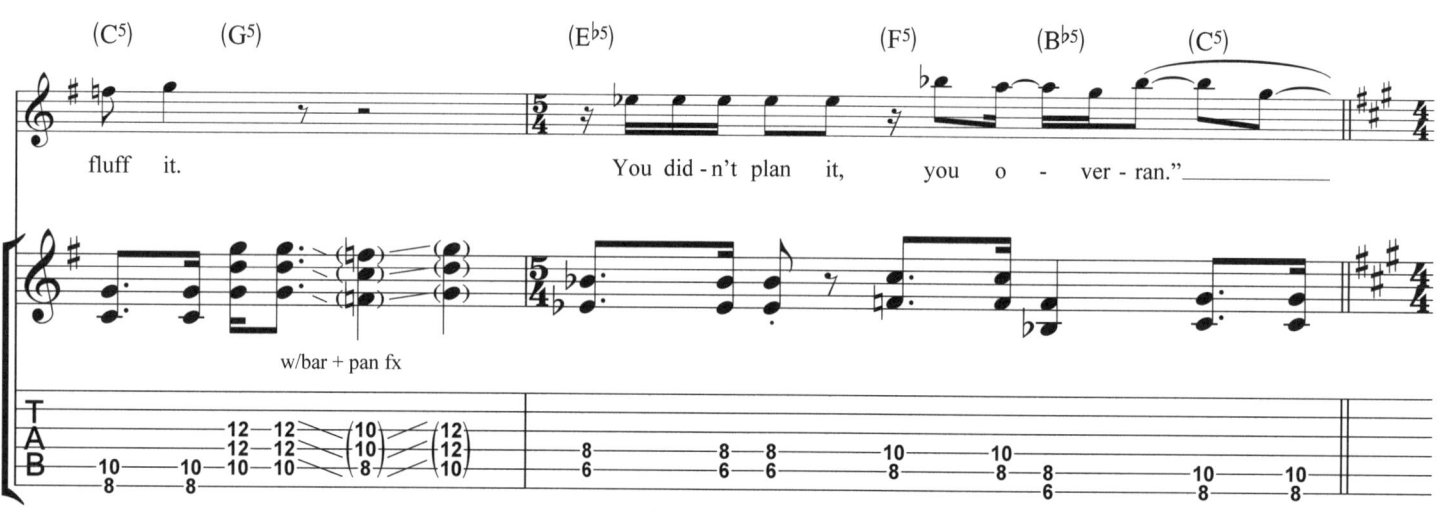

Interlude

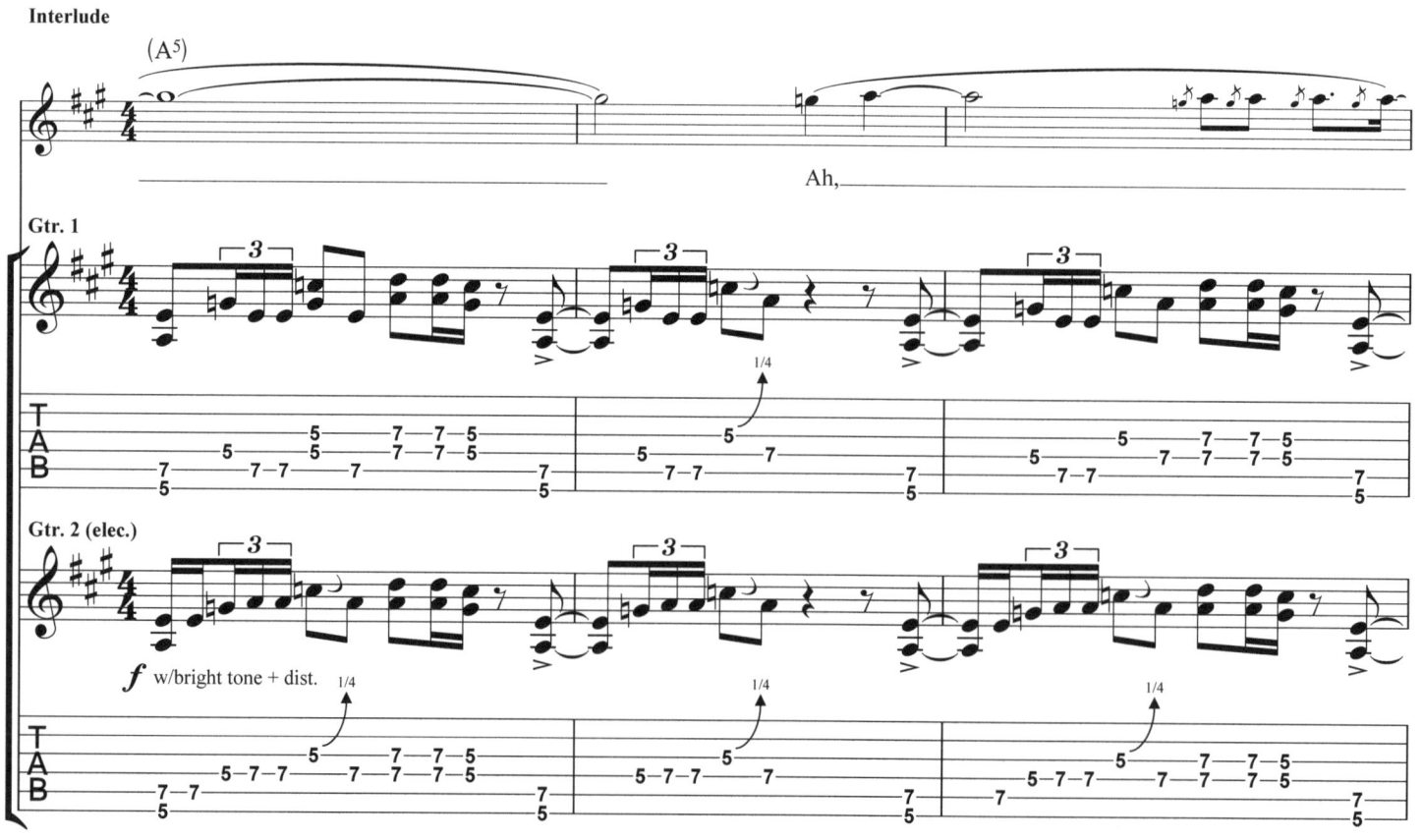

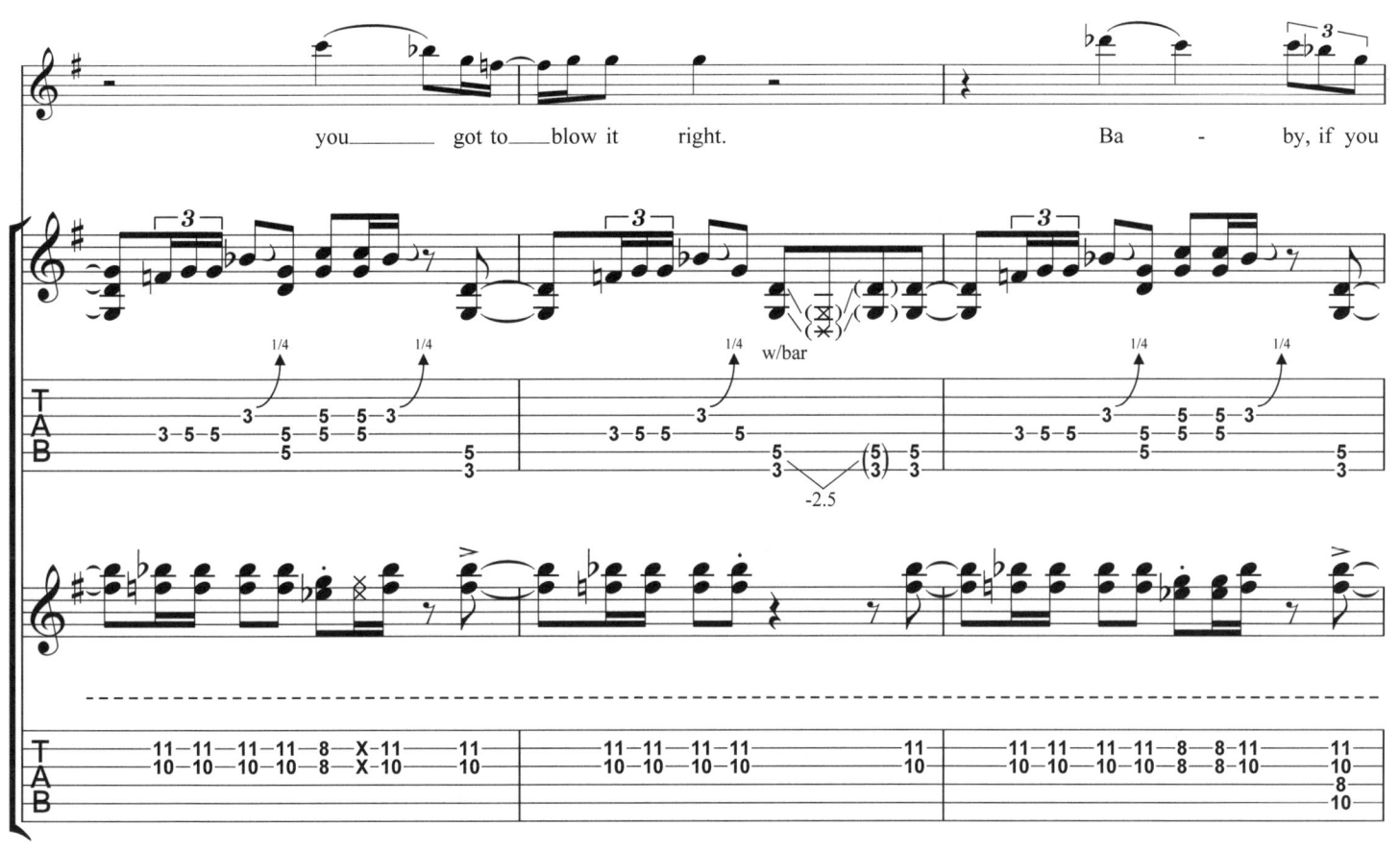

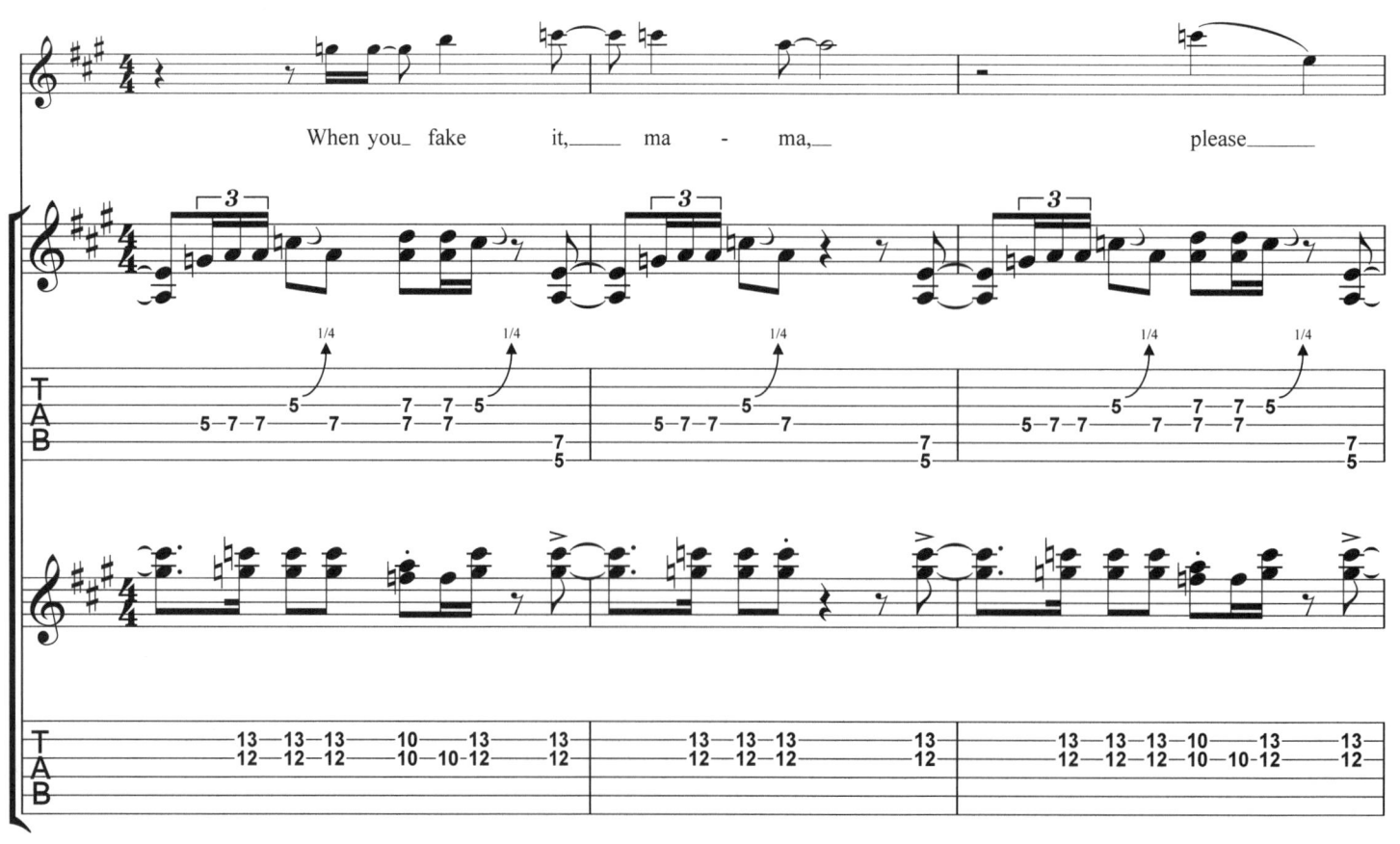

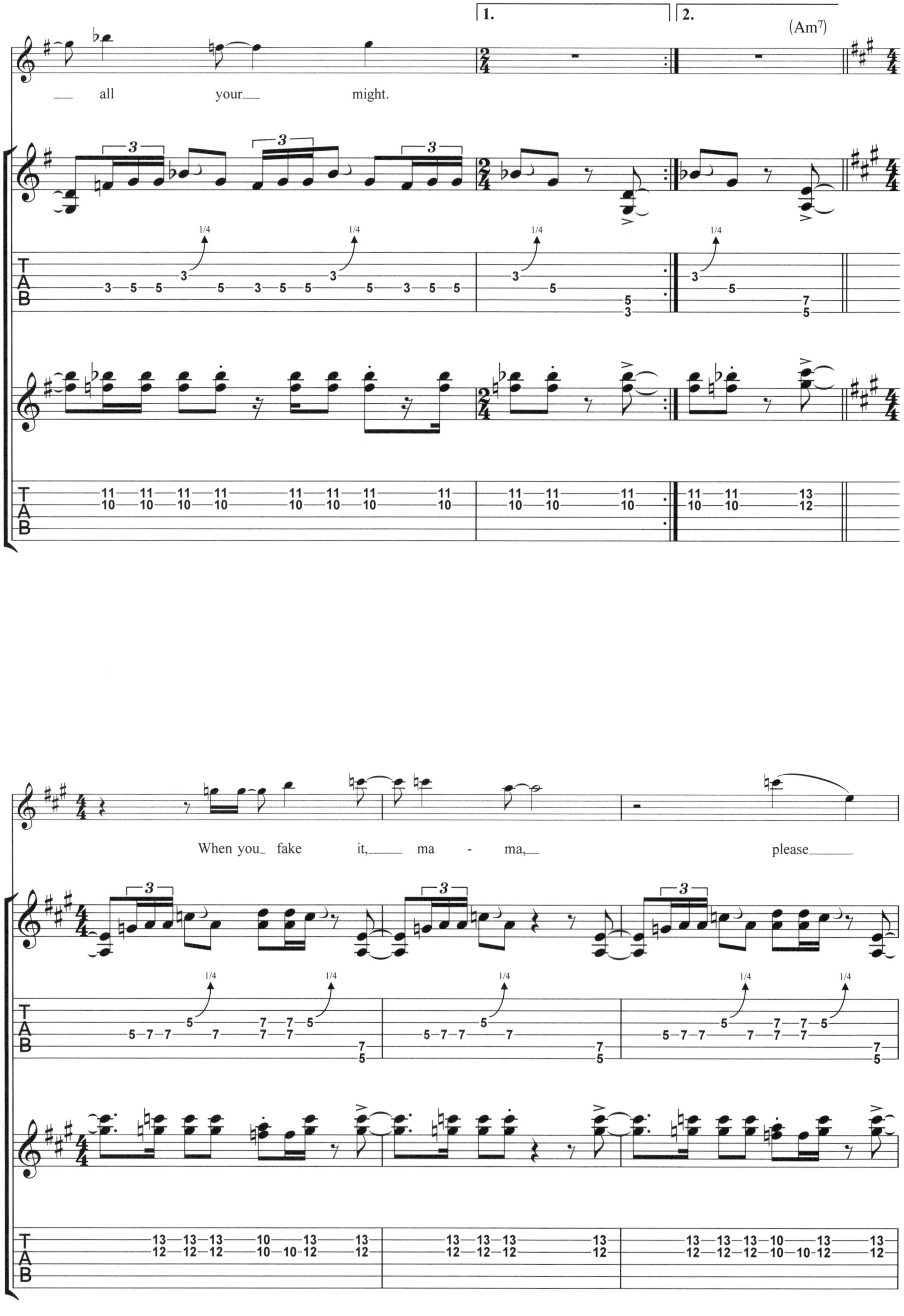
1.
2.
(Am7)
— all your— might.
When you fake it, — ma - ma, — please —

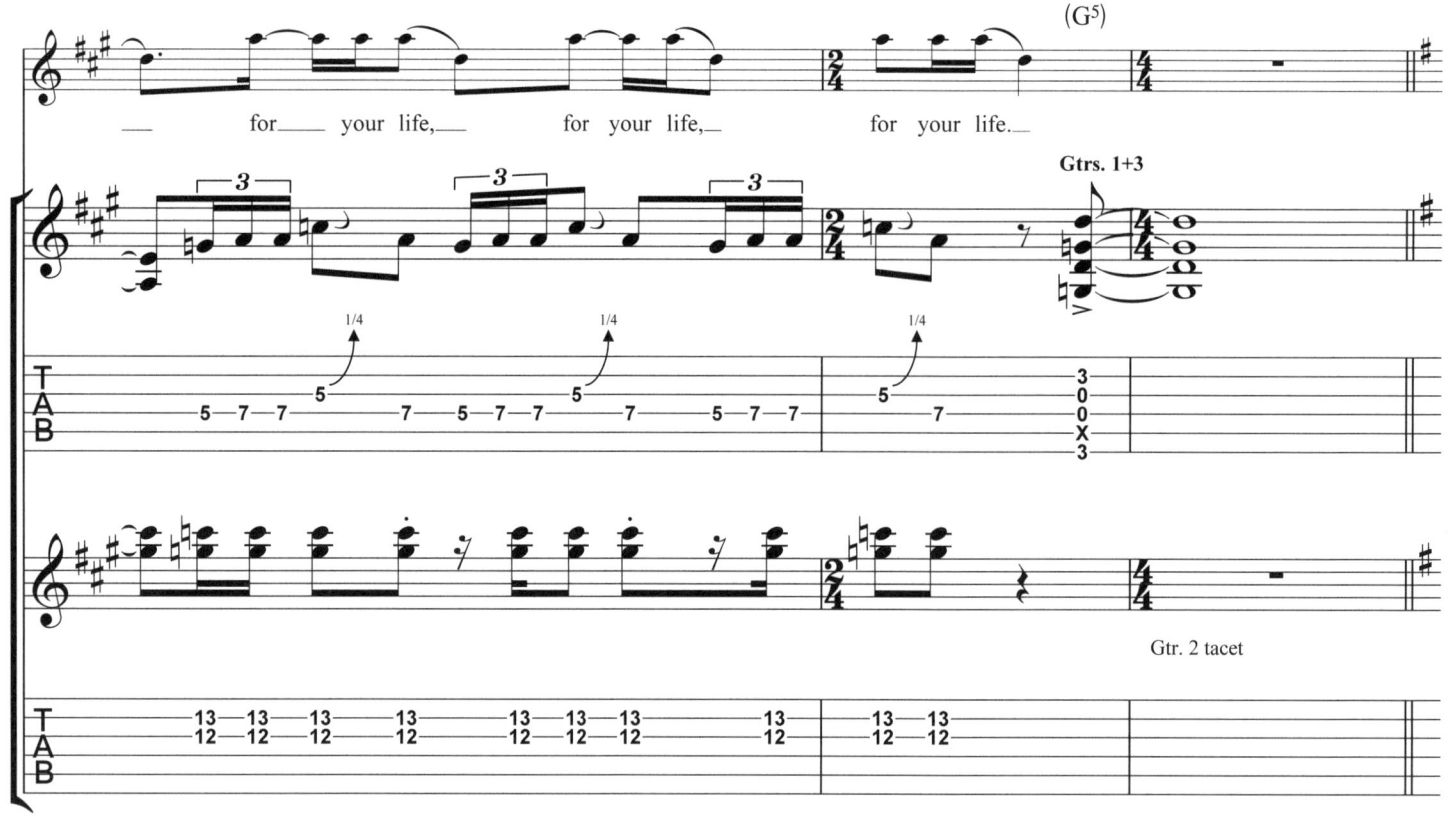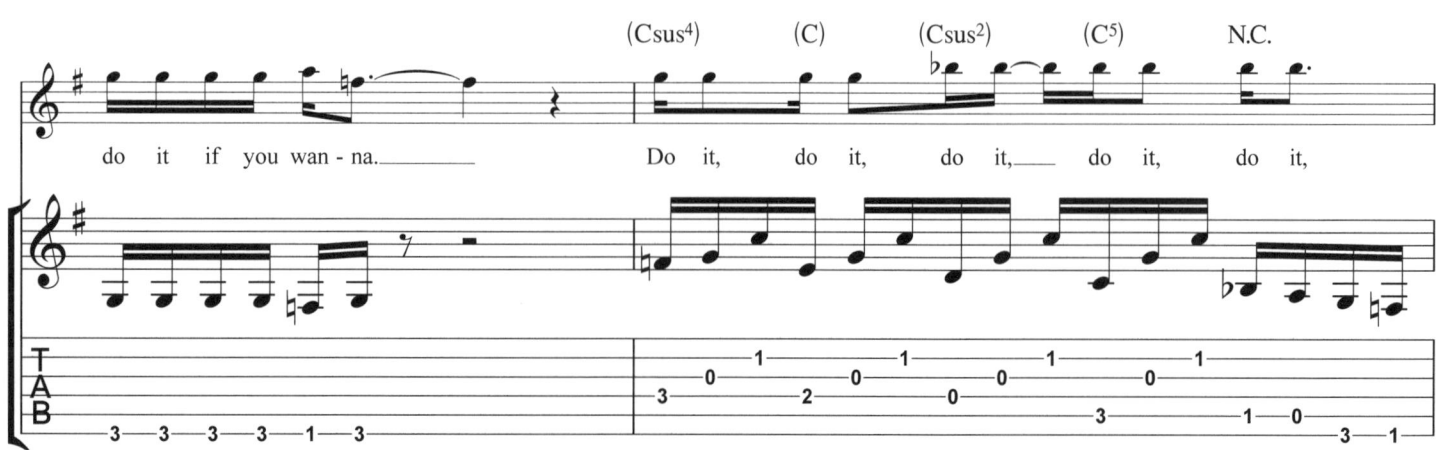

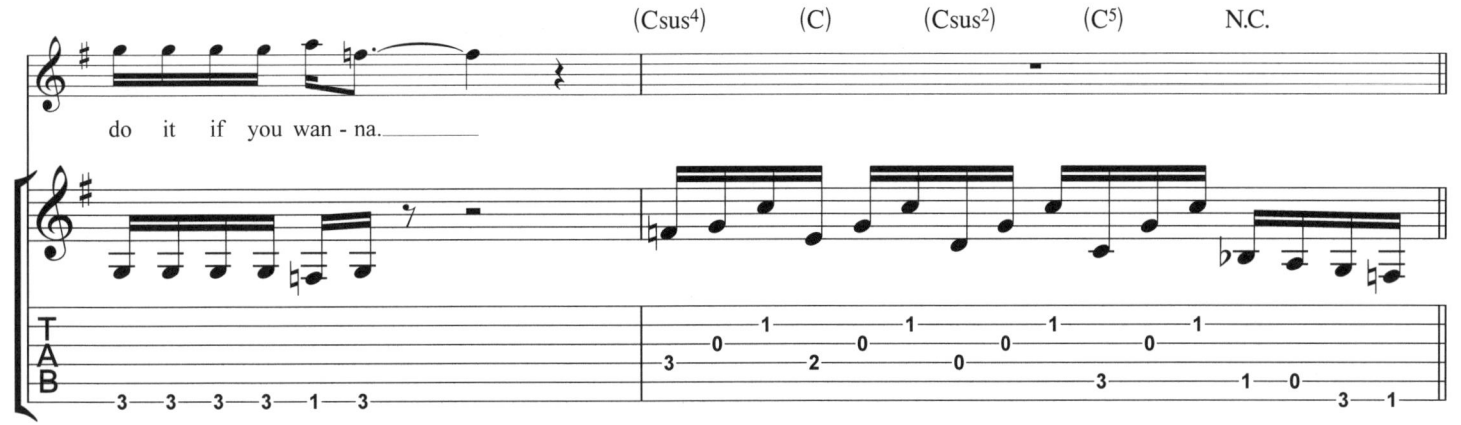
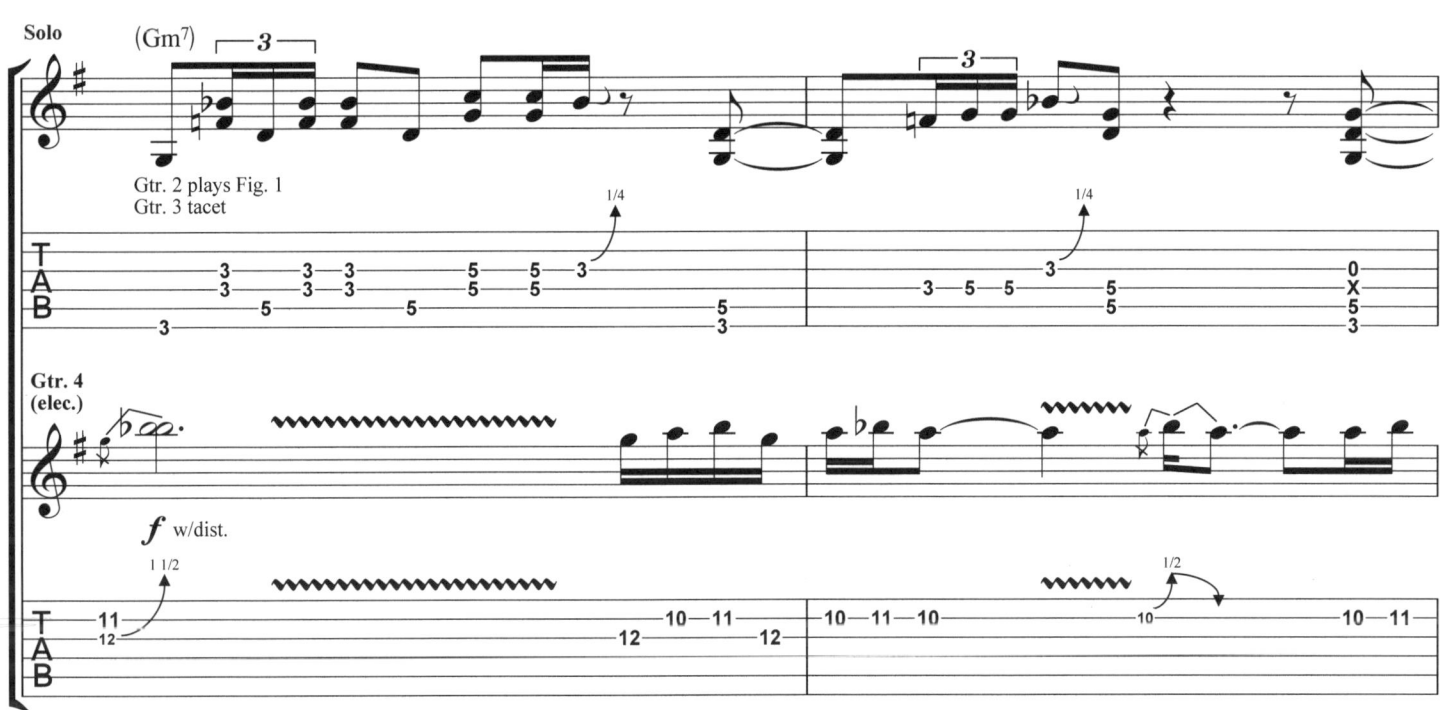

61

*B string gets caught under ring finger

62

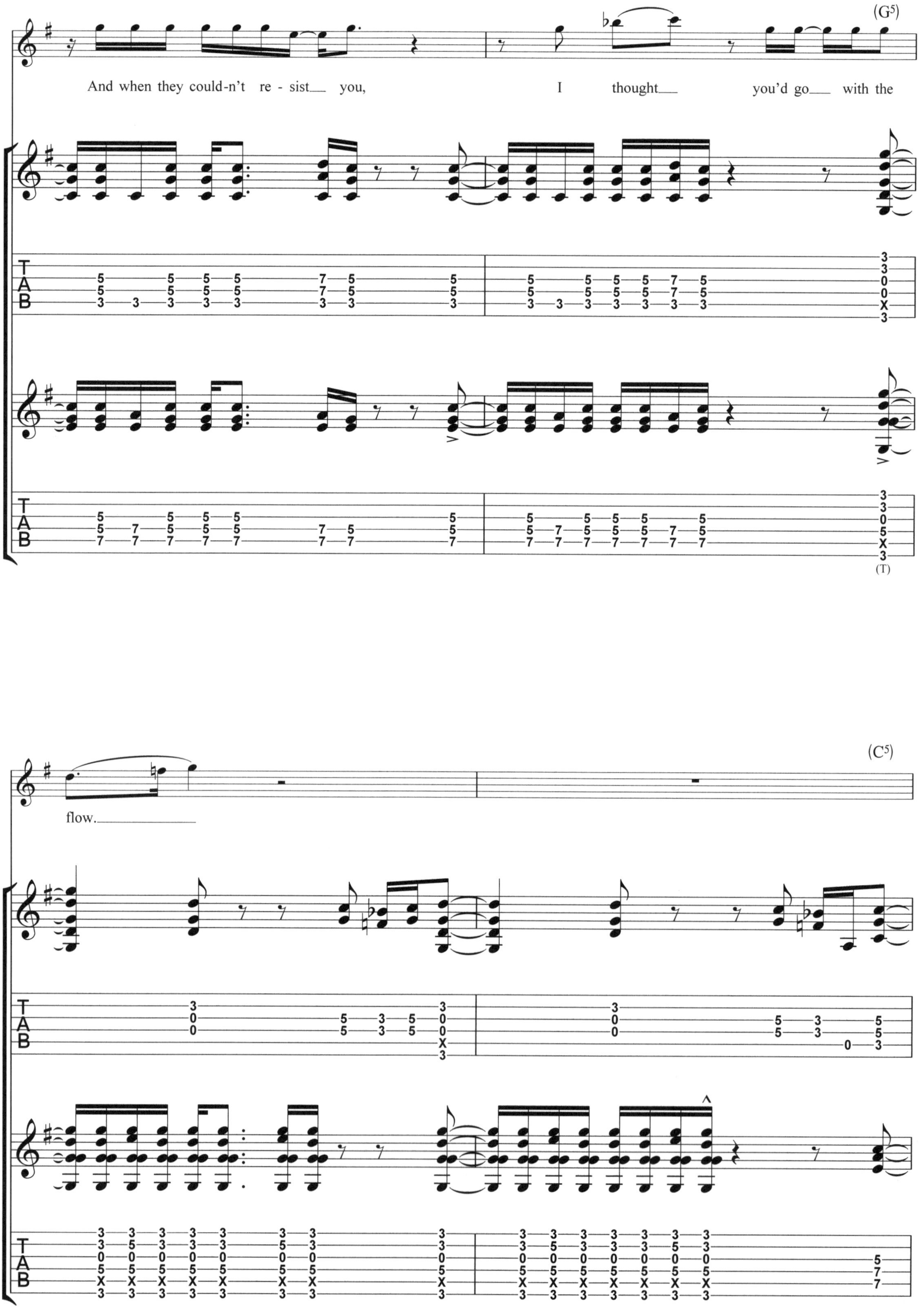
(G5)
And when they could-n't re - sist__ you,
I thought__ you'd go__ with the
(T)
(C5)
flow.

And now your stage is emp-ty, pull down the cur-tain, ba-by, please, fold up your show.

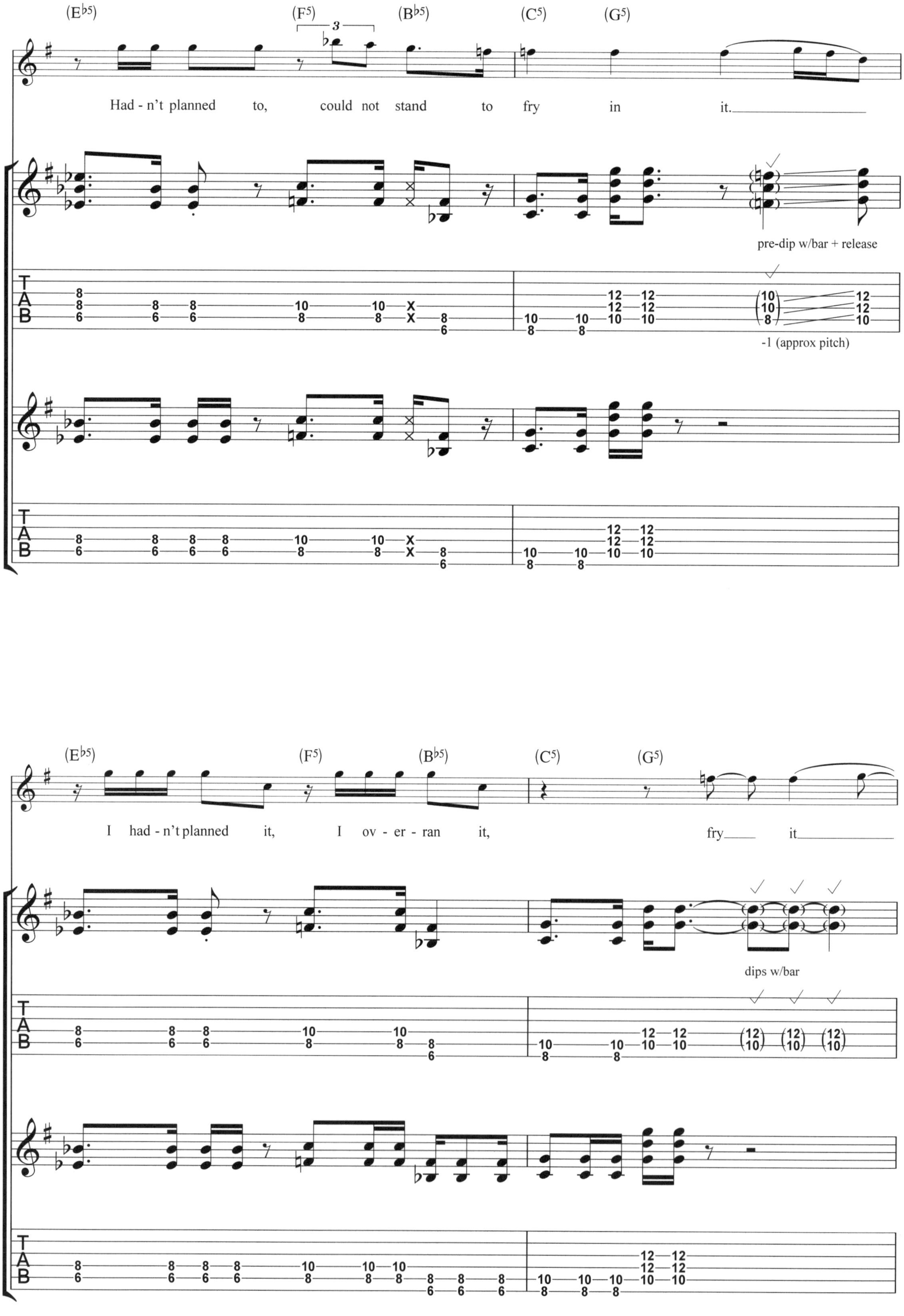
(E♭5) (F5) (B♭5) (C5) (G5)
Had - n't planned to, could not stand to fry in it.
pre-dip w/bar + release
-1 (approx pitch)
(E♭5) (F5) (B♭5) (C5) (G5)
I had - n't planned it, I ov - er - ran it, fry it
dips w/bar

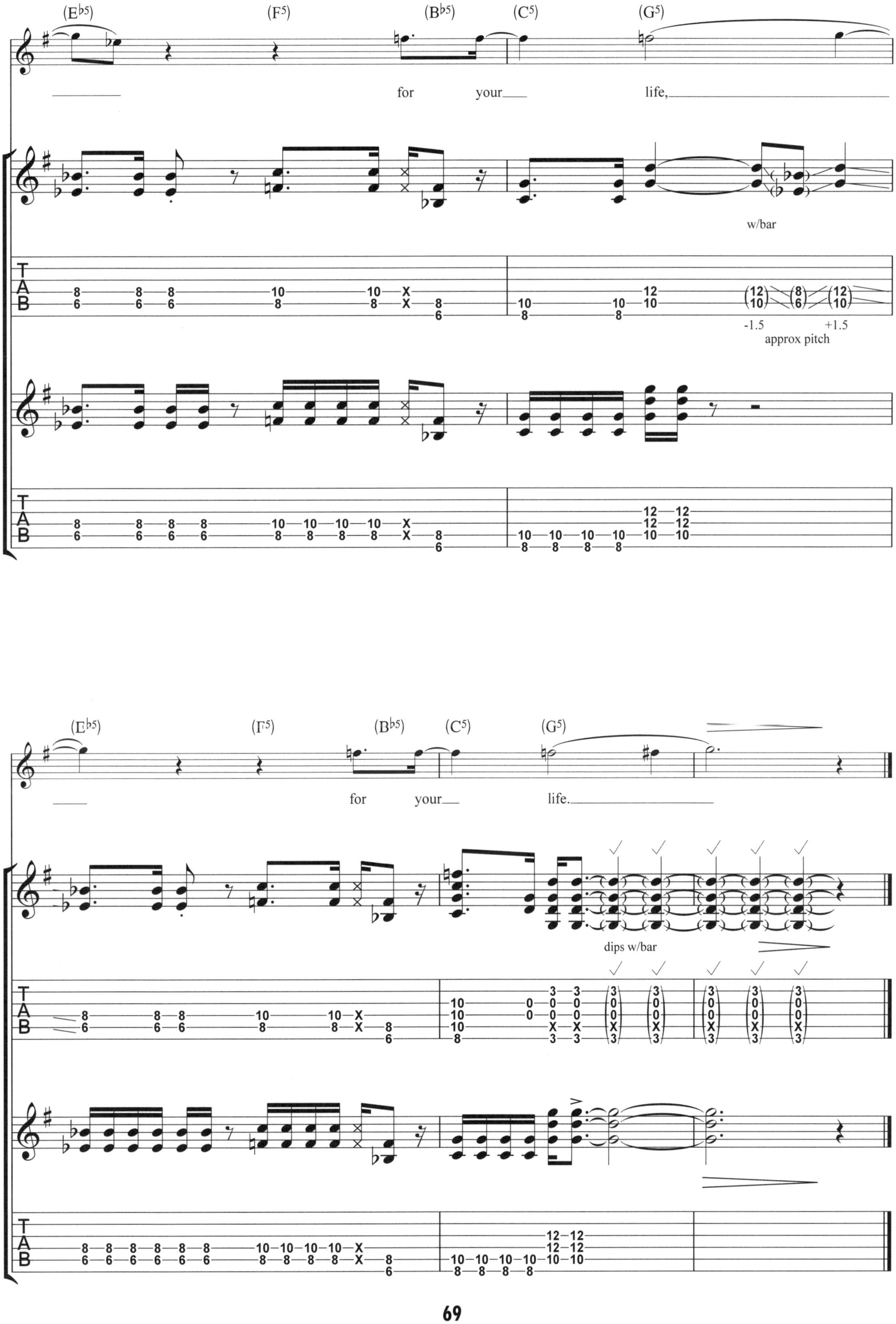
(E♭5) (F5) (B♭5) (C5) (G5)
for your life,
w/bar
-1.5 +1.5
approx pitch
(E♭5) (F5) (B♭5) (C5) (G5)
for your life.
dips w/bar

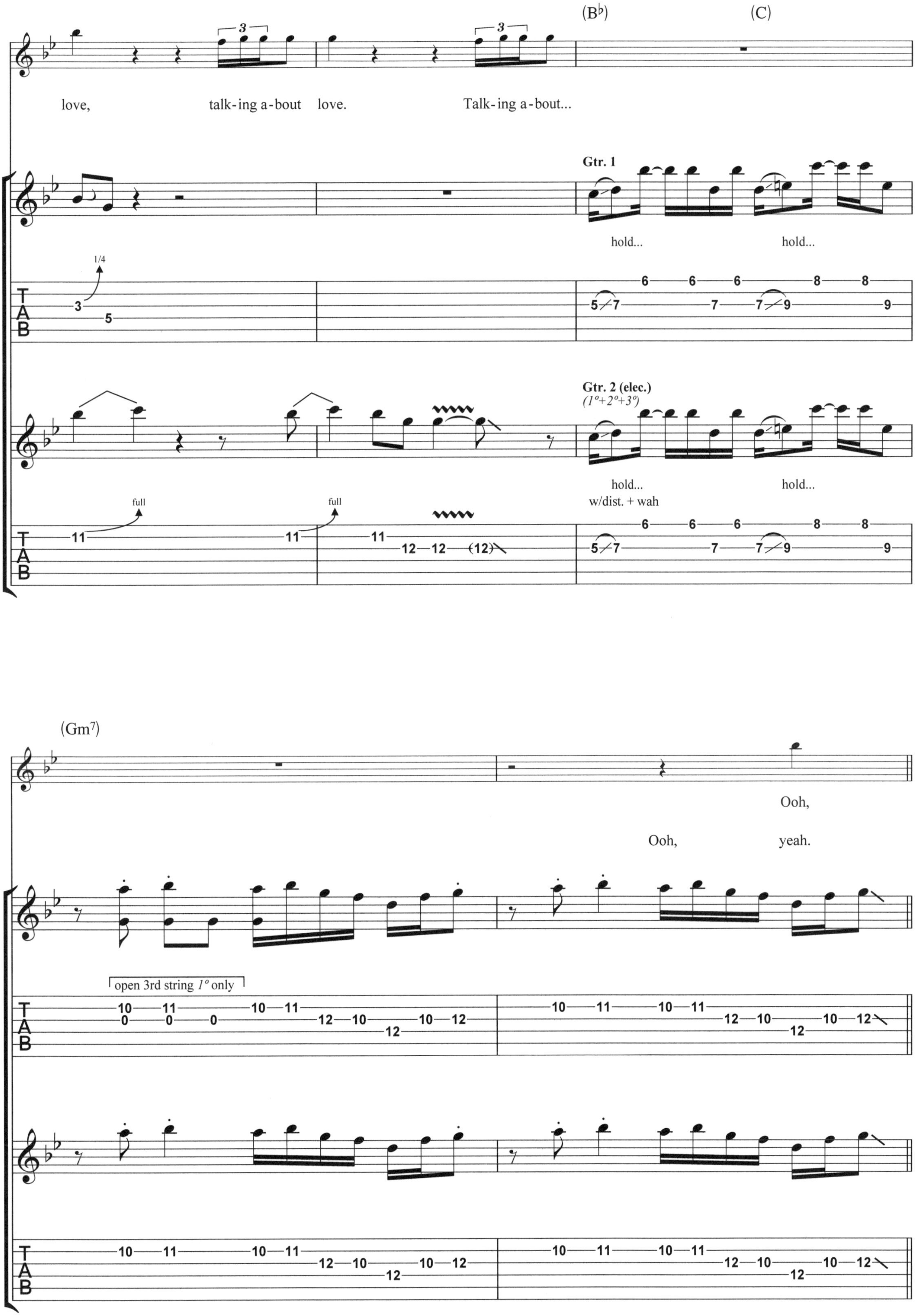
(B♭)
(C)
love,
talk-ing a-bout
love.
Talk-ing a-bout...
Gtr. 1
hold...
hold...
1/4
Gtr. 2 (elec.)
(1º+2º+3º)
hold...
hold...
w/dist. + wah
full
full
(Gm7)
Ooh,
Ooh,
yeah.
open 3rd string 1º only

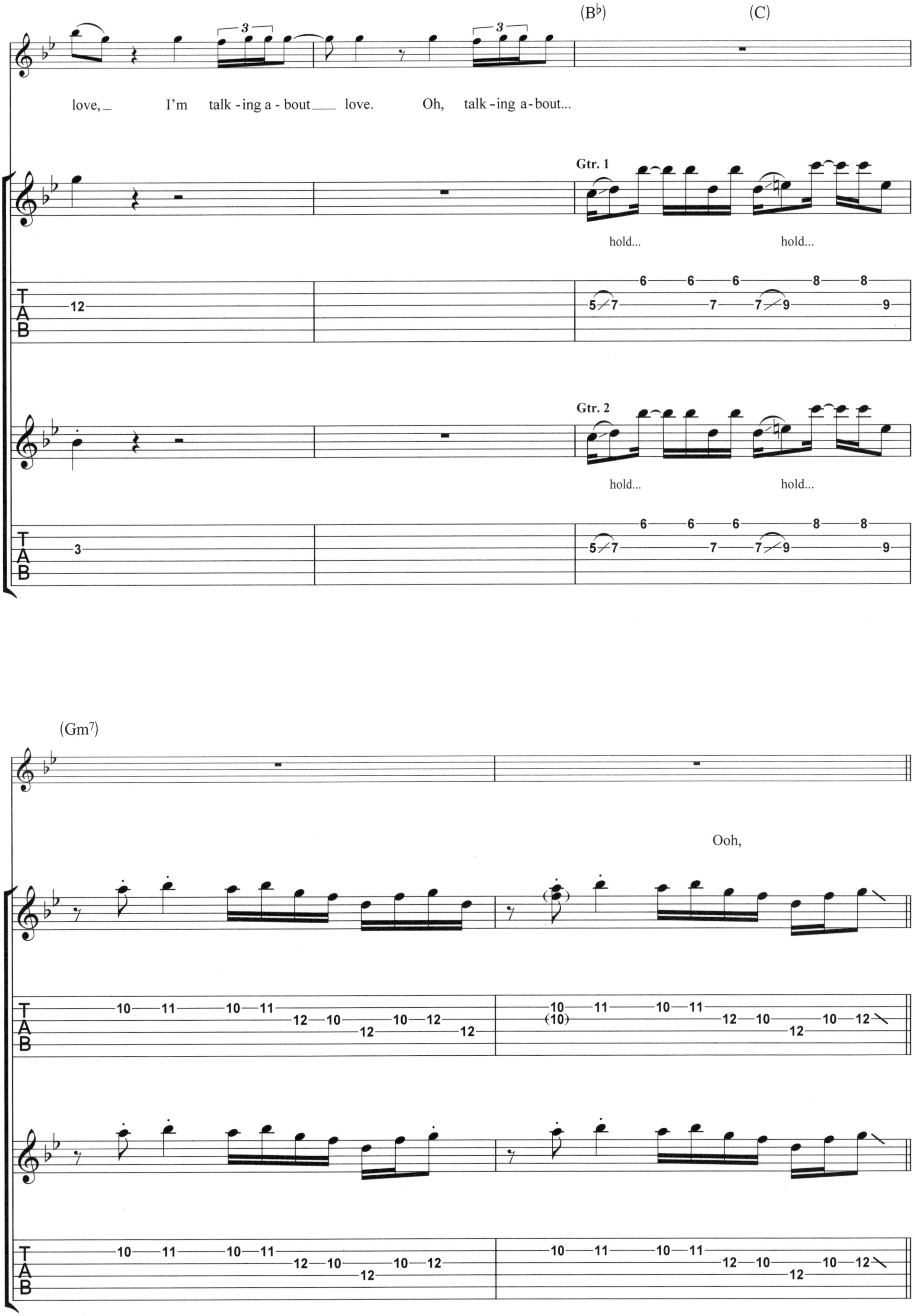
(B♭)
(C)
love, I'm talk-ing a-bout love. Oh, talk-ing a-bout...
Gtr. 1
hold...
hold...
Gtr. 2
hold...
hold...
(Gm7)
Ooh,

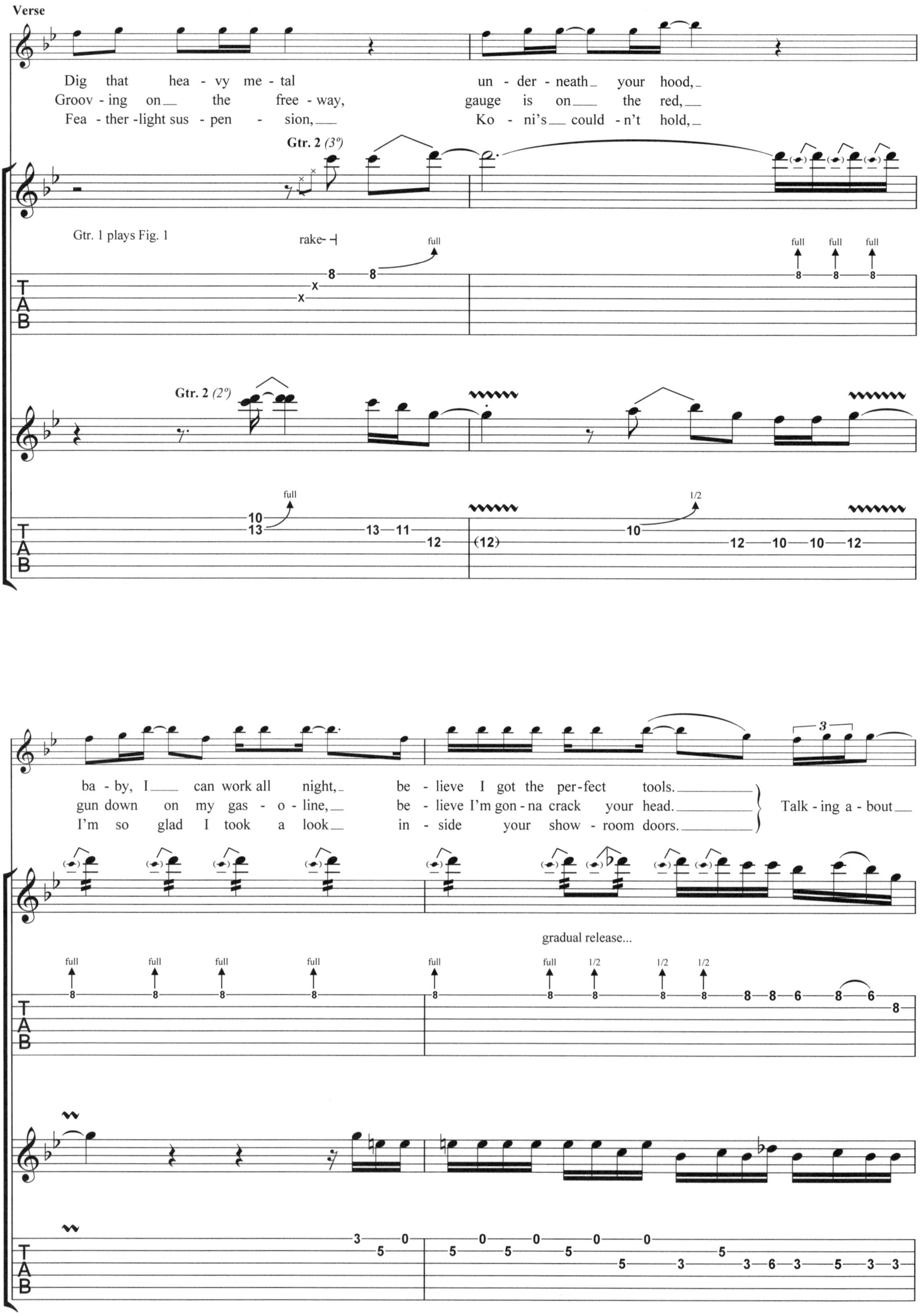
Verse
Dig that hea - vy me - tal un - der - neath your hood,
Groov - ing on the free - way, gauge is on the red,
Fea - ther -light sus - pen - sion, Ko - ni's could - n't hold,
Gtr. 2 (3º)
Gtr. 1 plays Fig. 1
rake
full
Gtr. 2 (2º)
1/2
ba - by, I can work all night, be - lieve I got the per-fect tools.
gun down on my gas - o - line, be - lieve I'm gon - na crack your head.
I'm so glad I took a look in - side your show - room doors.
Talk - ing a - bout
gradual release...

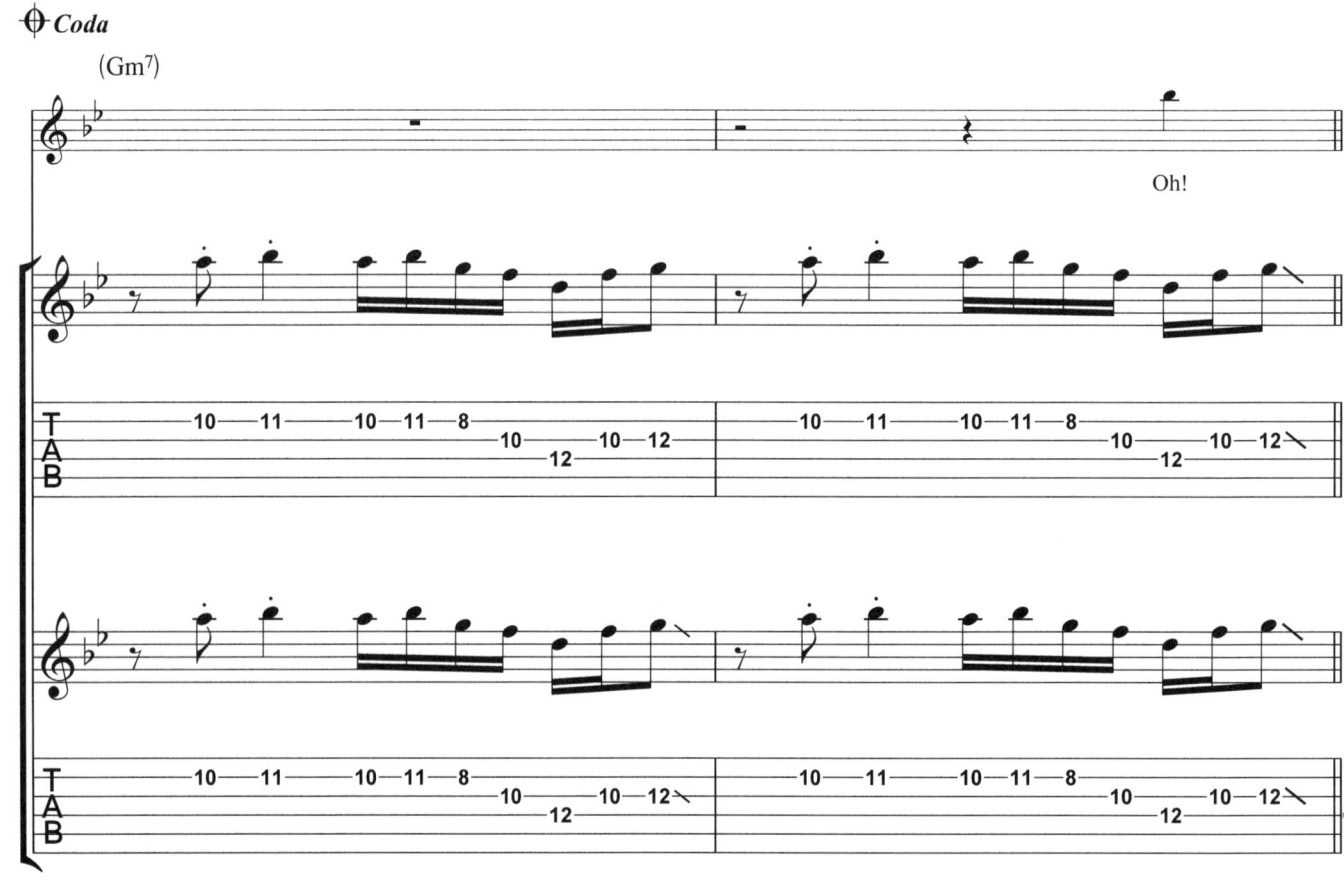

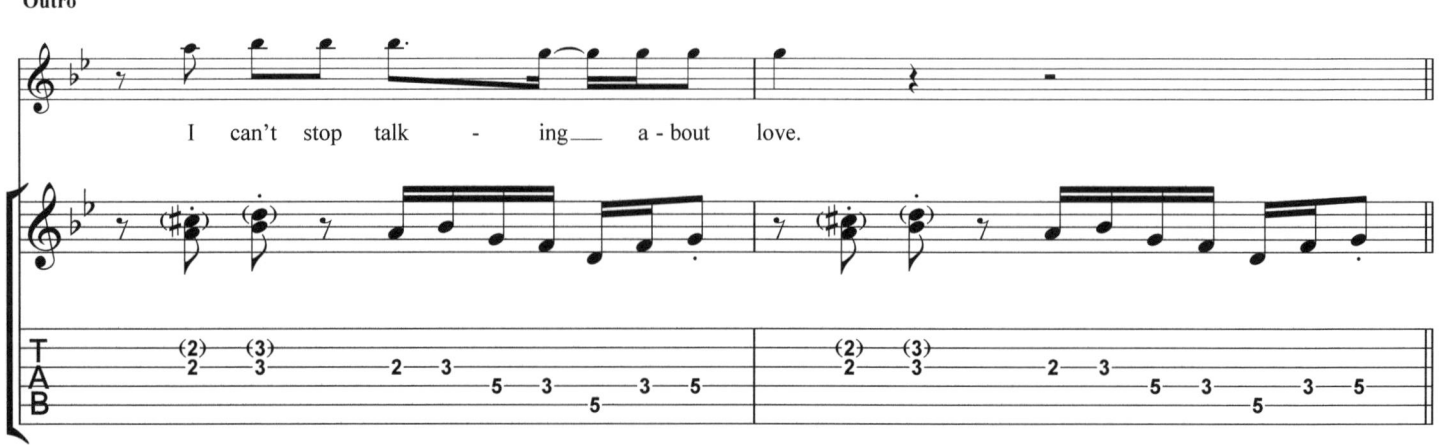

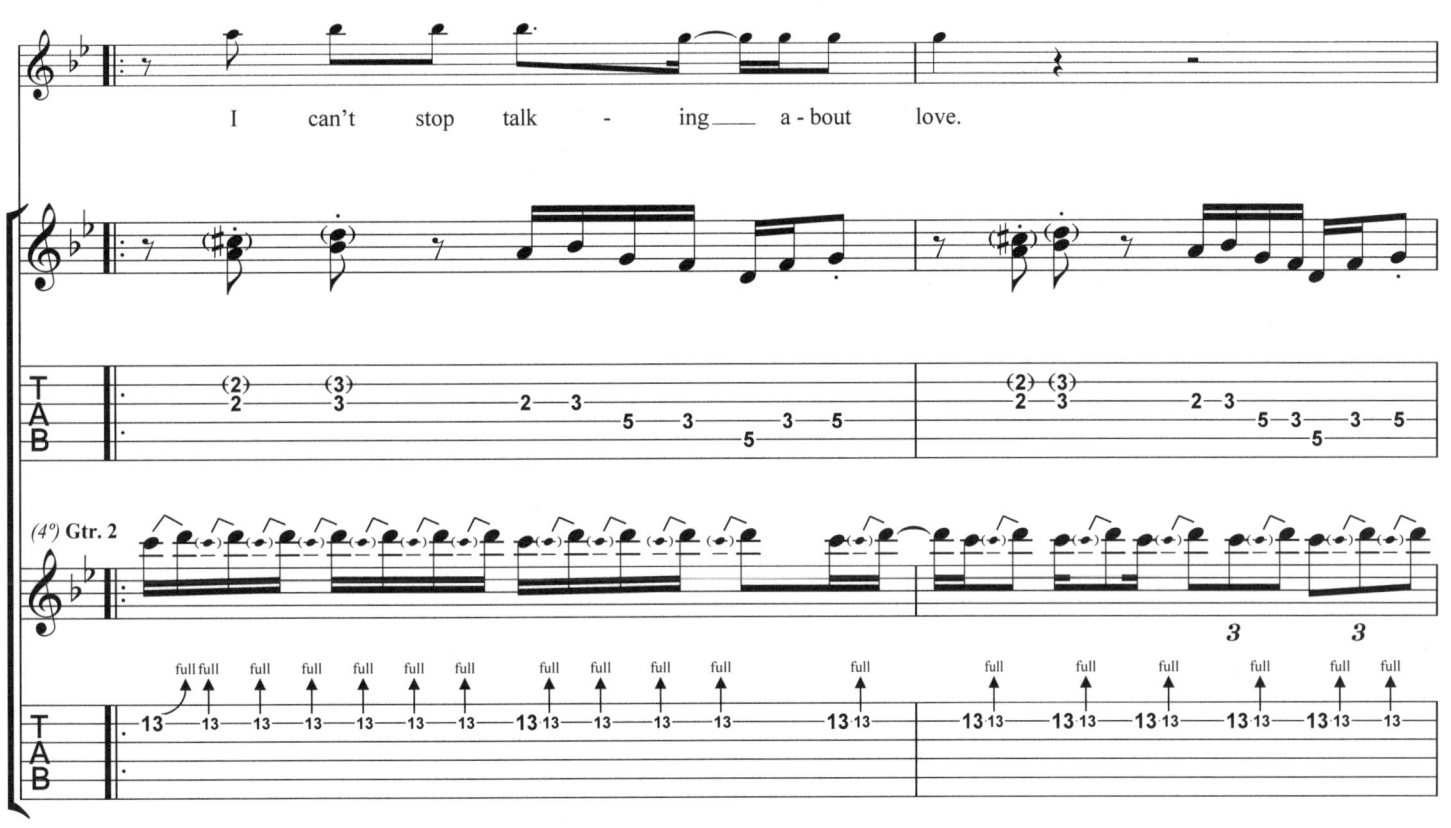

NOBODY'S FAULT BUT MINE

Words & Music by Jimmy Page & Robert Plant

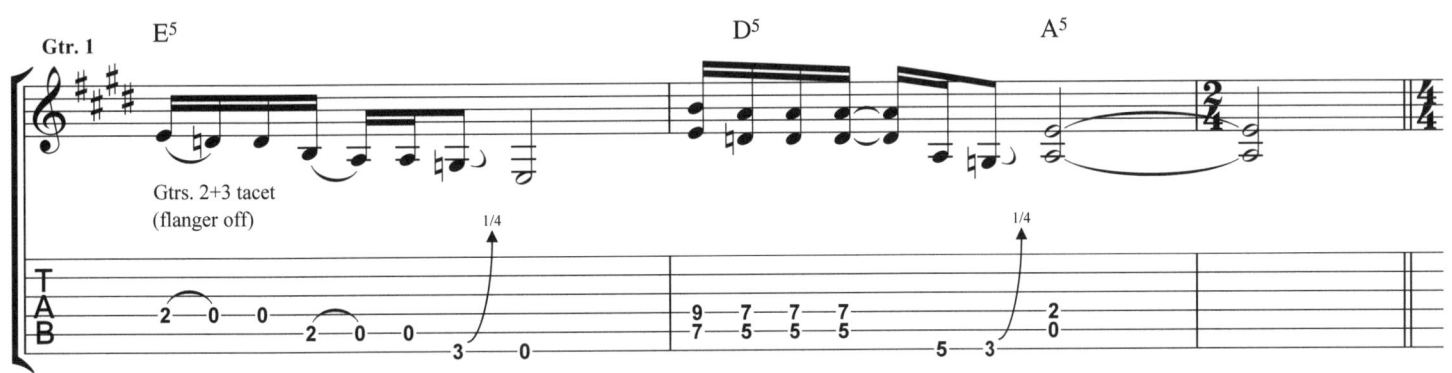
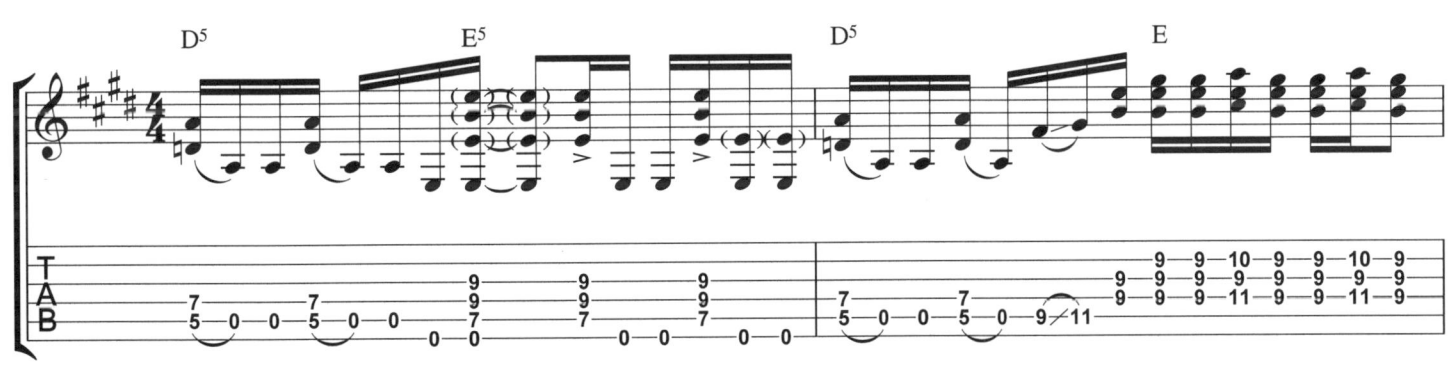

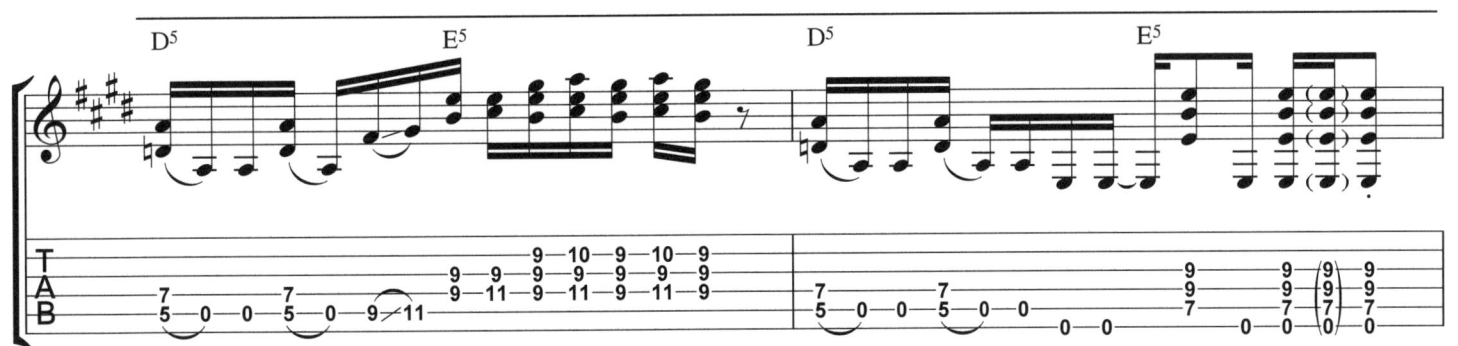
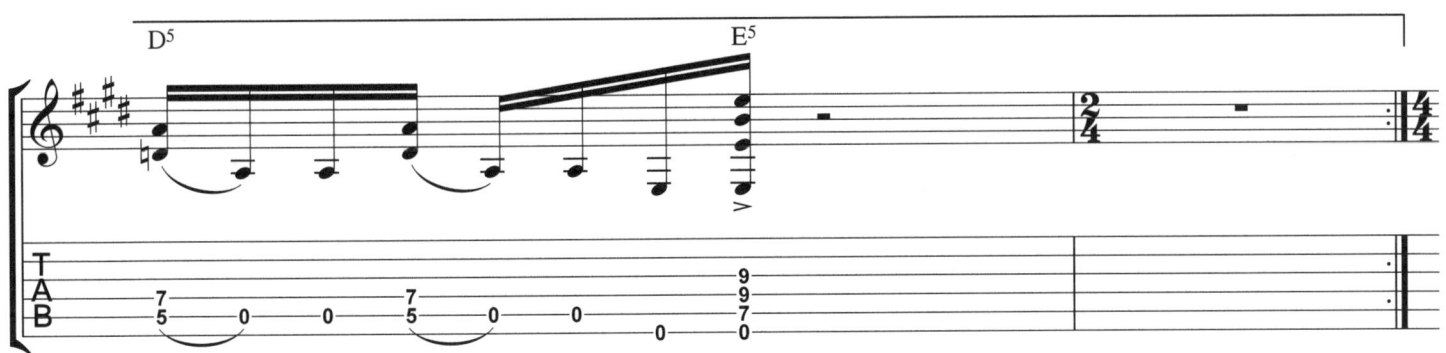
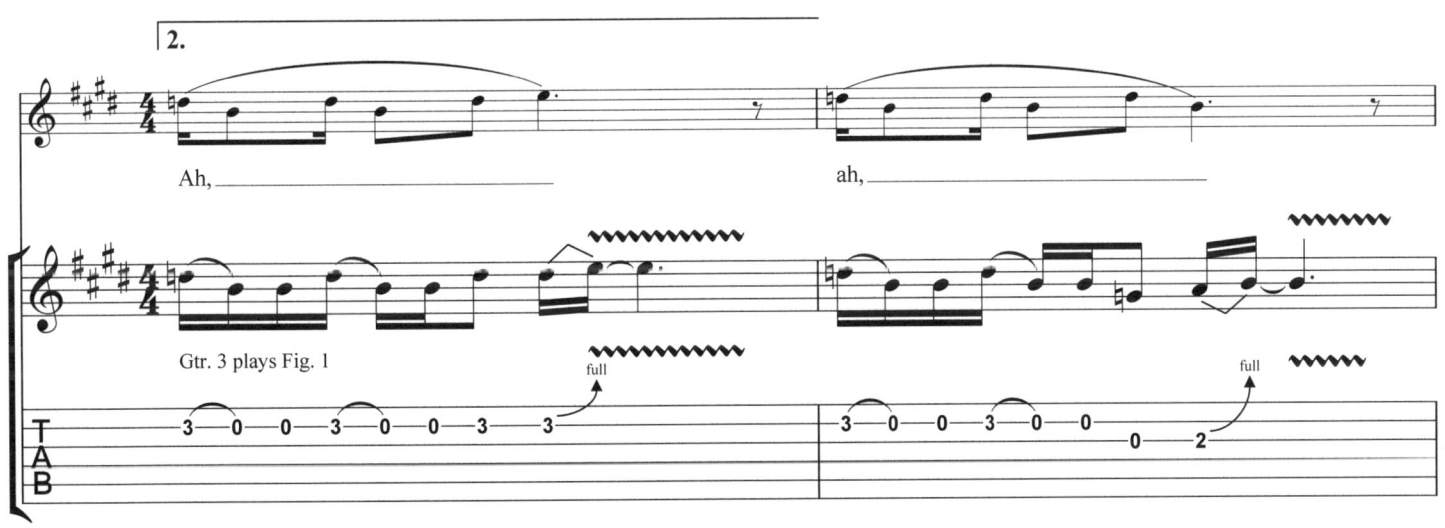

83

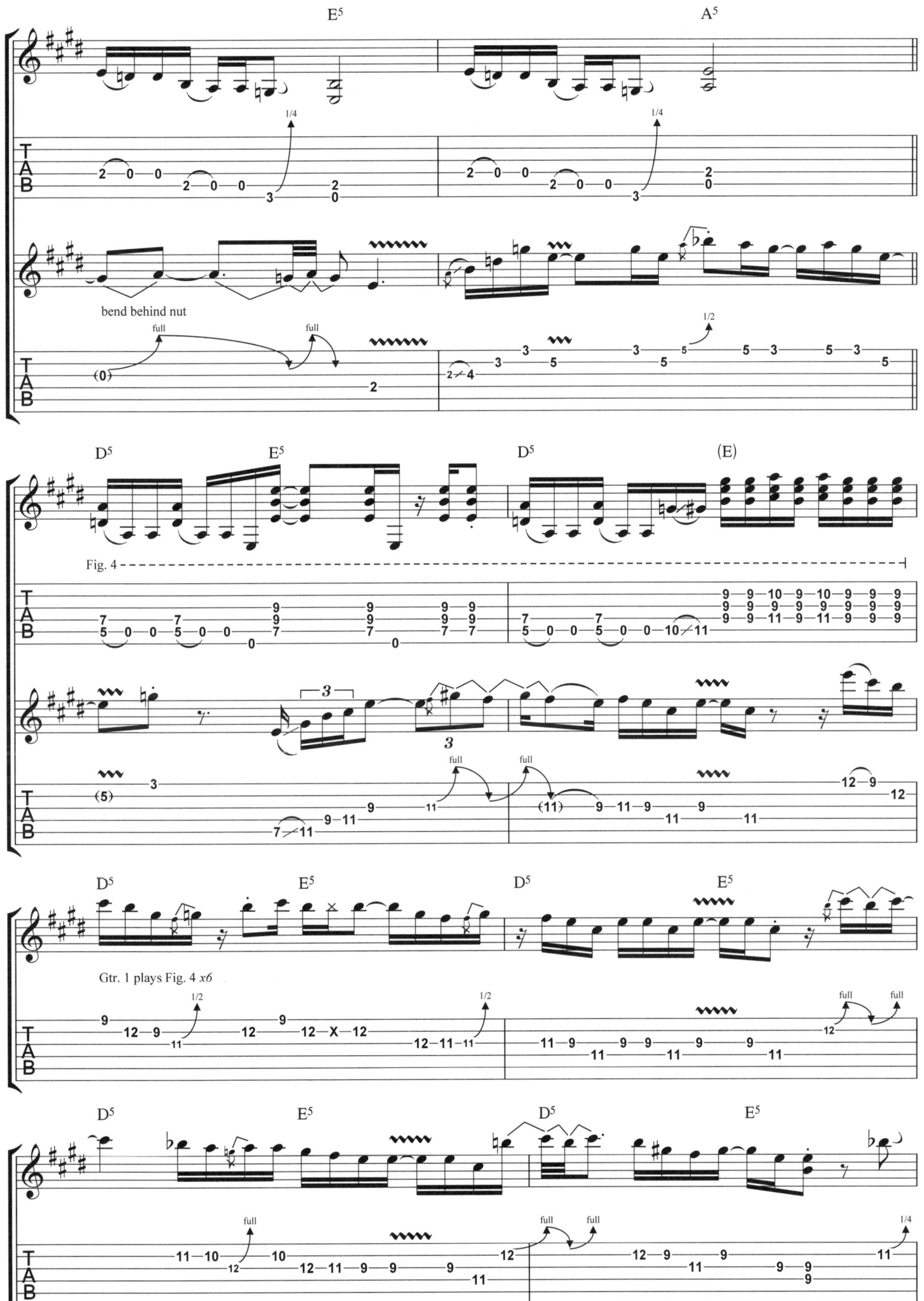

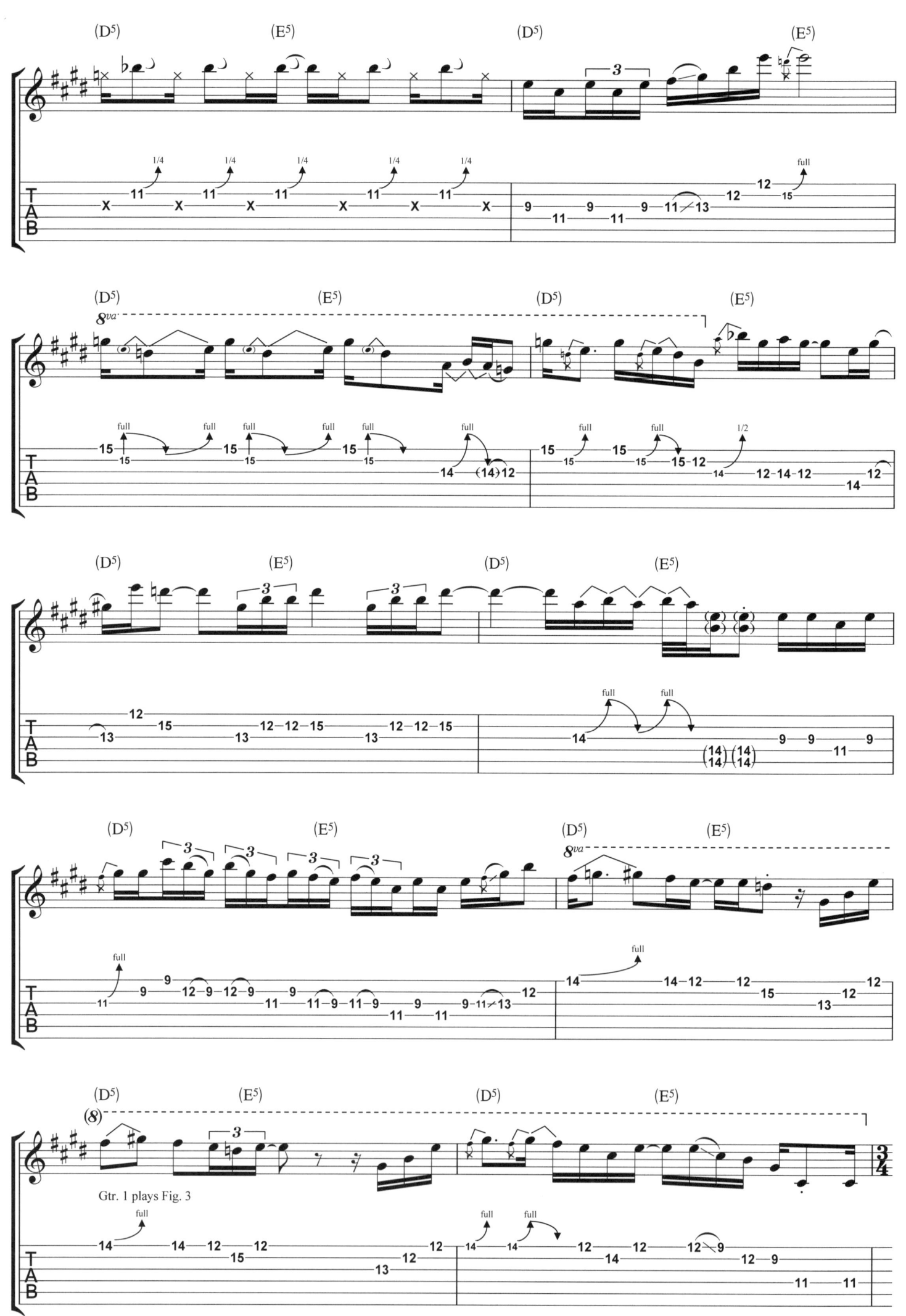

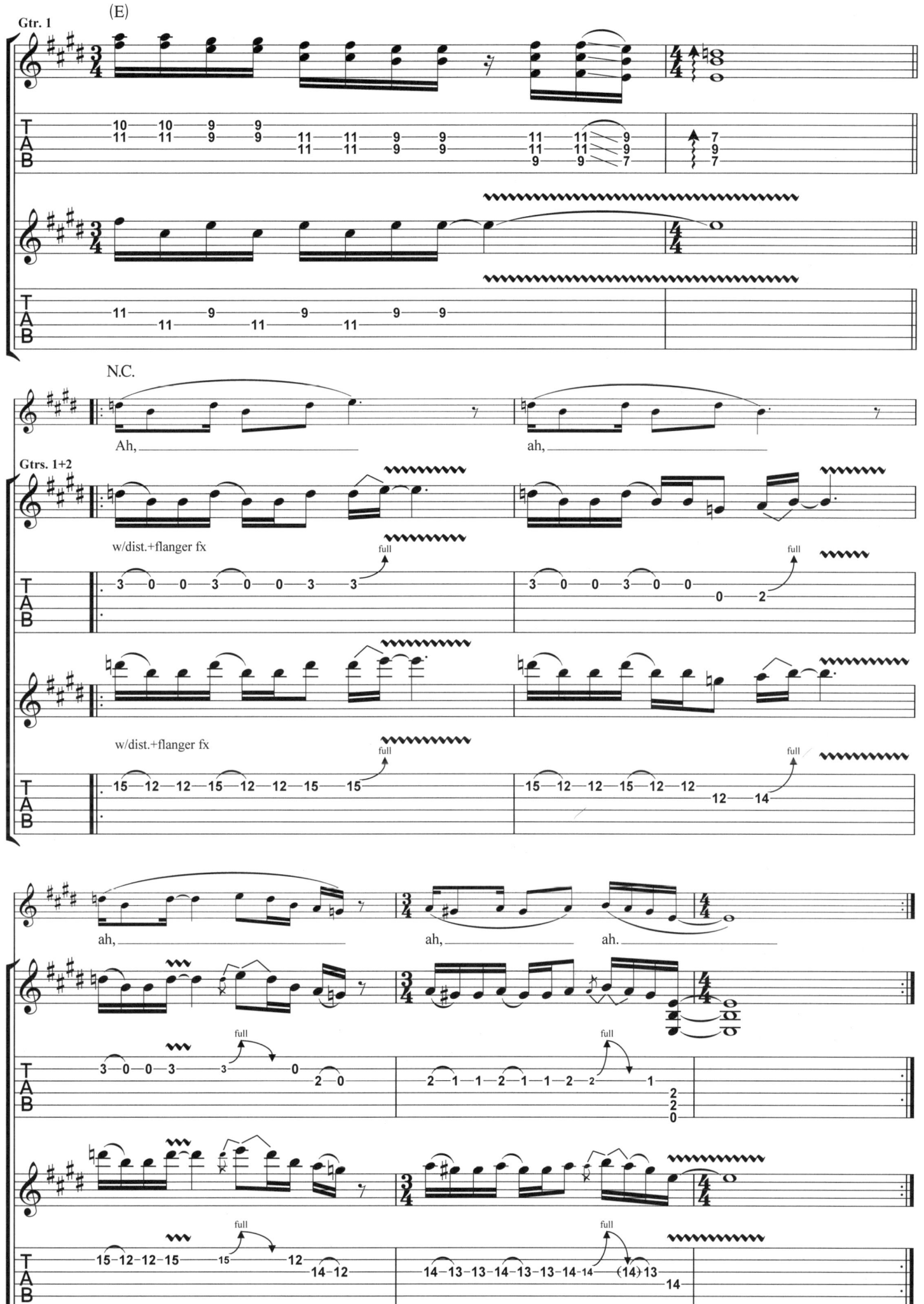

NO QUARTER

Words & Music by Jimmy Page, Robert Plant & John Paul Jones

© Copyright 1973 Succubus Music Limited/Sons Of Einion Limited/Cap Three Limited.
Print Rights Administered by Music Sales Limited.
All Rights Reserved. International Copyright Secured.

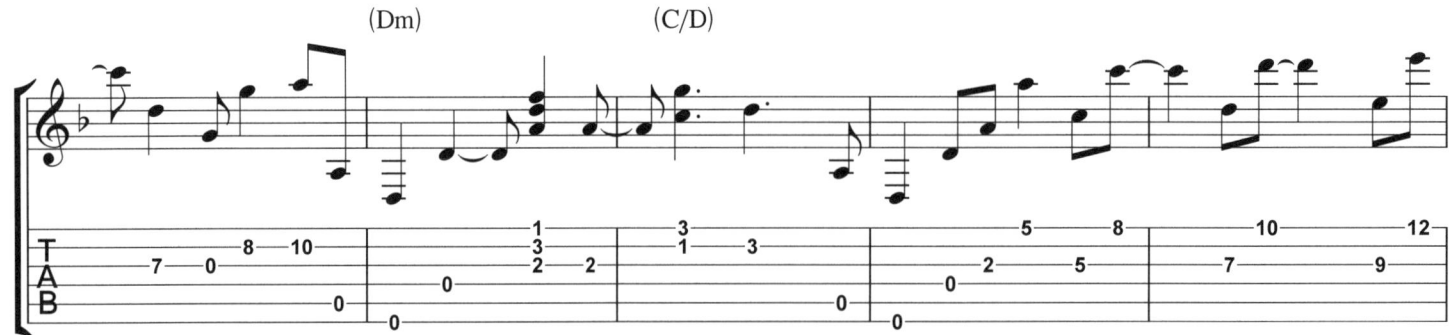
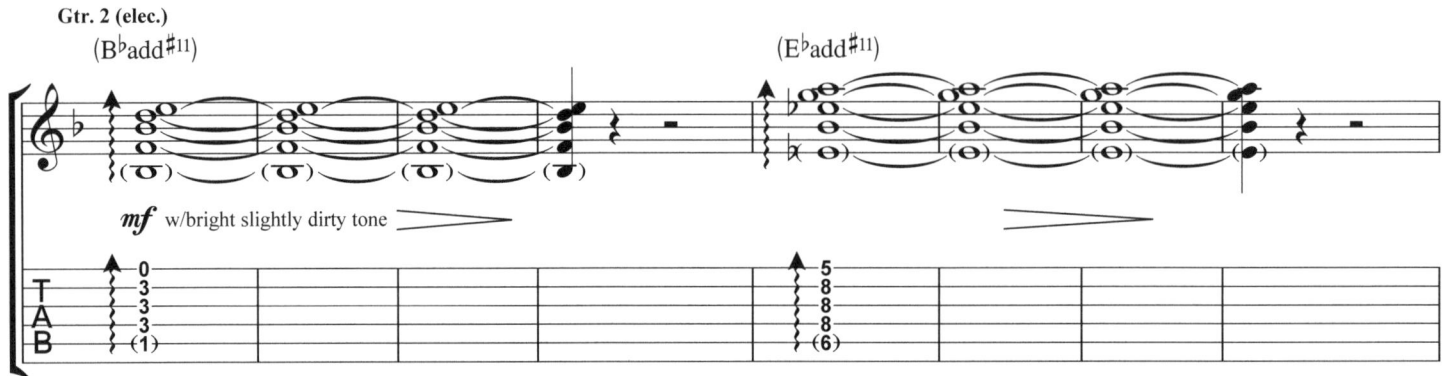
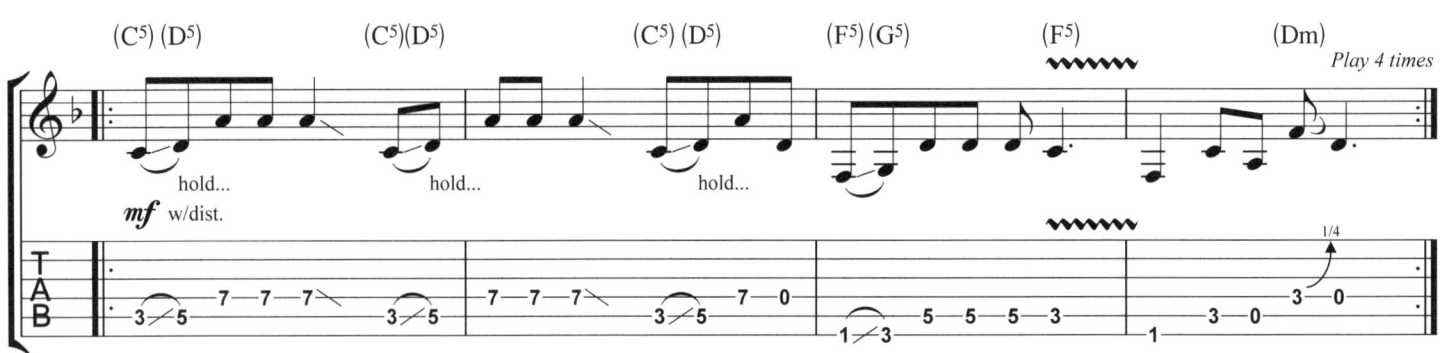
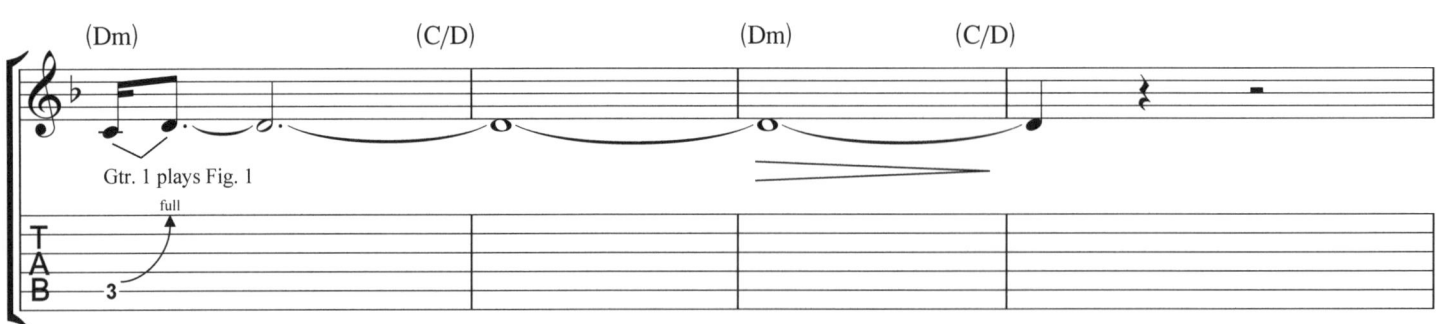
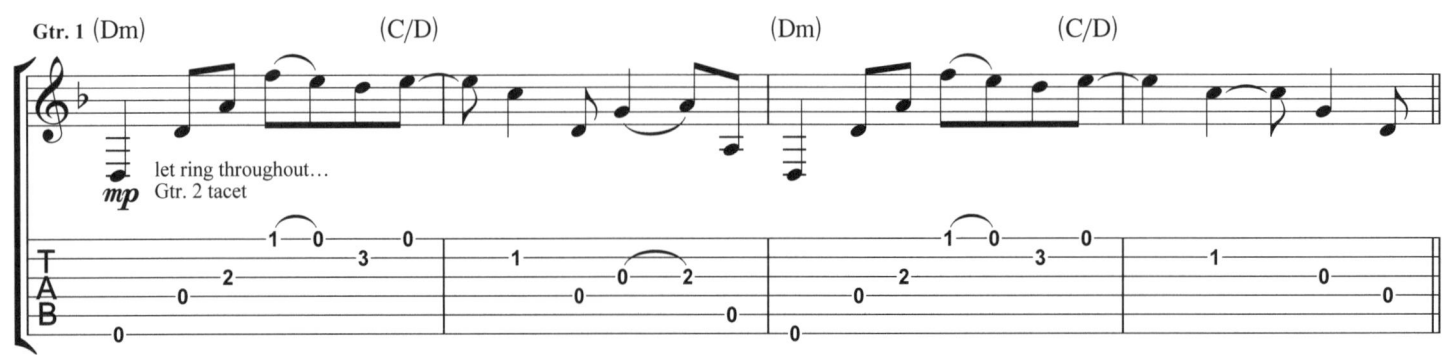

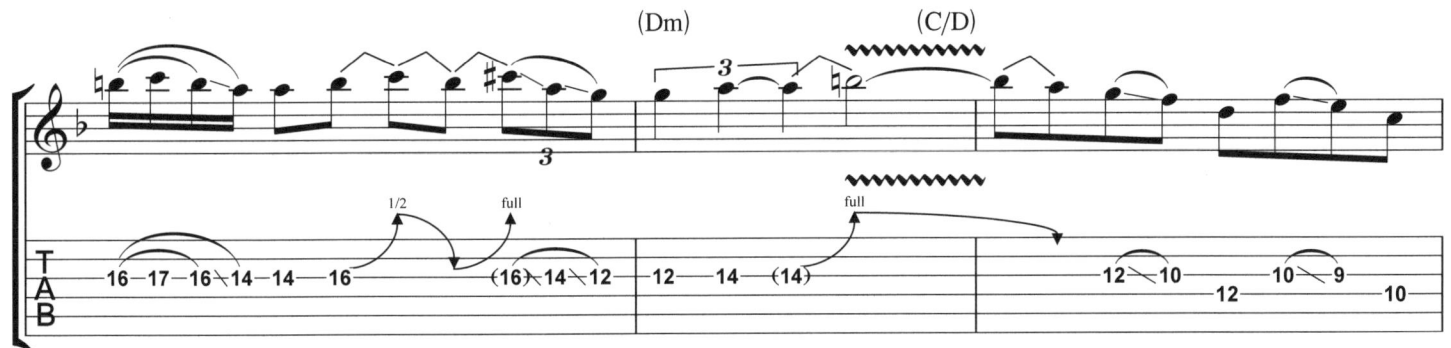
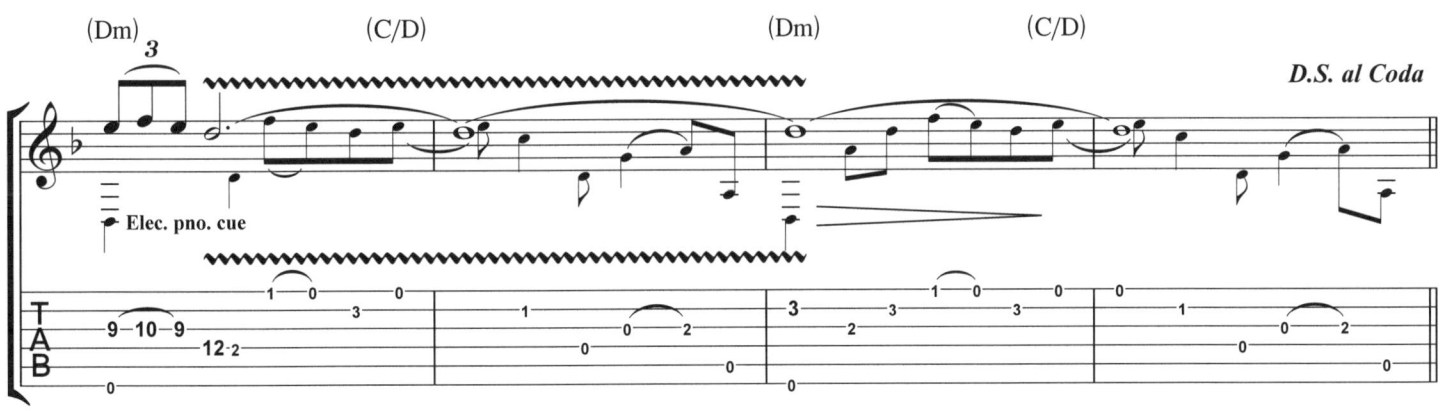

SINCE I'VE BEEN LOVING YOU

Words & Music by Jimmy Page, Robert Plant & John Paul Jones

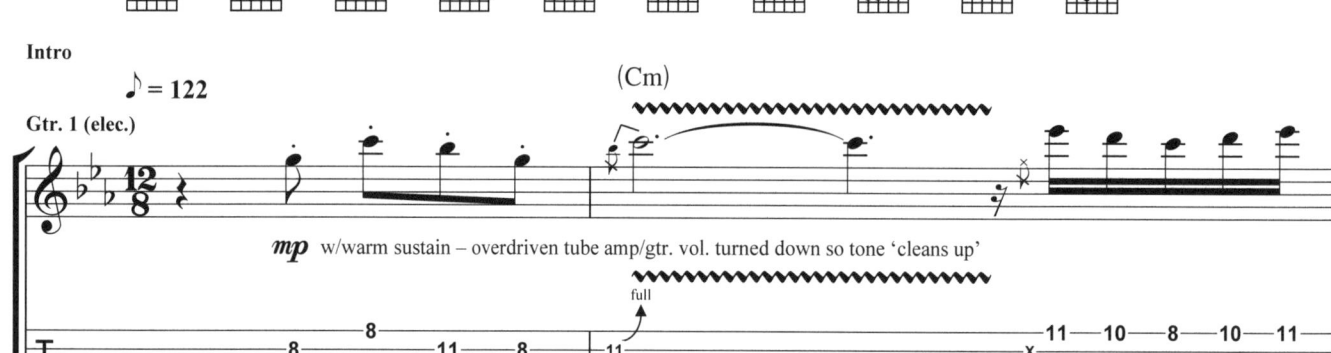
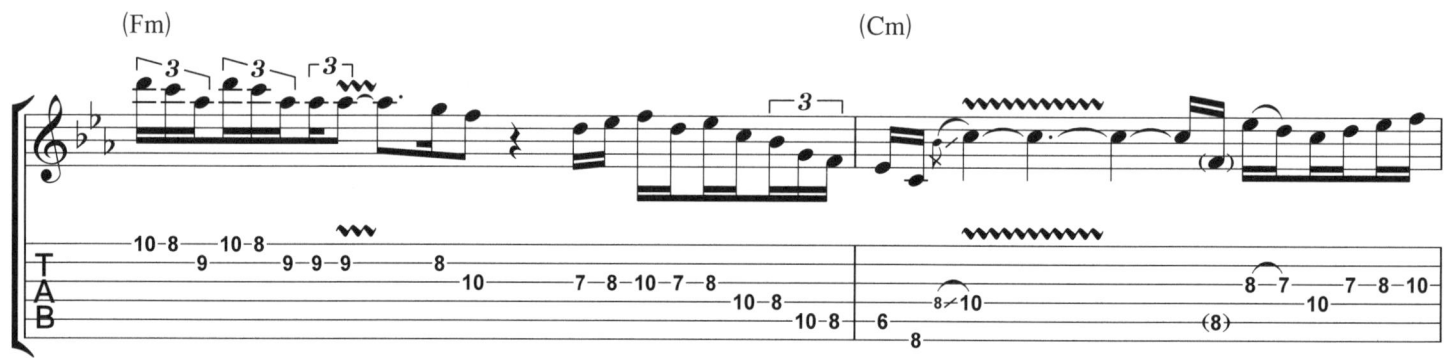
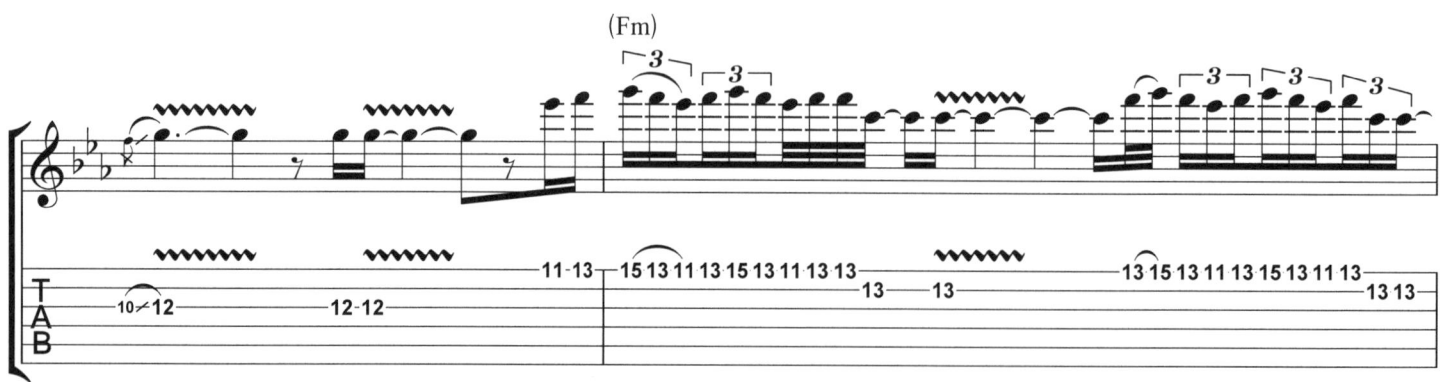
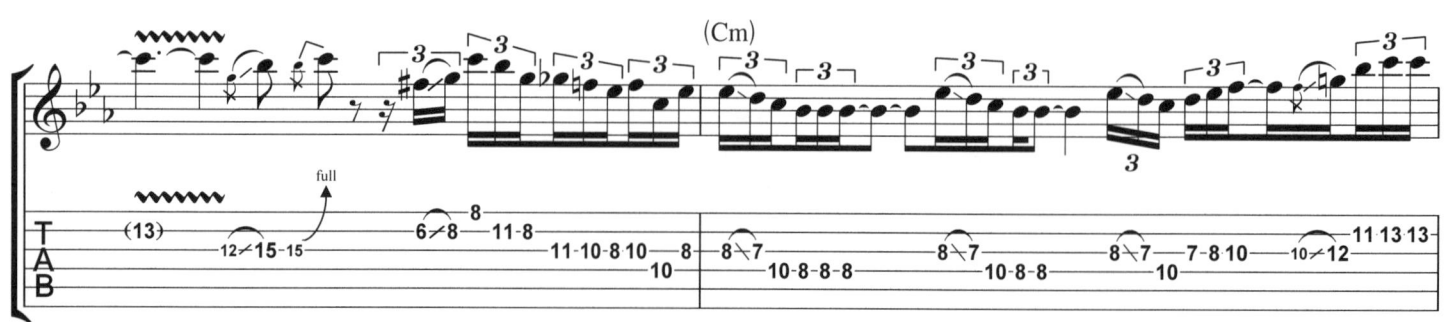

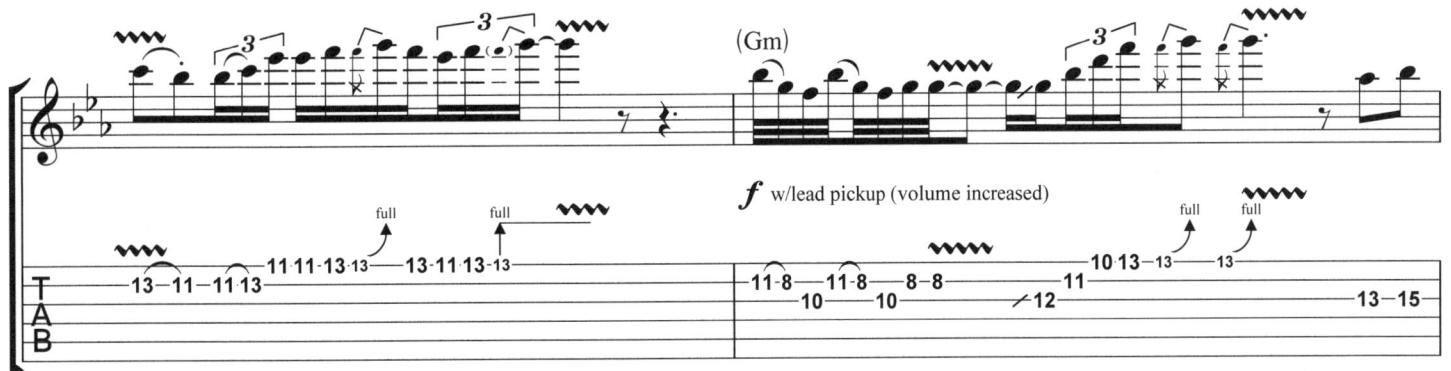
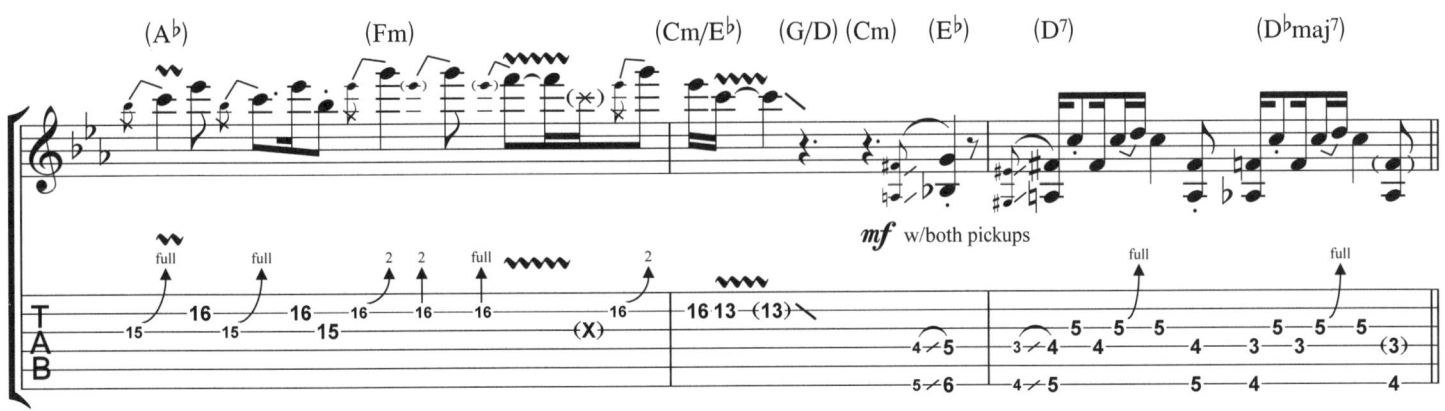

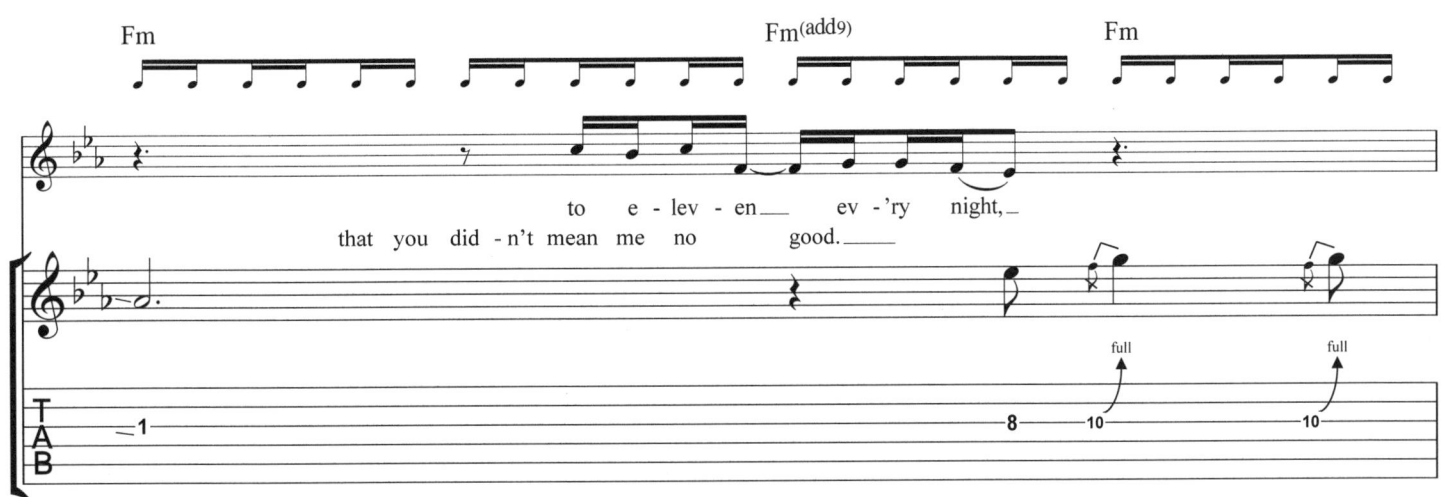

99

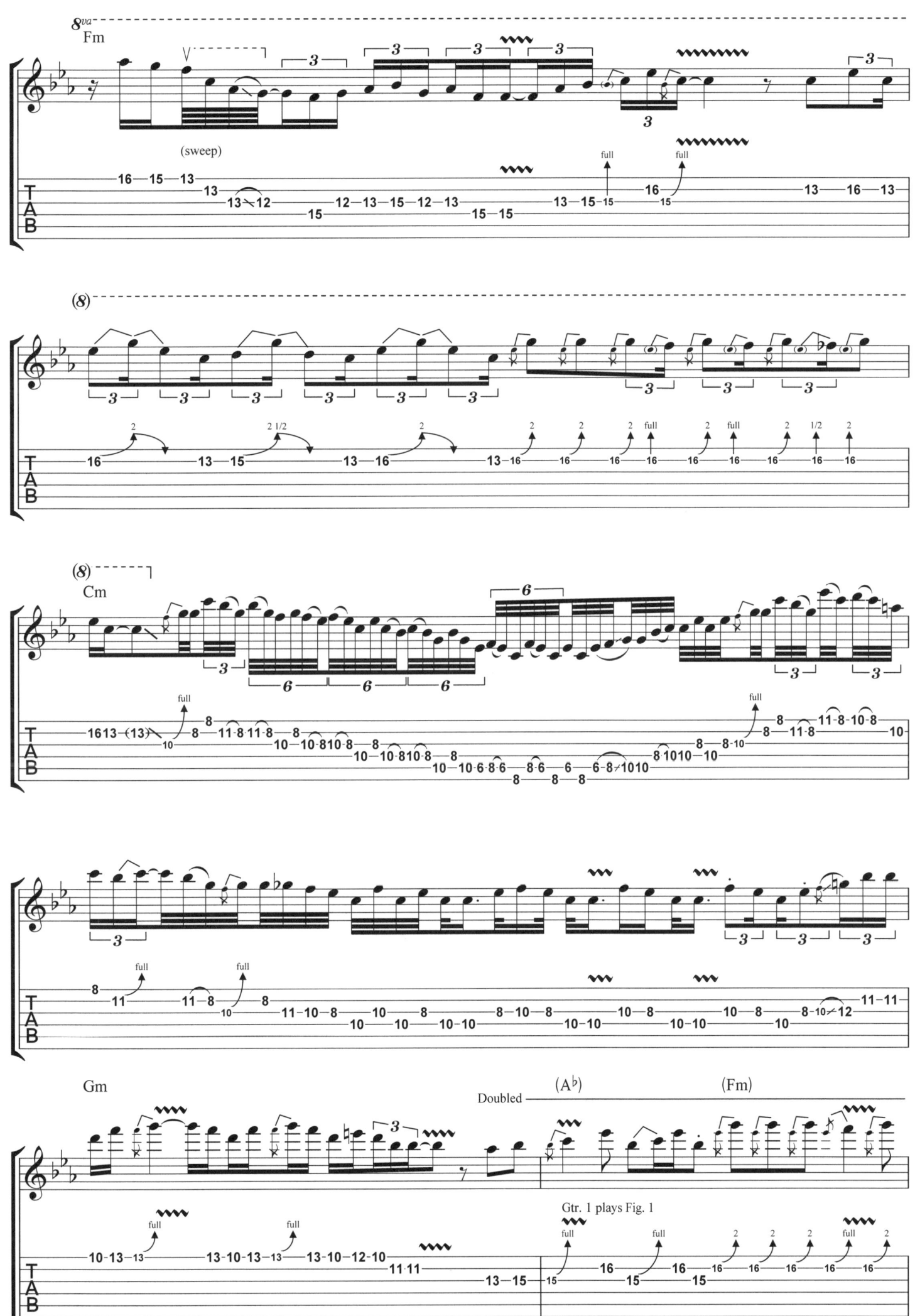

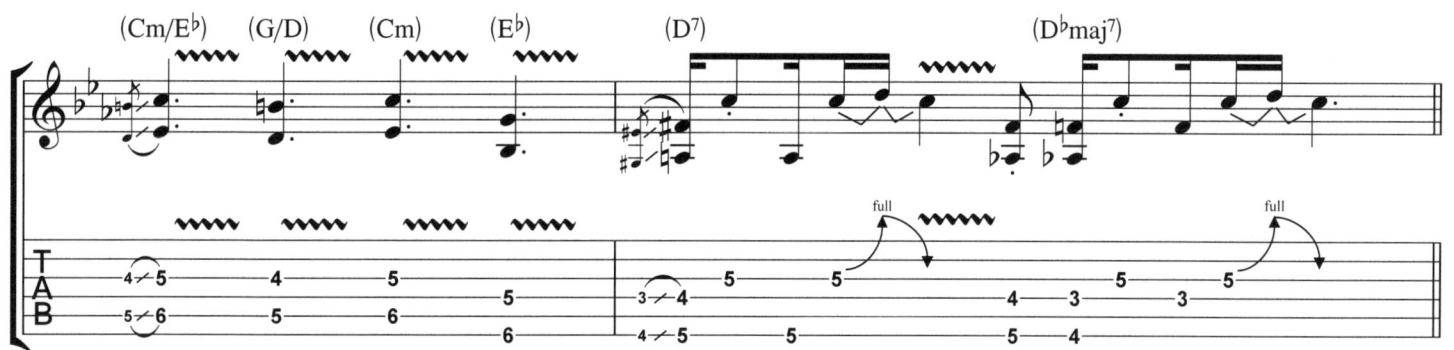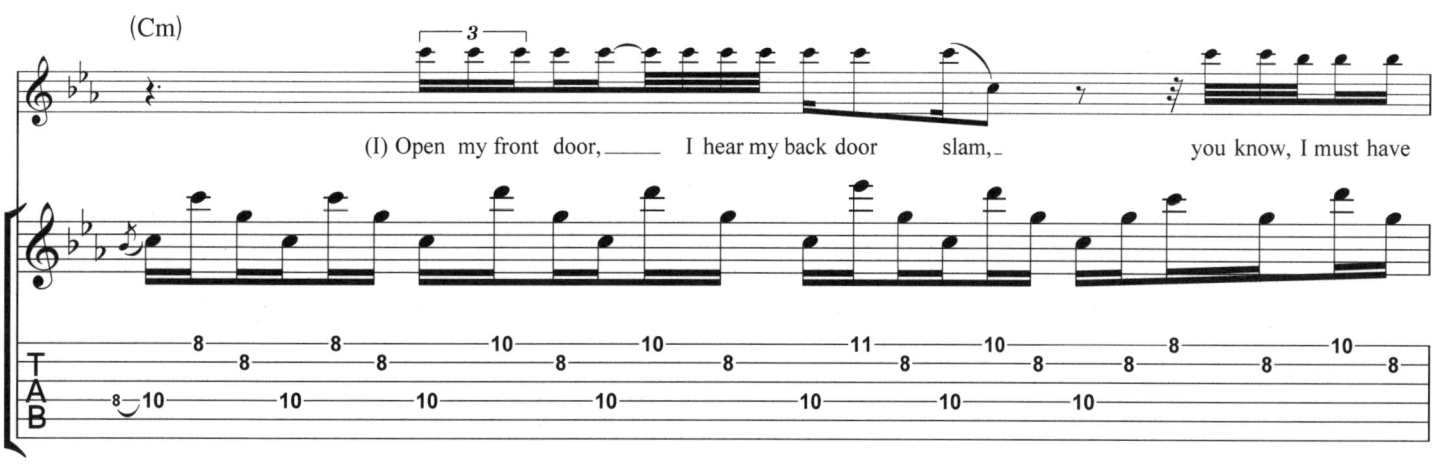

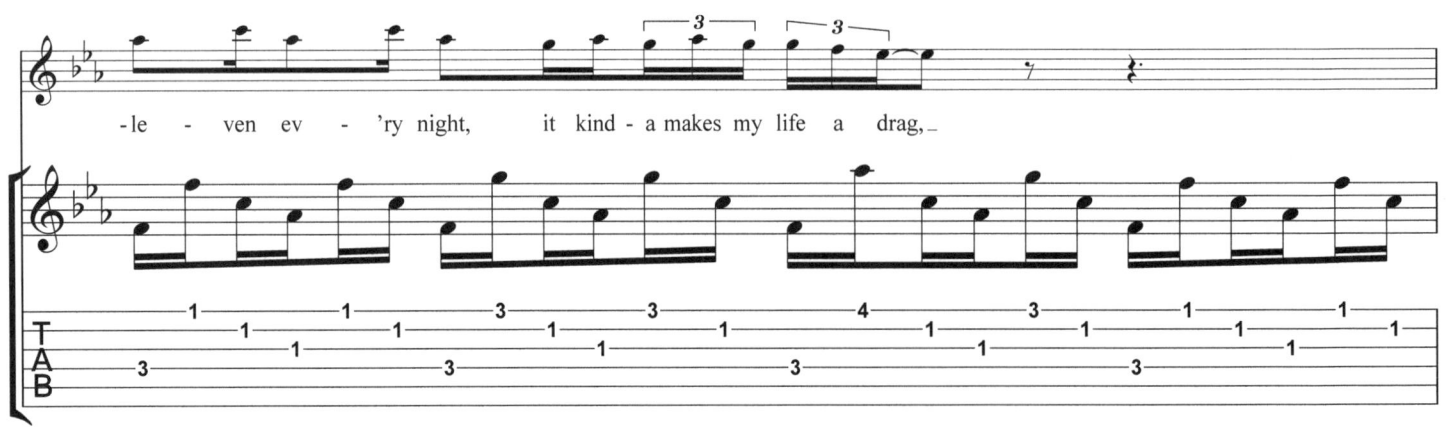
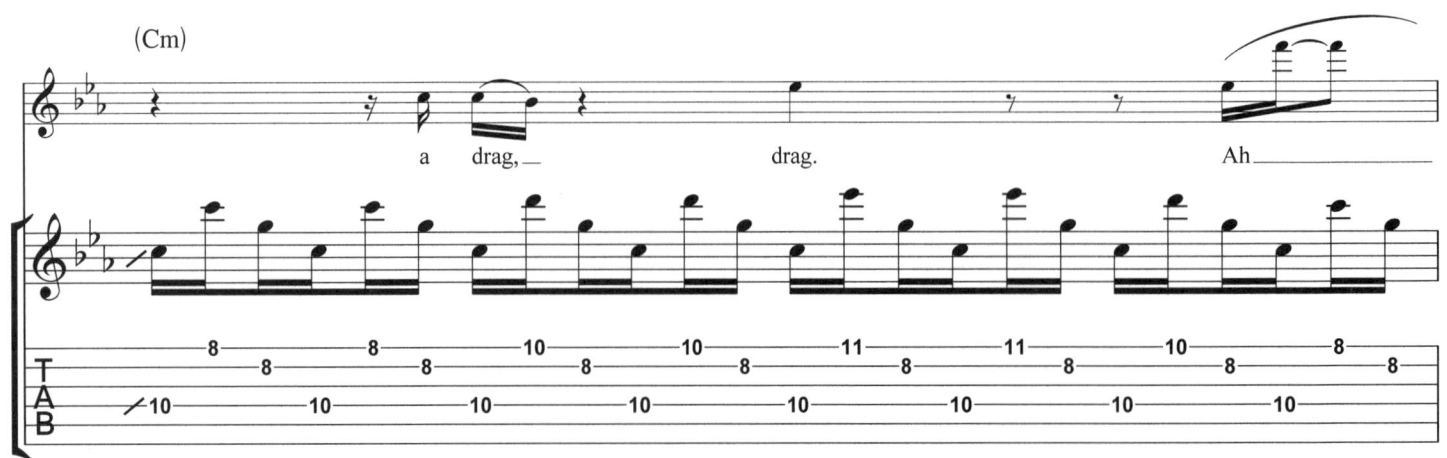

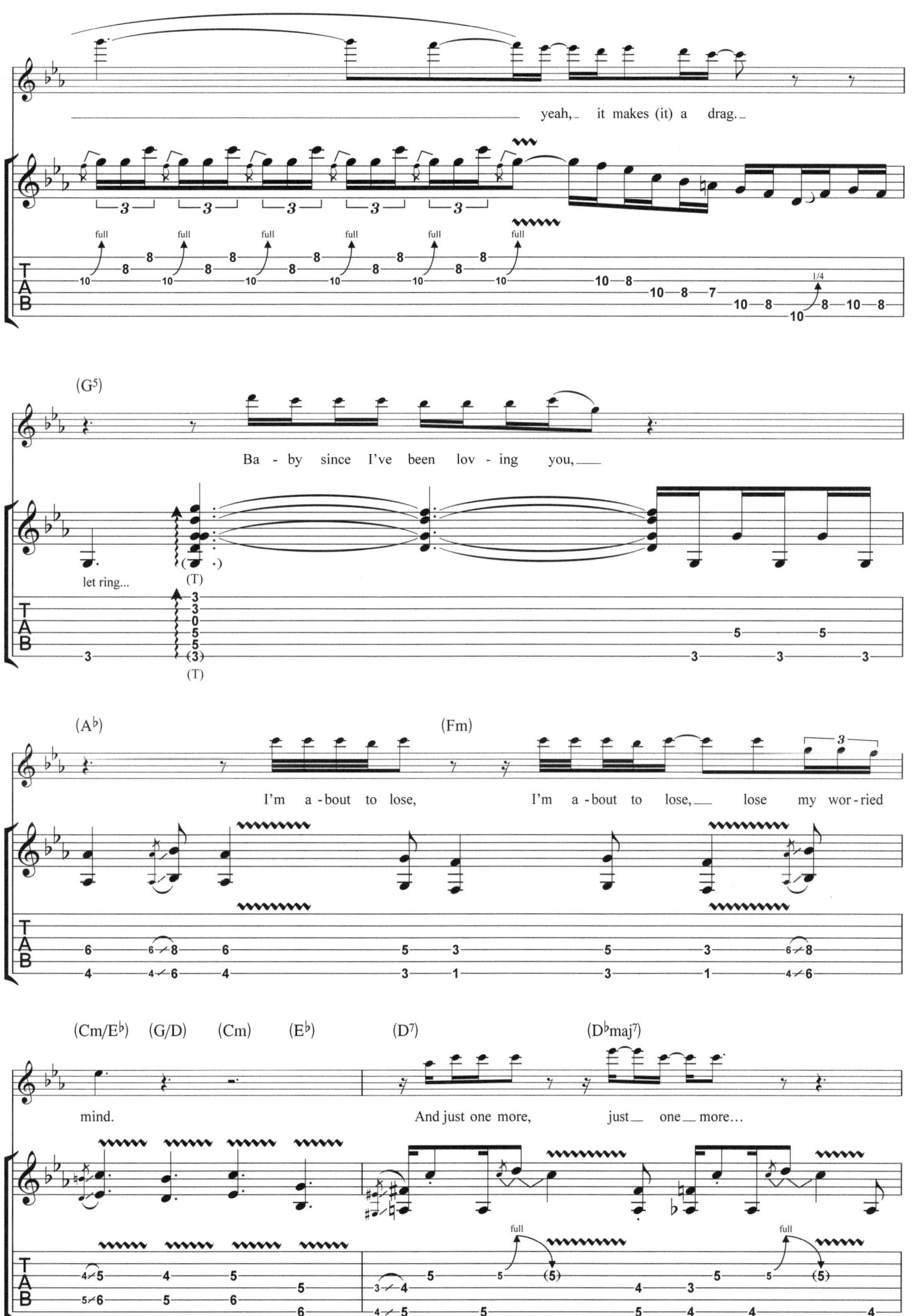

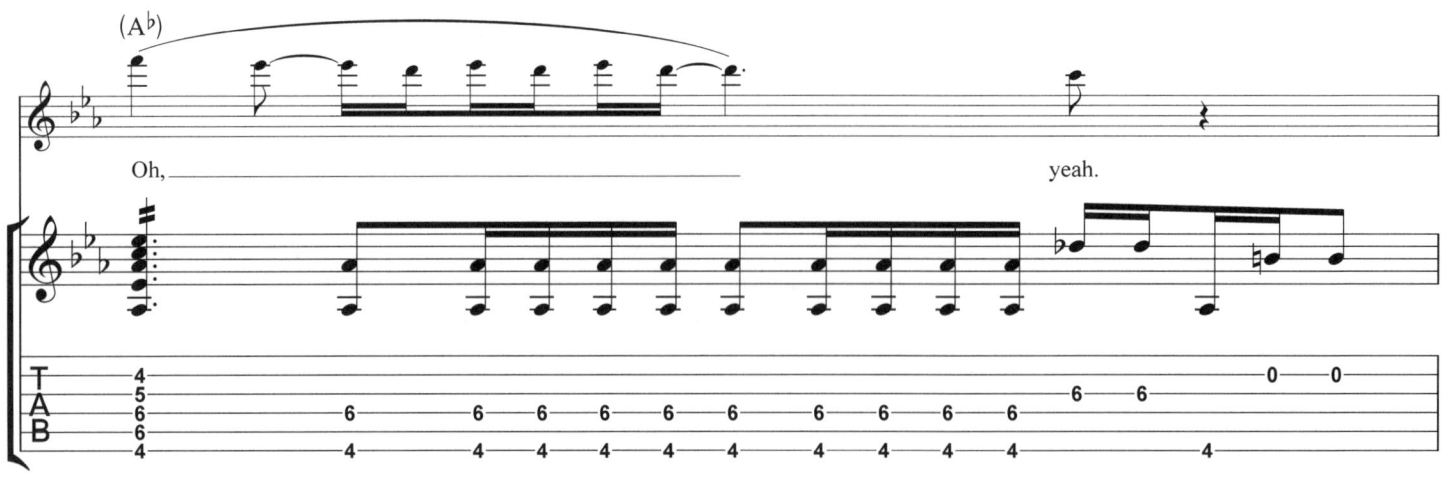

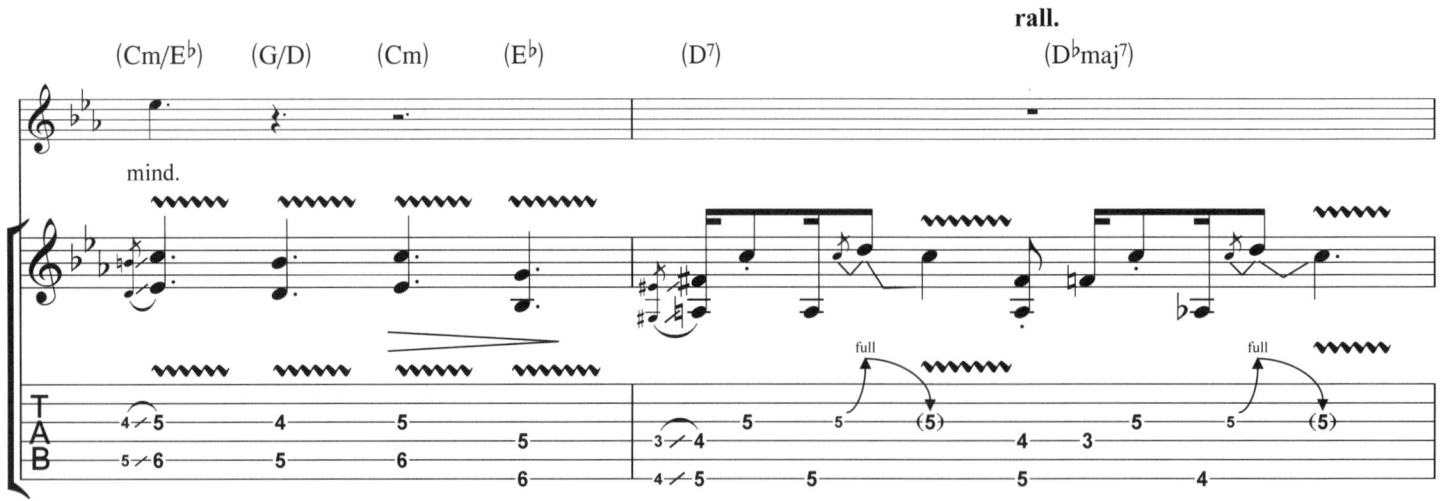
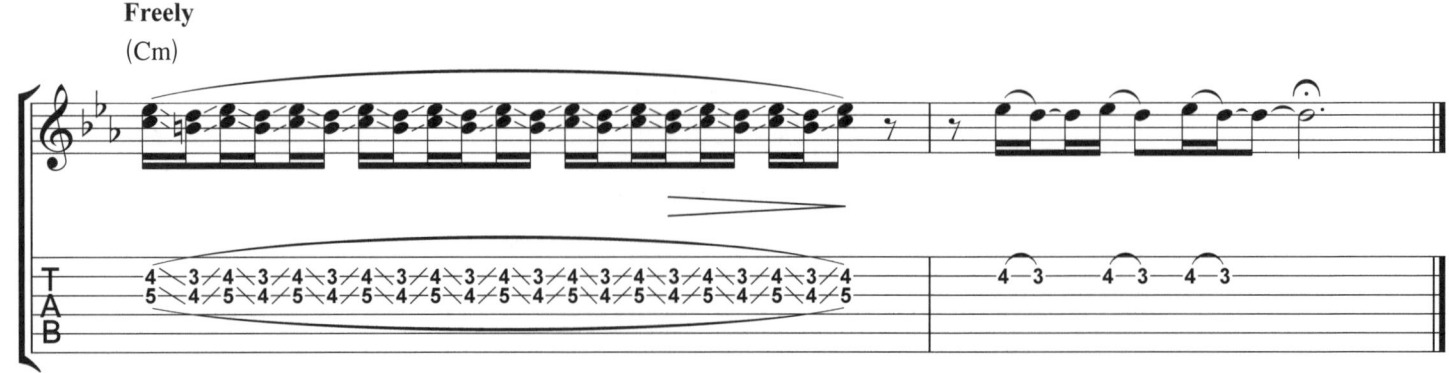

DAZED AND CONFUSED

Words & Music by Jimmy Page; inspired by Jake Holmes

© Copyright 1969 Succubus Music Limited.
Print Rights Administered by Music Sales Limited.
All Rights Reserved. International Copyright Secured.

yeah.
2. You hurt
Gtrs. 1+2
sim.
1/2
T A B
9 9 7 7 0 4 4 2 2 0 9 9 7 7 0 4 4 2 2 0
Gtr. 3 (elec.)
8va
19 19 17 17 14 14 12 12 19 19 17 17 14 14 12 12
Verse
and a - buse, tell -ing all of your lies,
run round, sweet ba - by, Lord, how you hyp -no - tize.
Gtr. 1
sim.
mf Gtrs. 2+3 tacet
9 9 7 7 0 4 4 2 2 0
Sweet lit - tle ba - by, I don't know where you been,
gon - na love you, ba - by, here I come a -
9/8
6/8
9 9 7 7 0 4 4 2

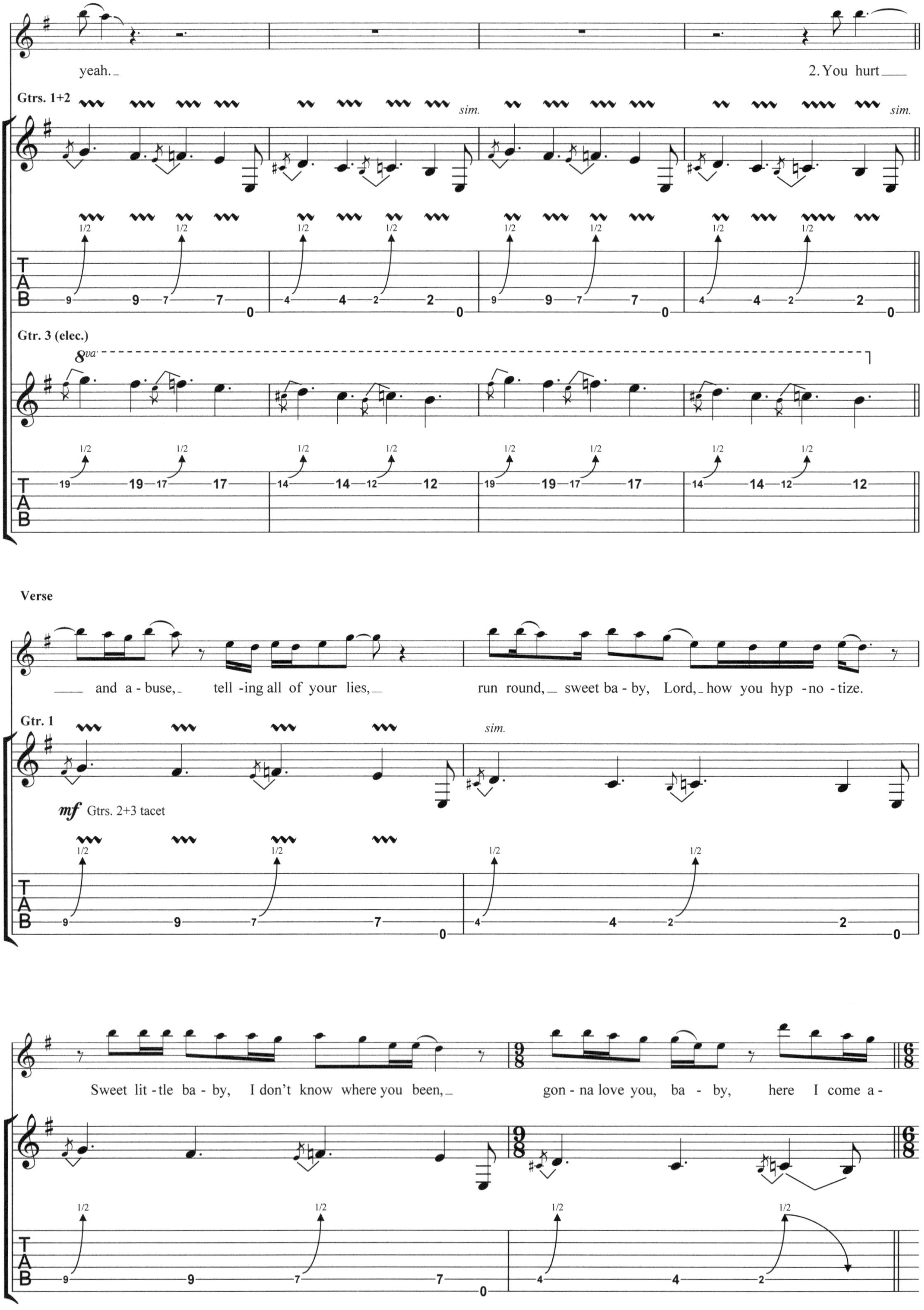

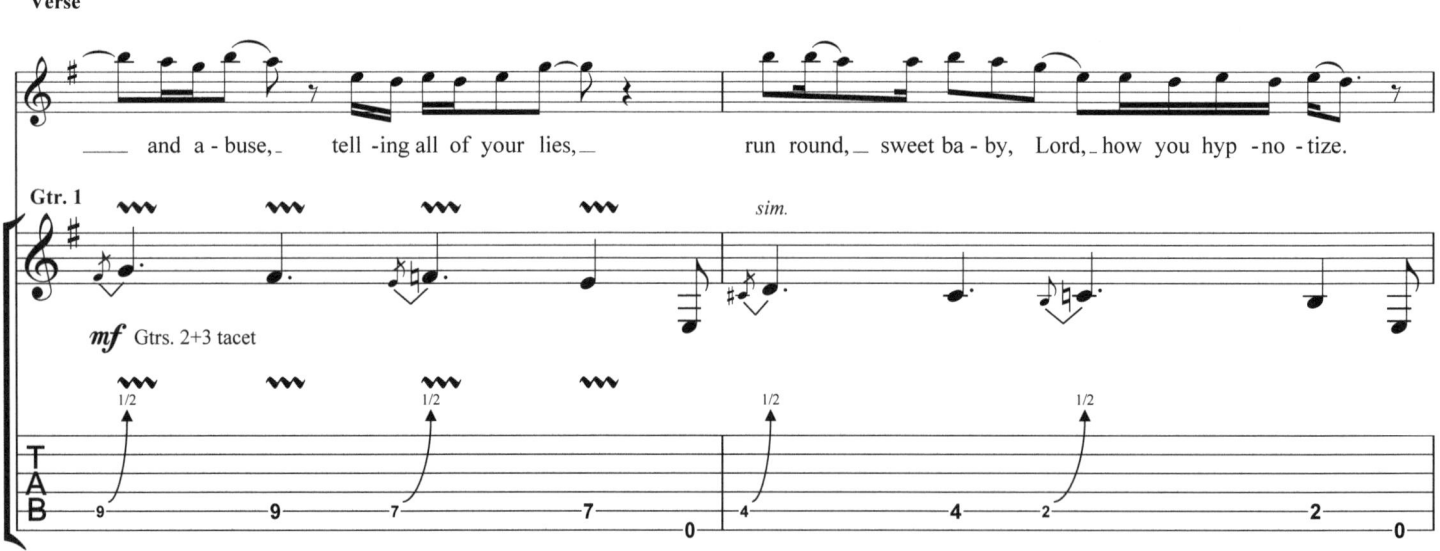

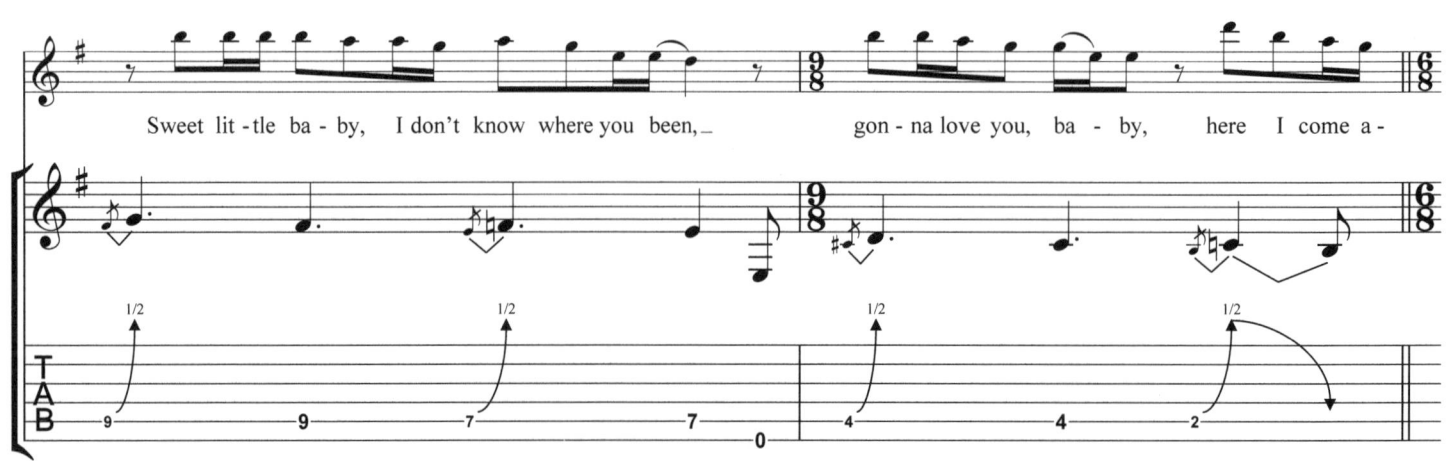

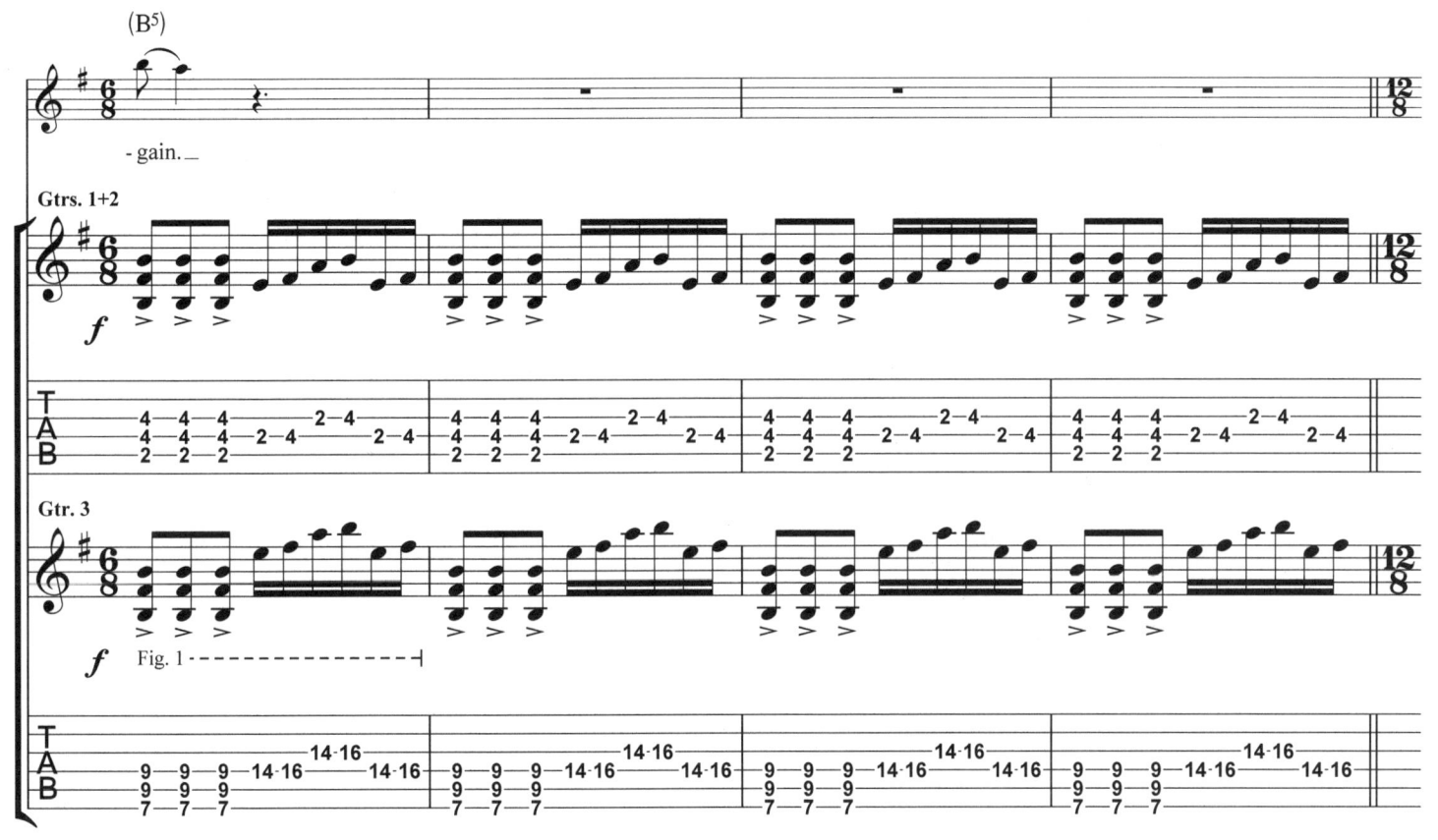
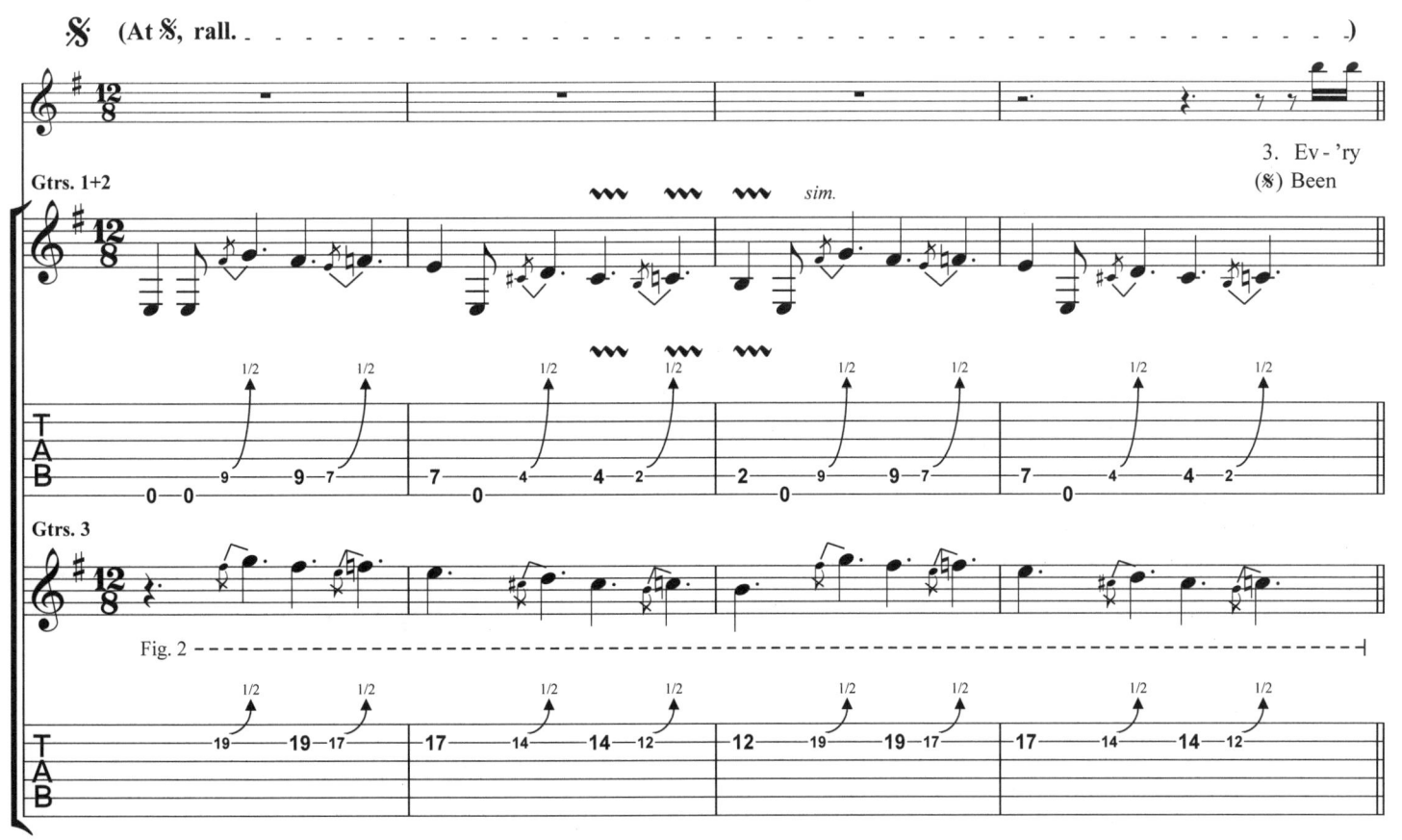

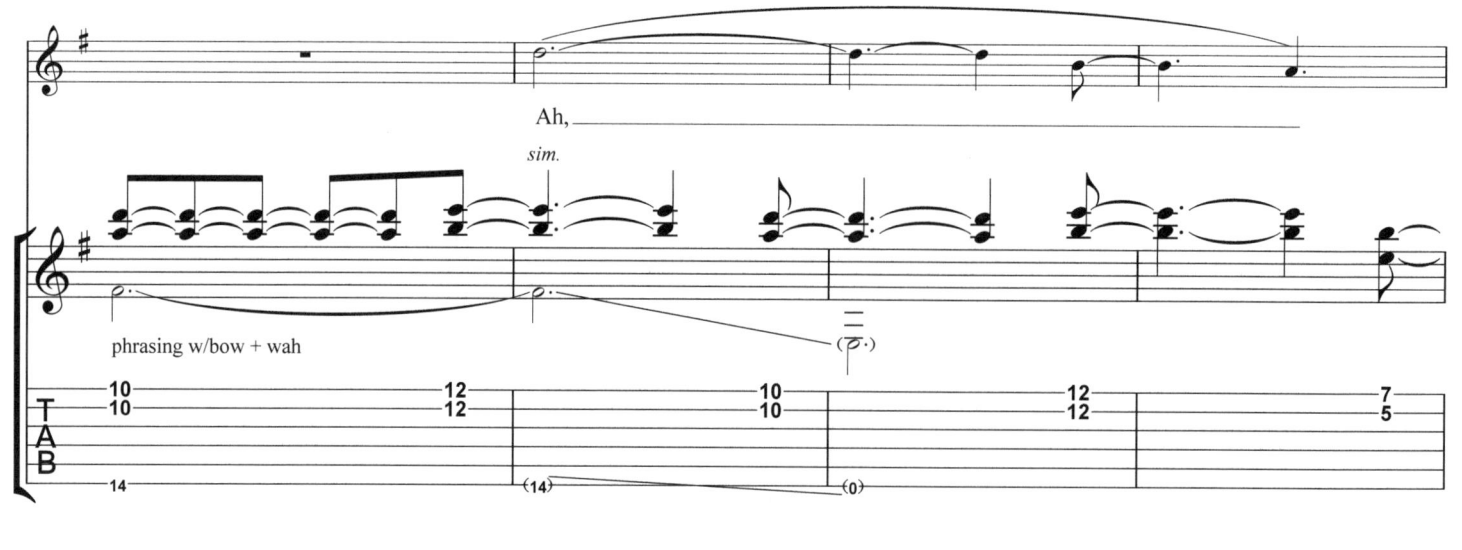

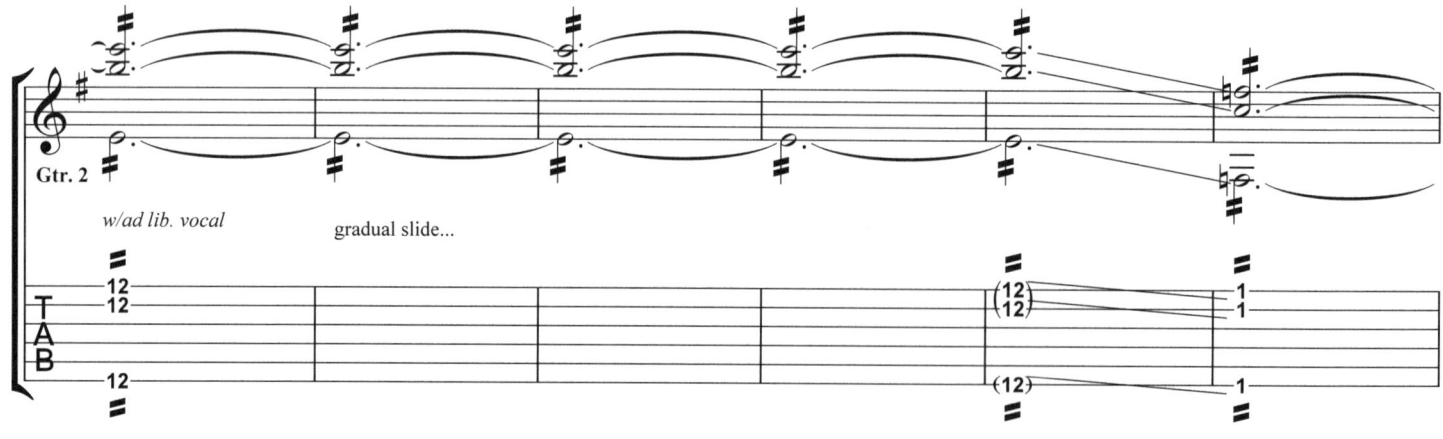
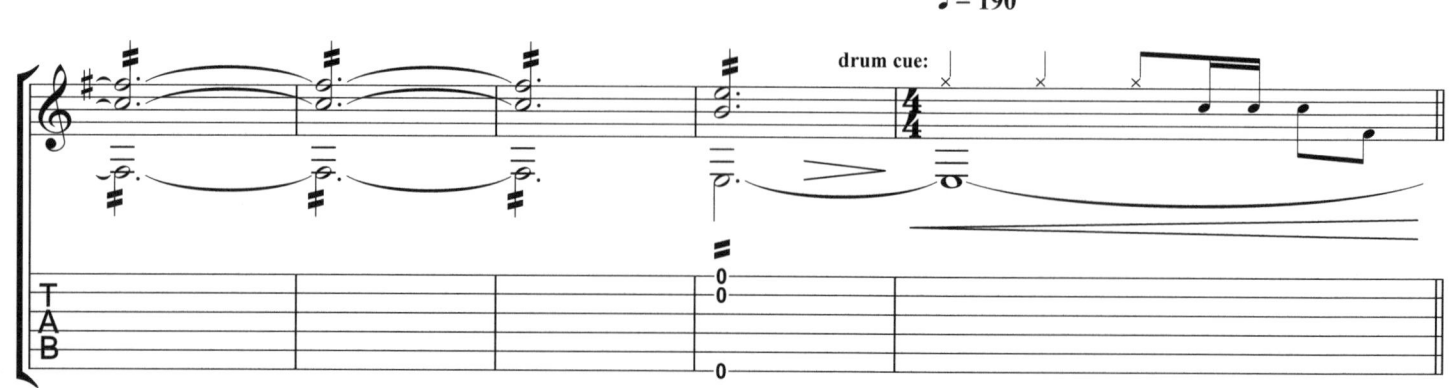

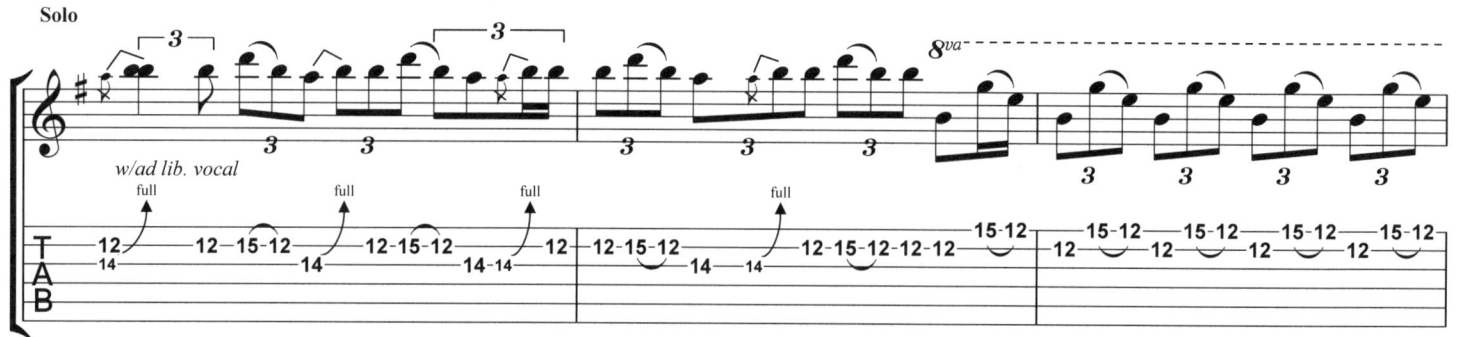
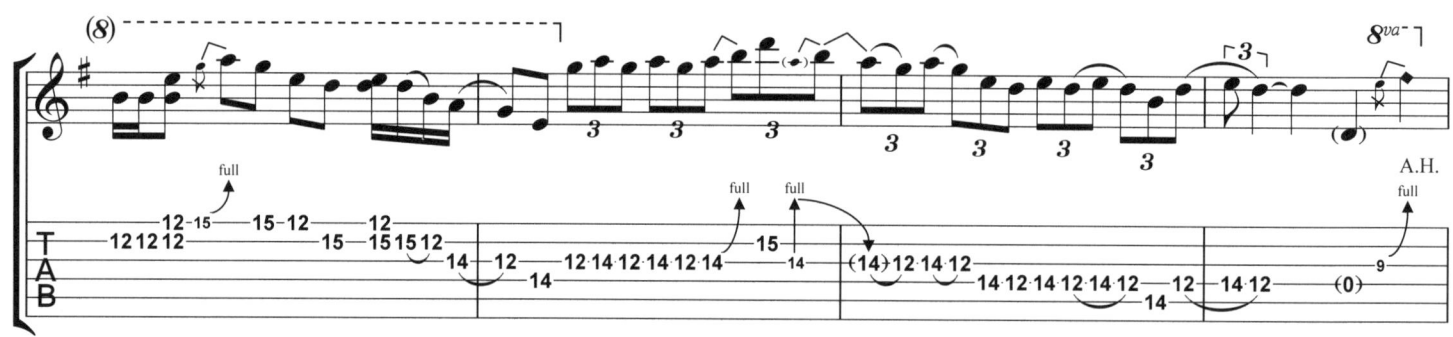
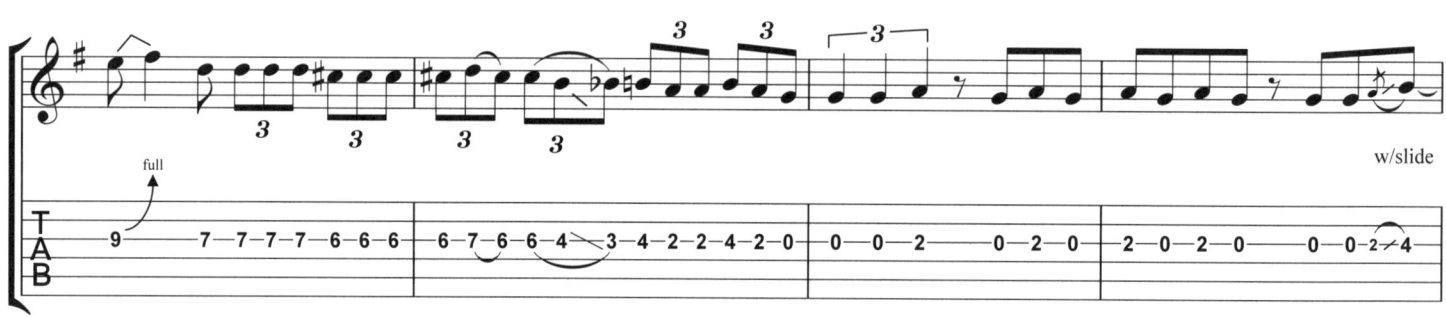

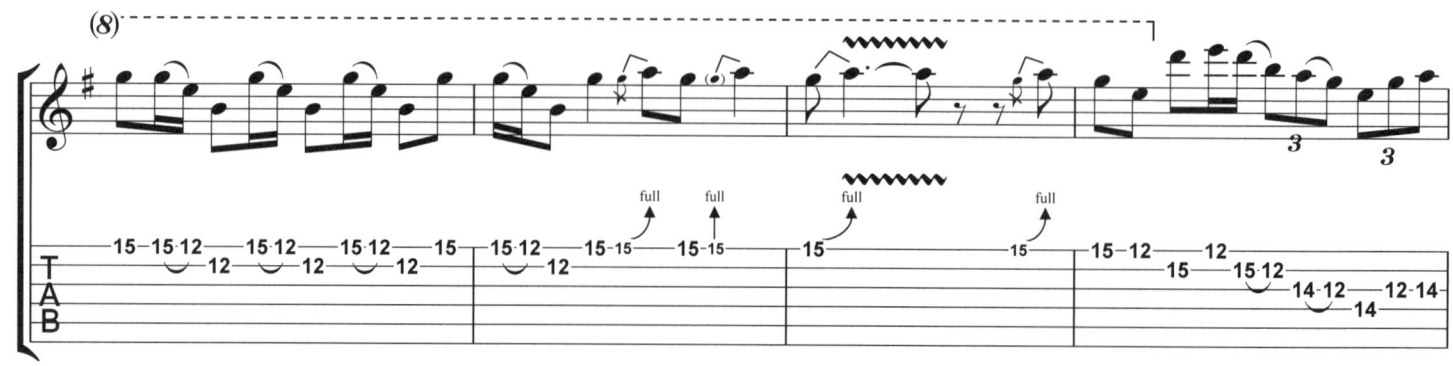

116

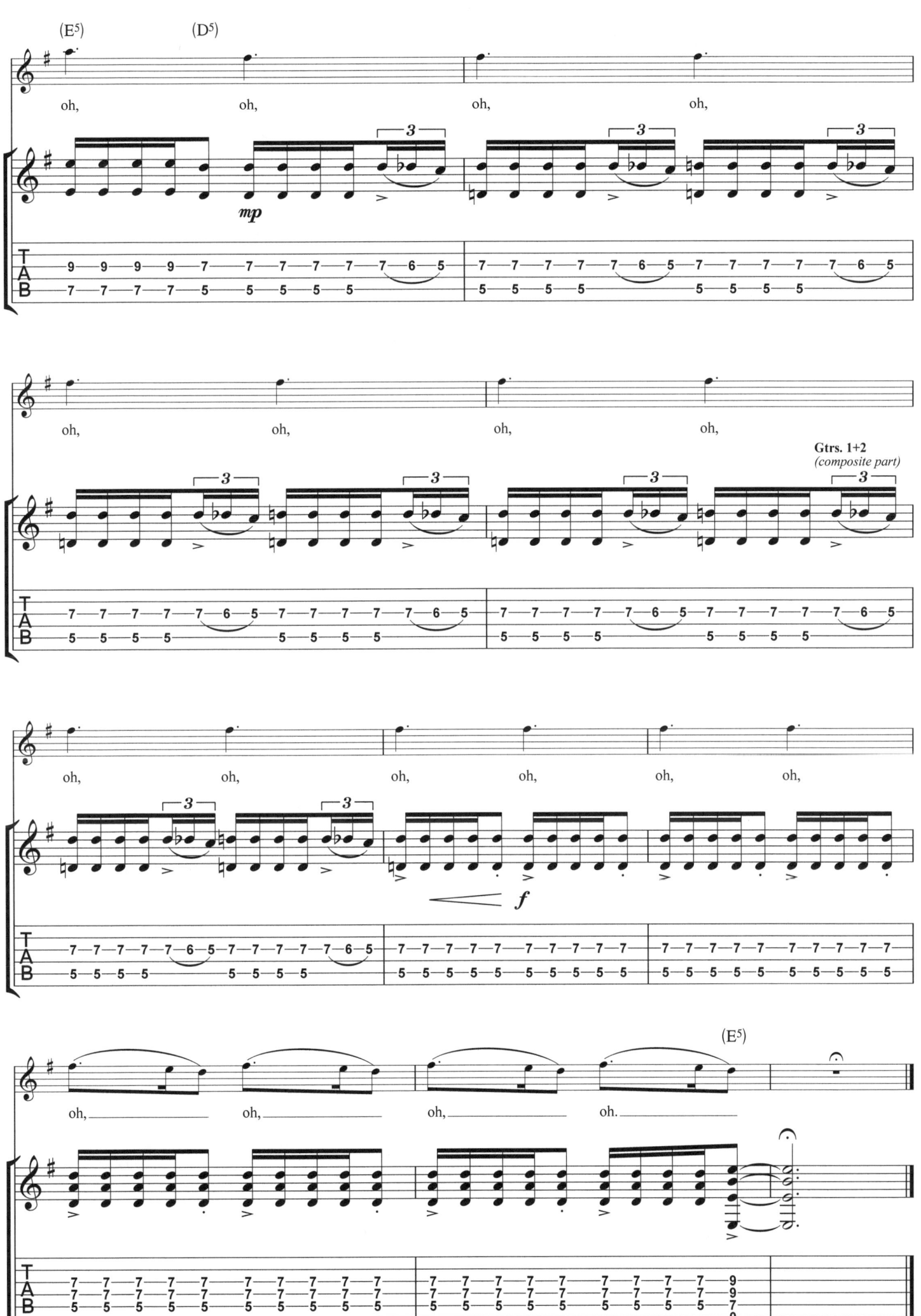

STAIRWAY TO HEAVEN

Words & Music by Jimmy Page & Robert Plant

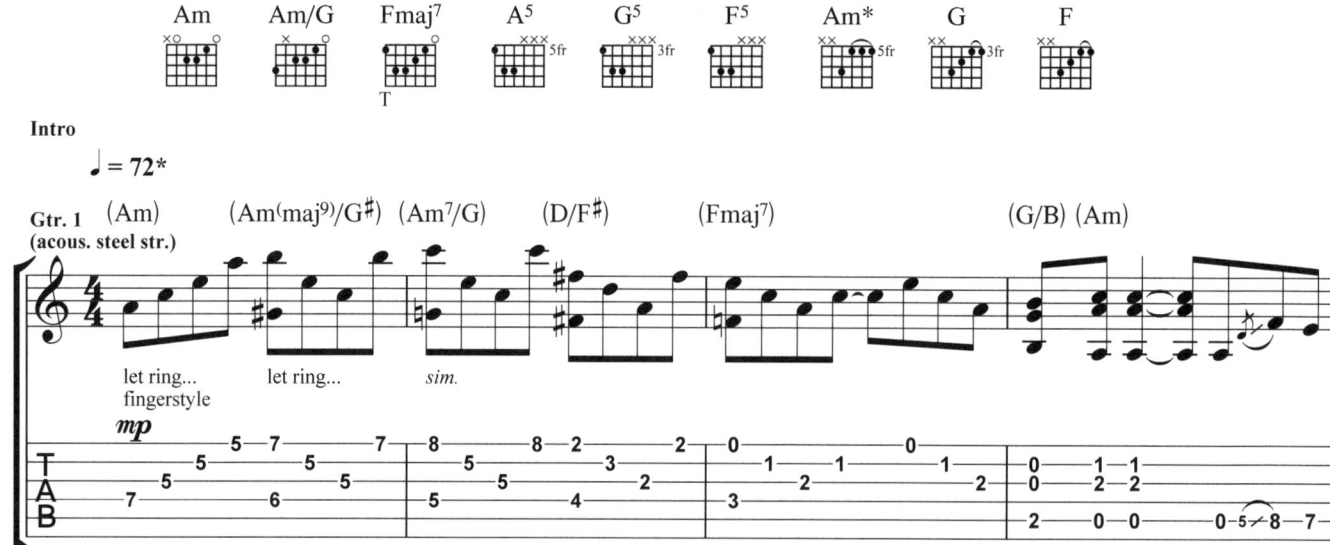

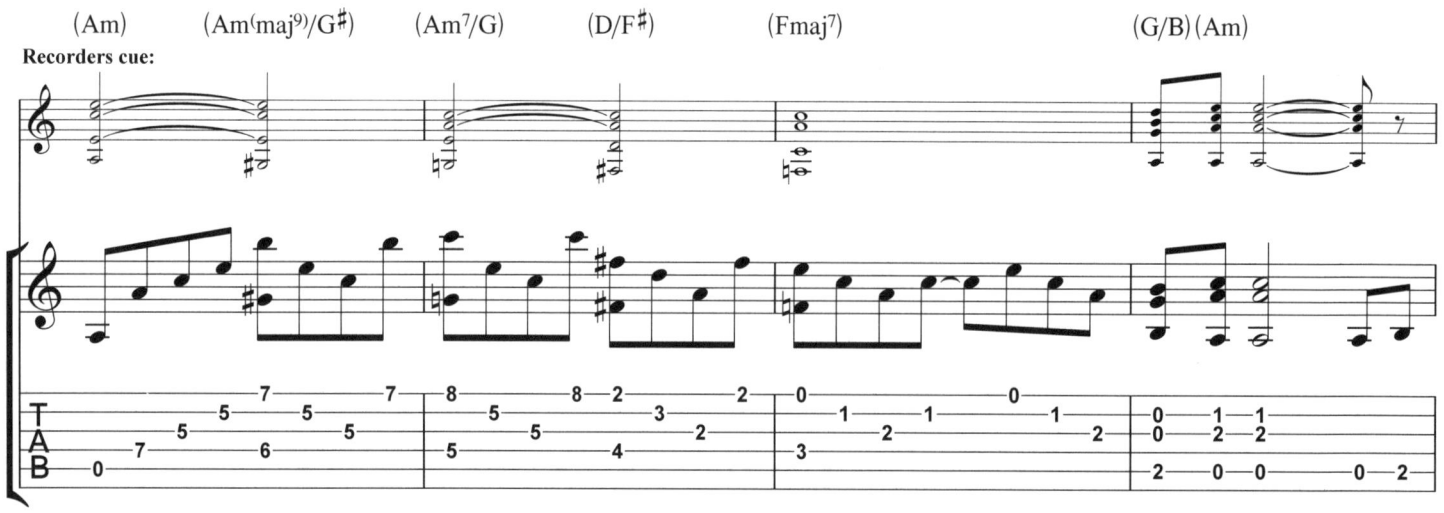

© Copyright 1972 Succubus Music Limited/Sons Of Einion Limited.
Print Rights Administered by Music Sales Limited.
All Rights Reserved. International Copyright Secured.

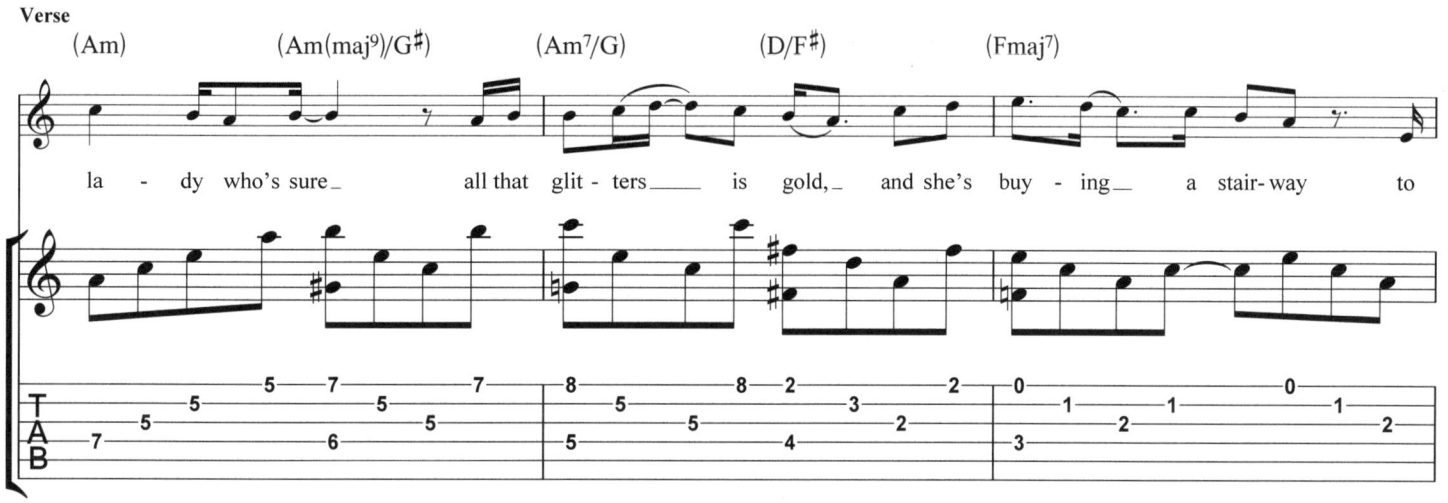
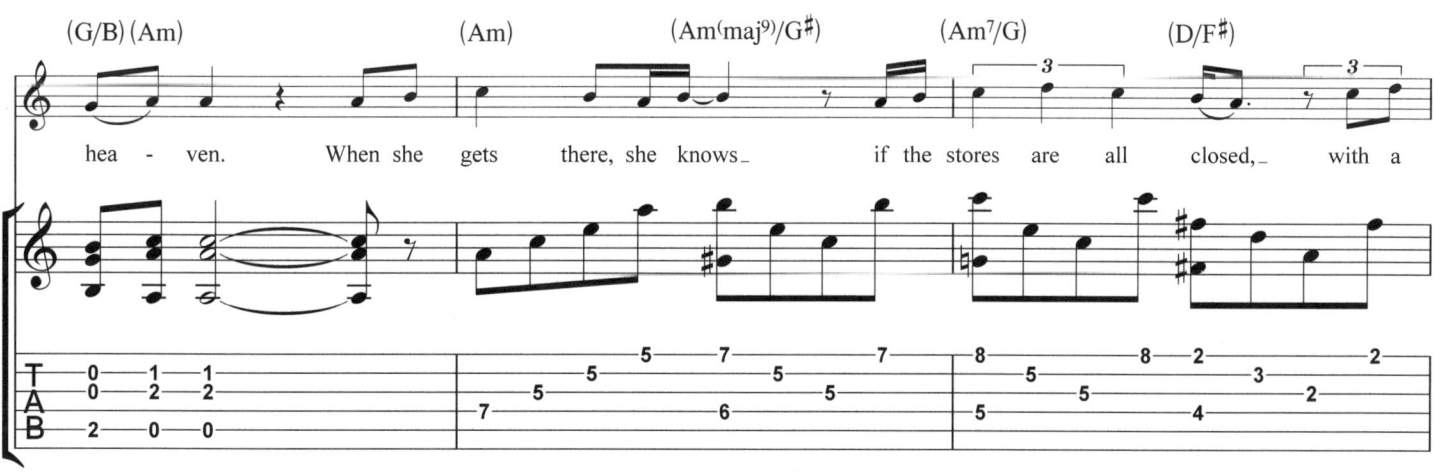
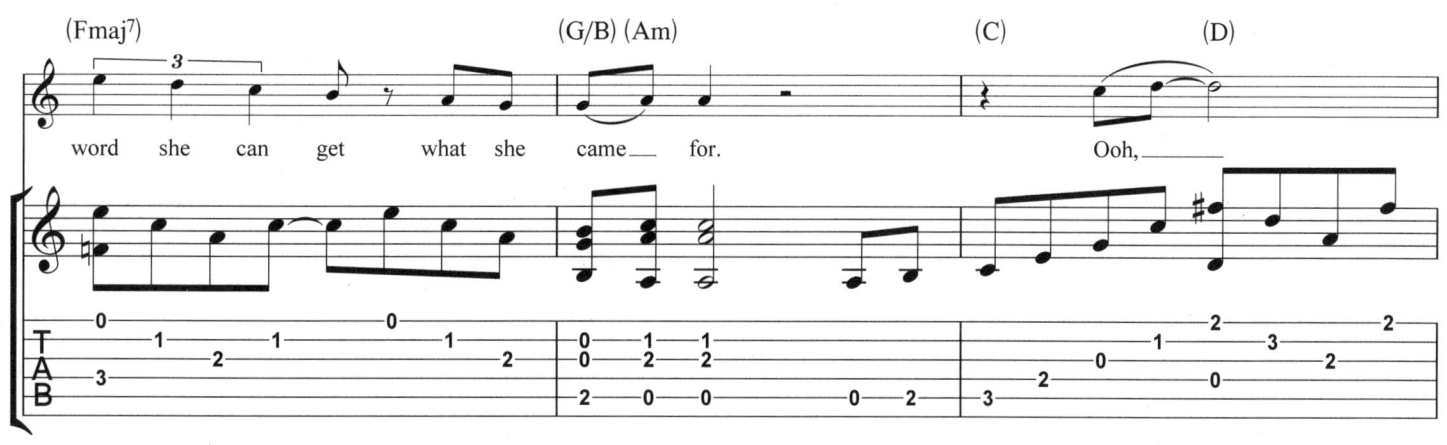

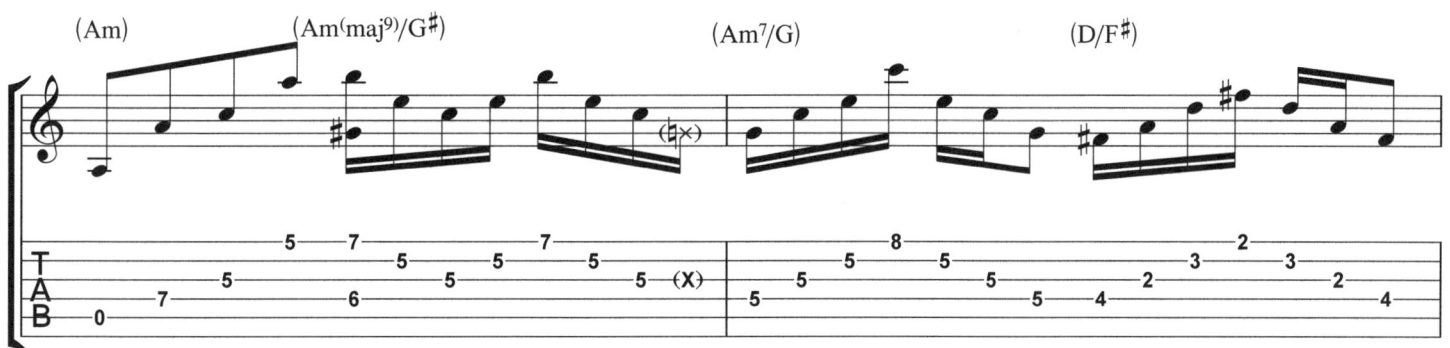

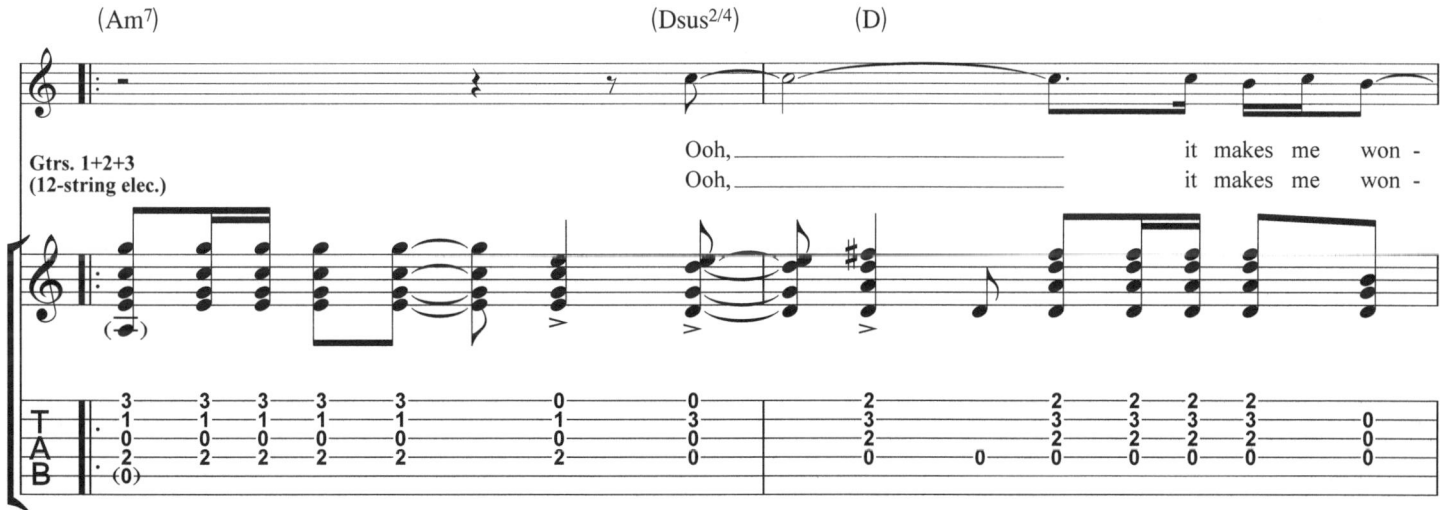
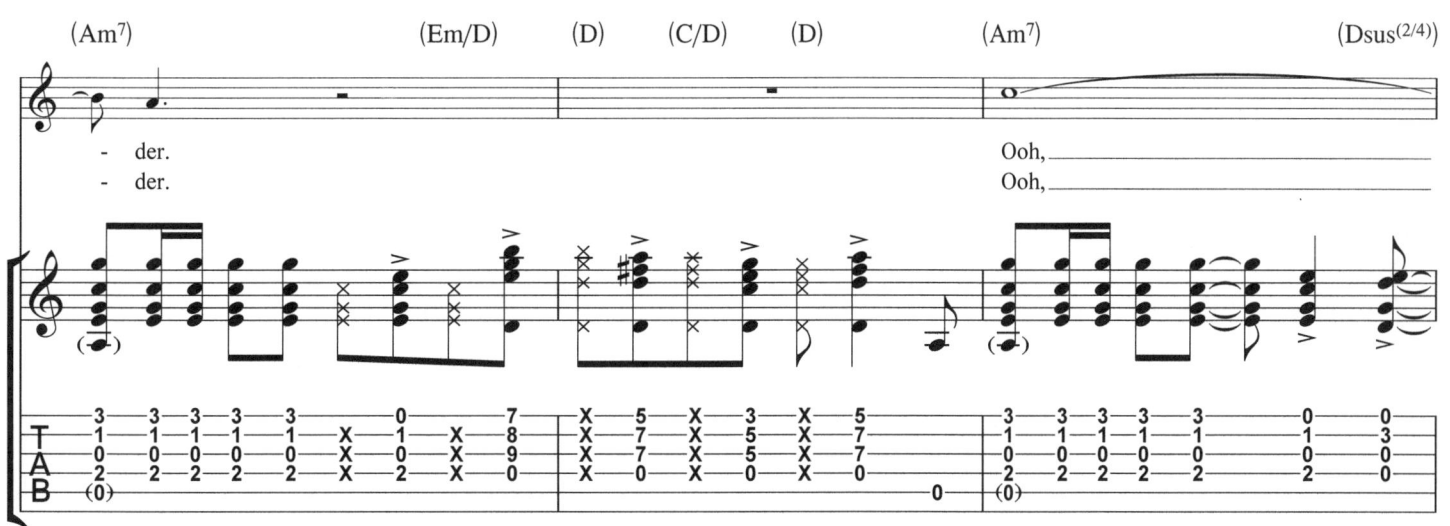

123

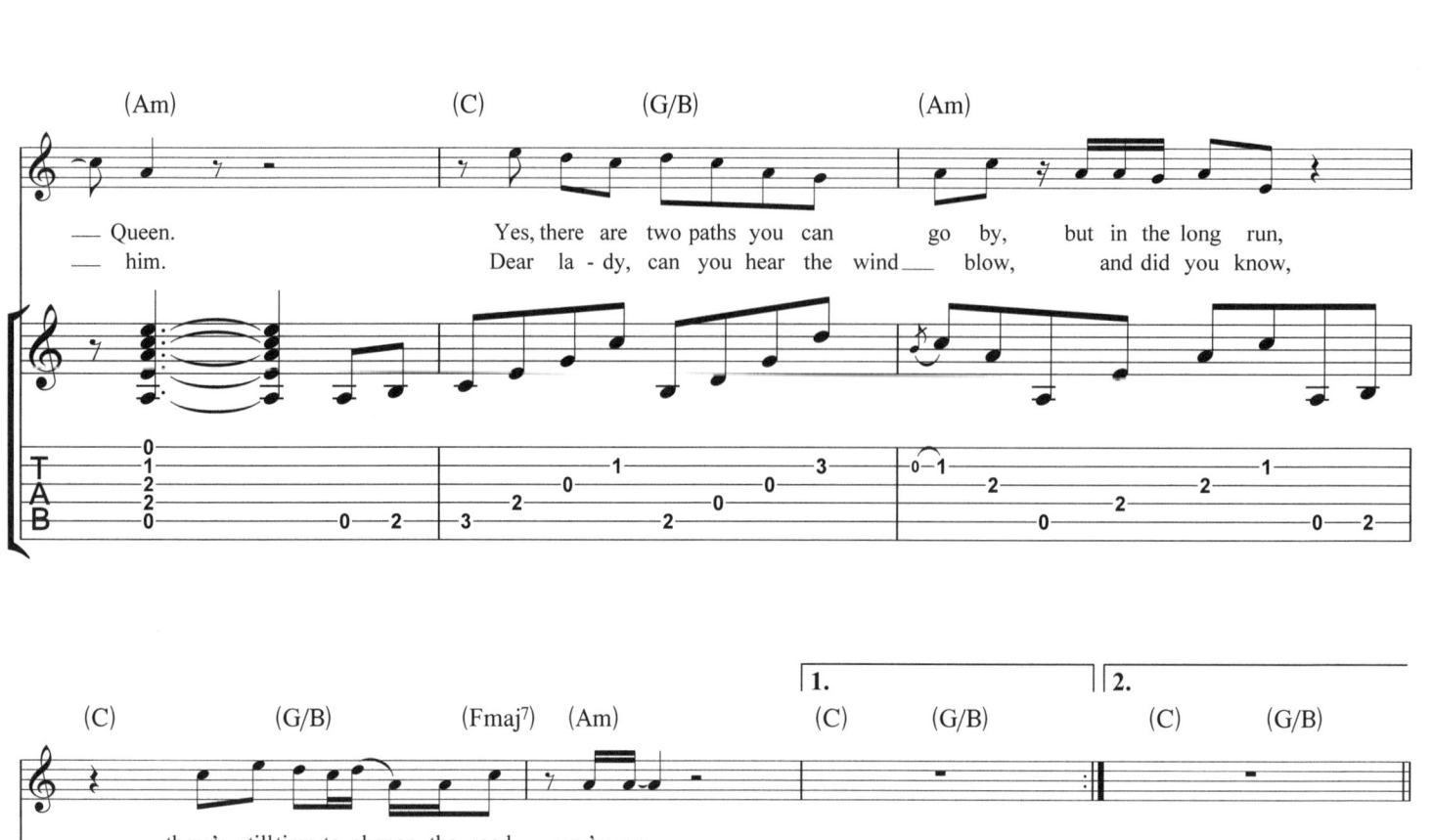
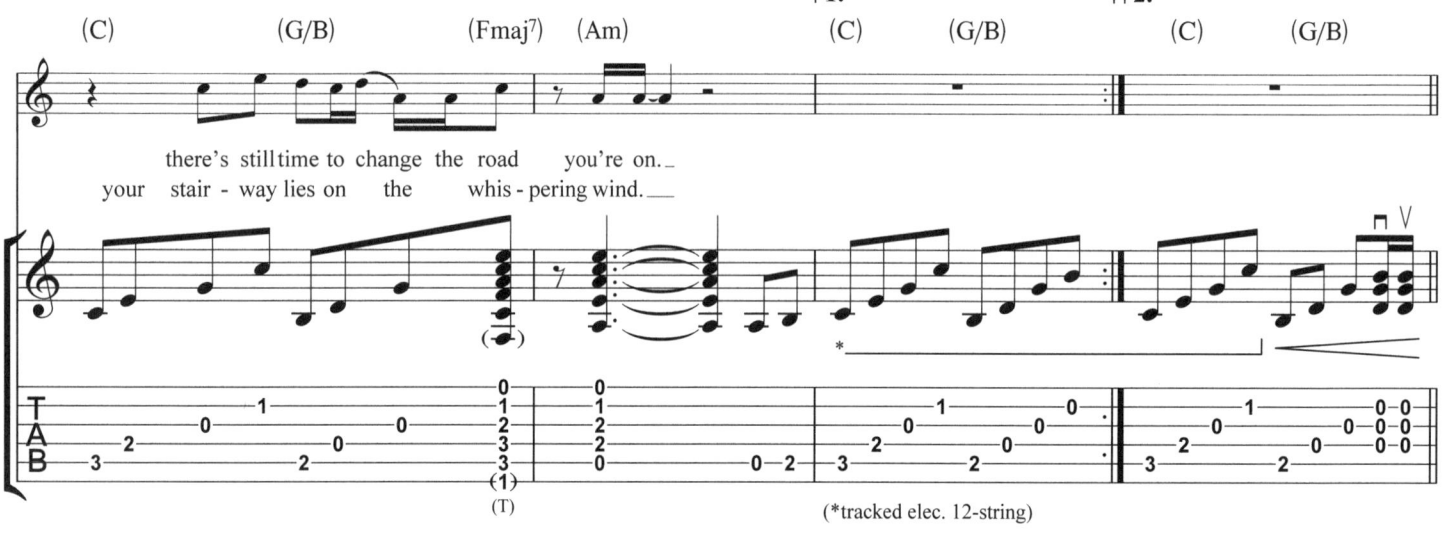
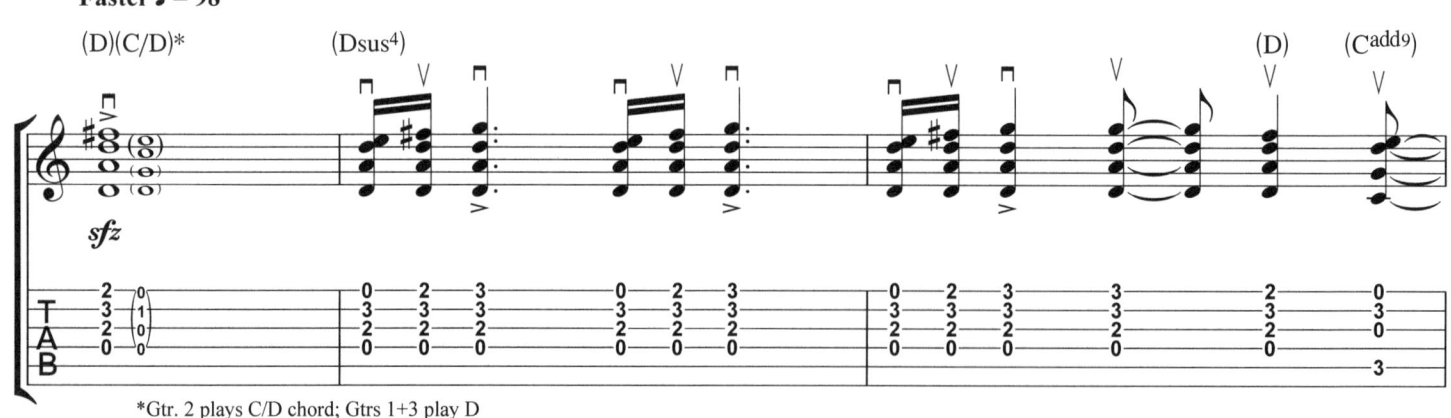
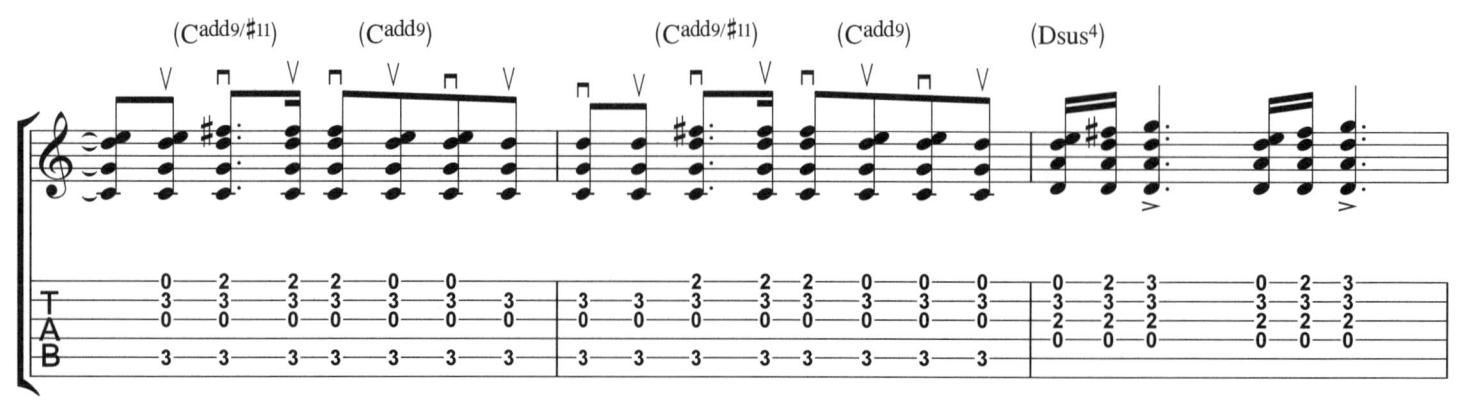

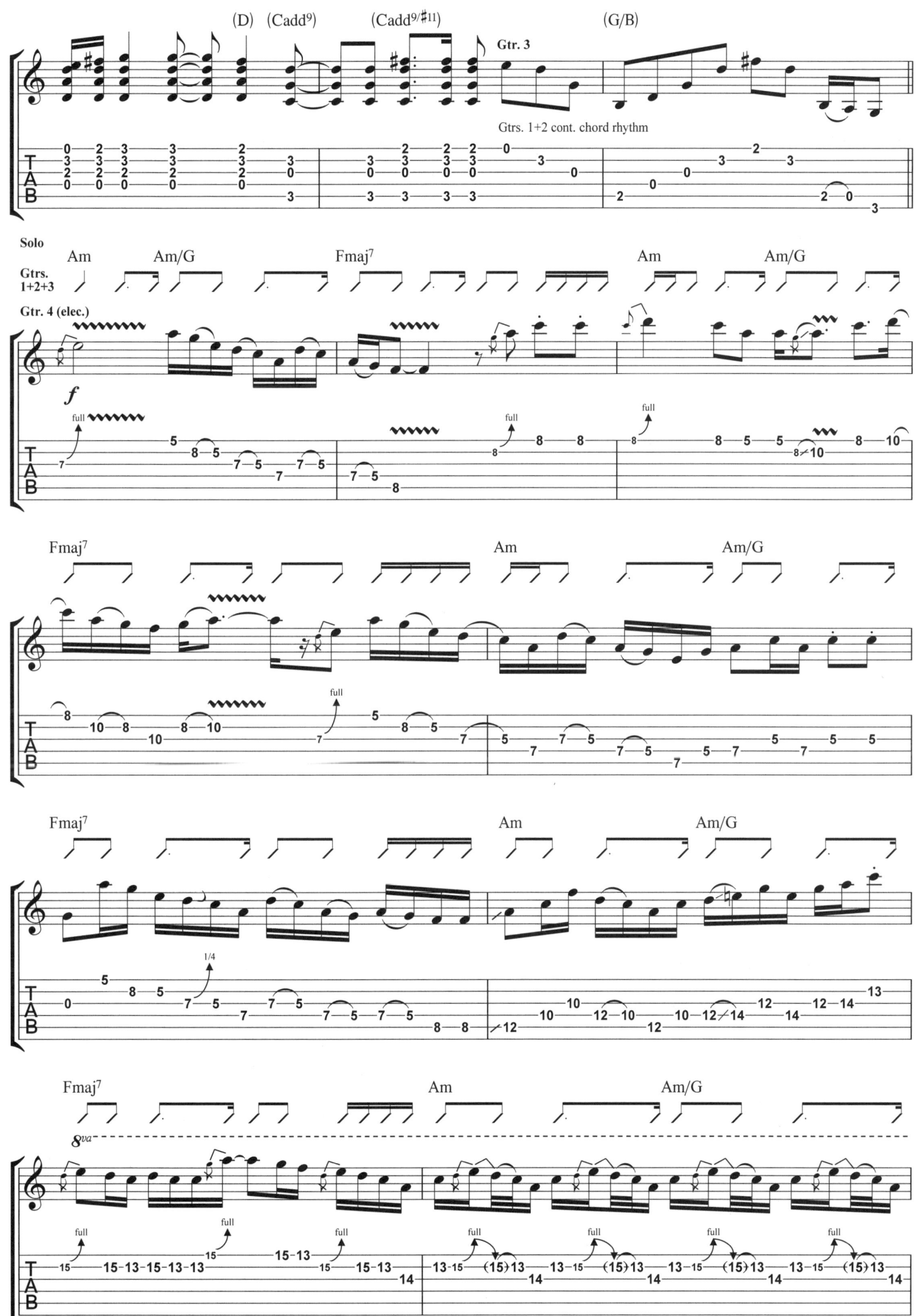

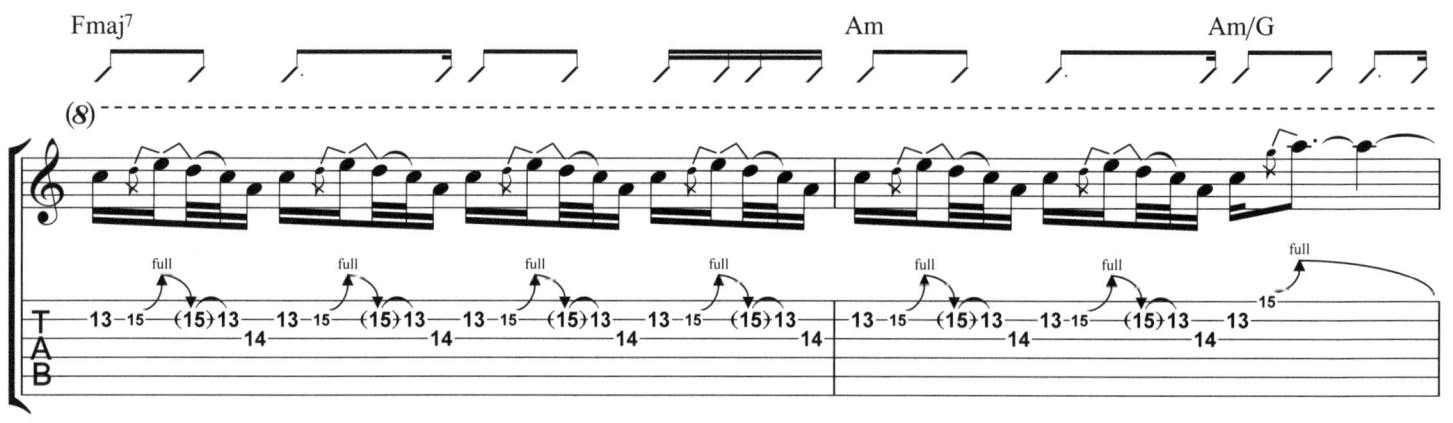
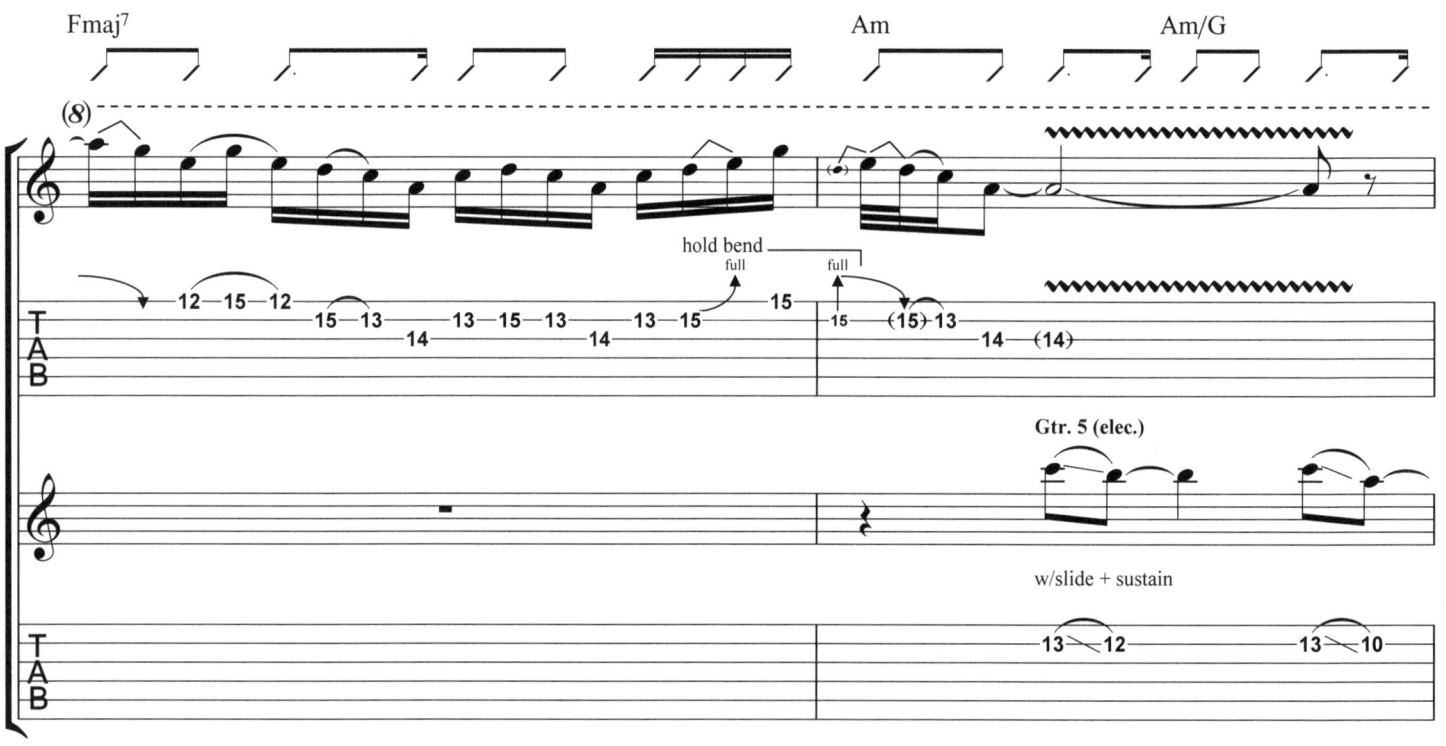
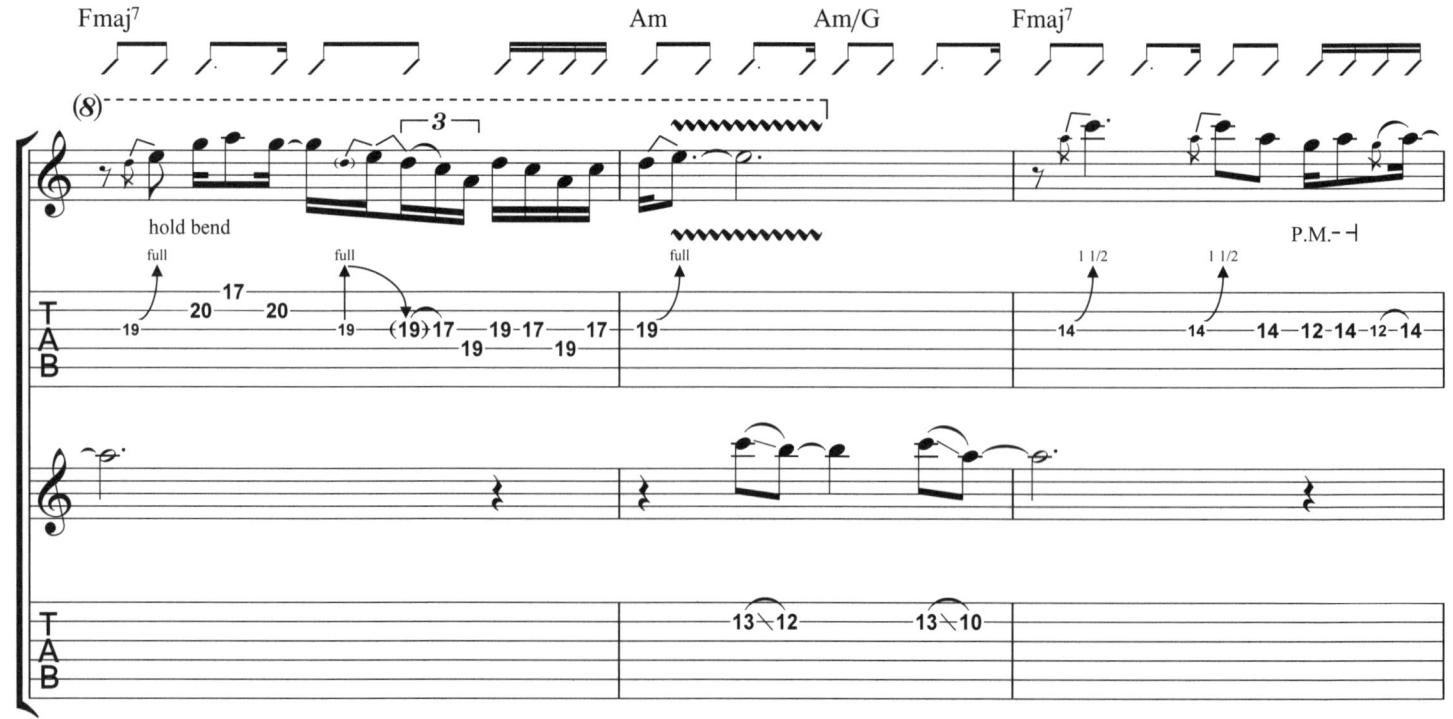

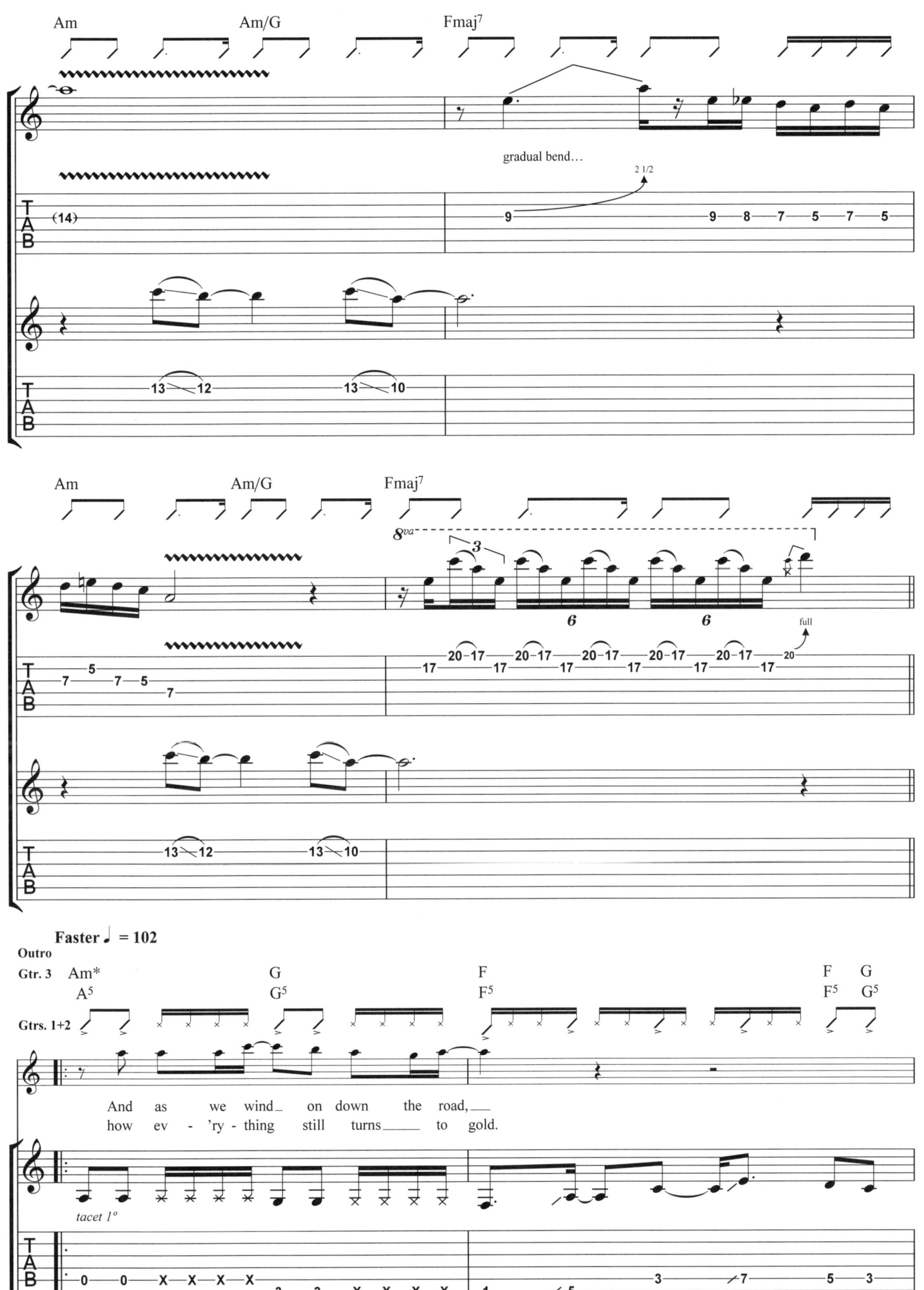

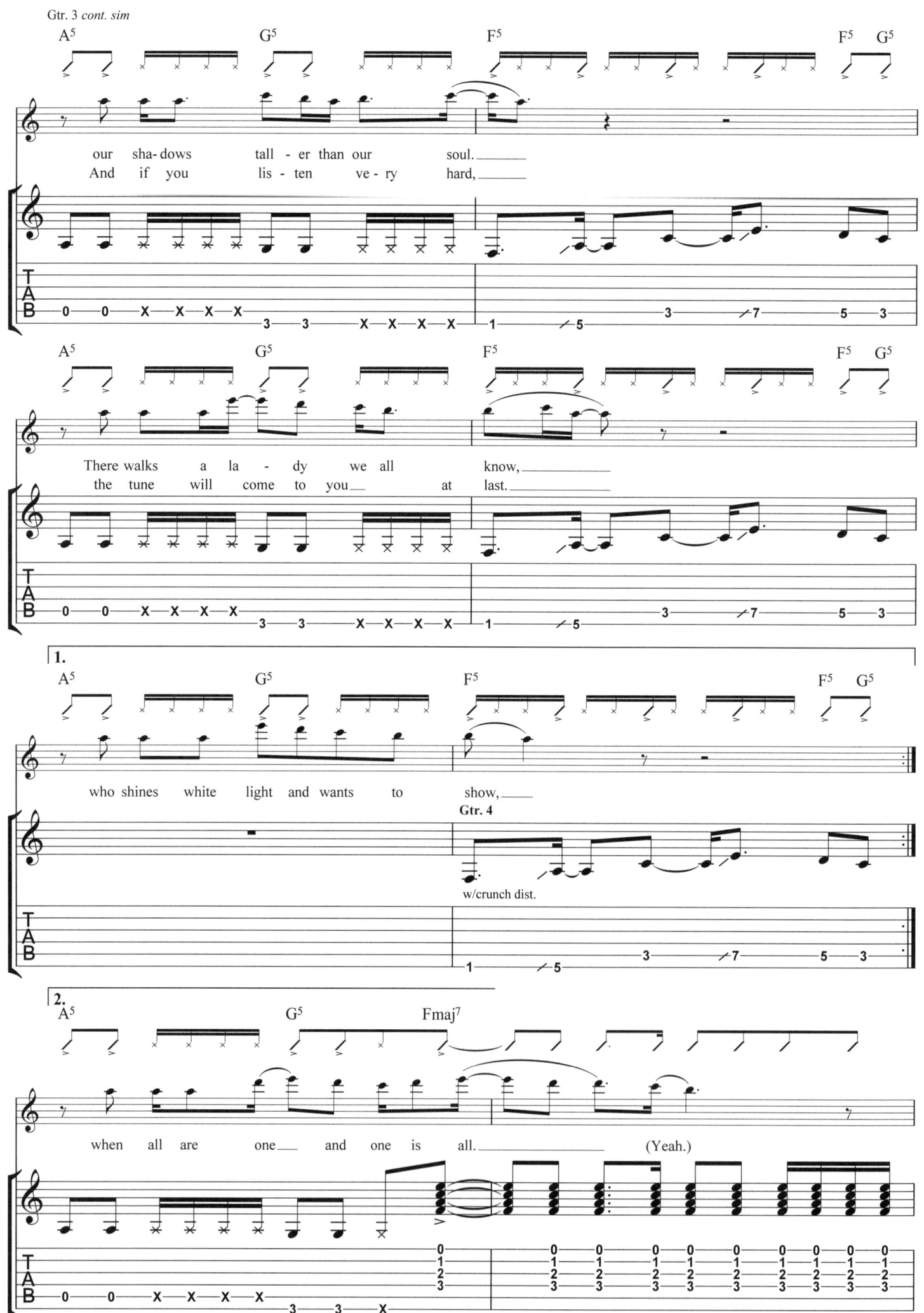

THE SONG REMAINS THE SAME

Words & Music by Jimmy Page & Robert Plant

132

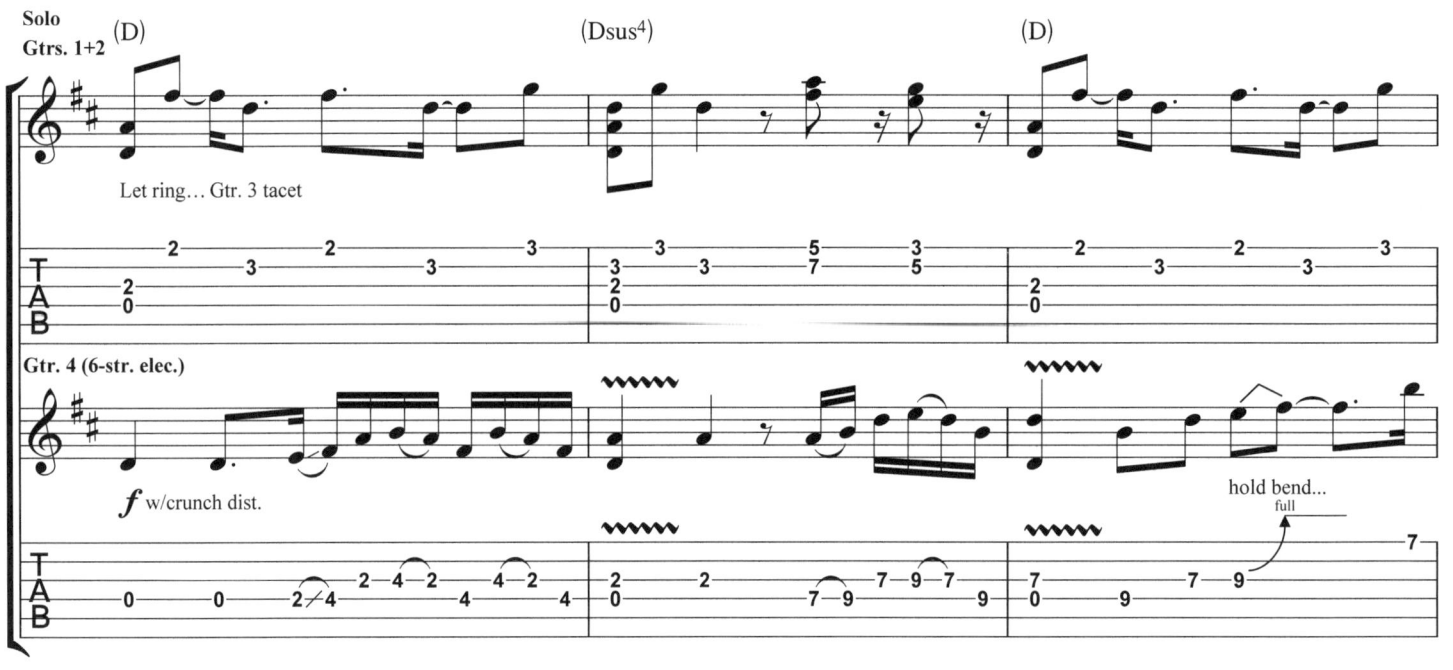
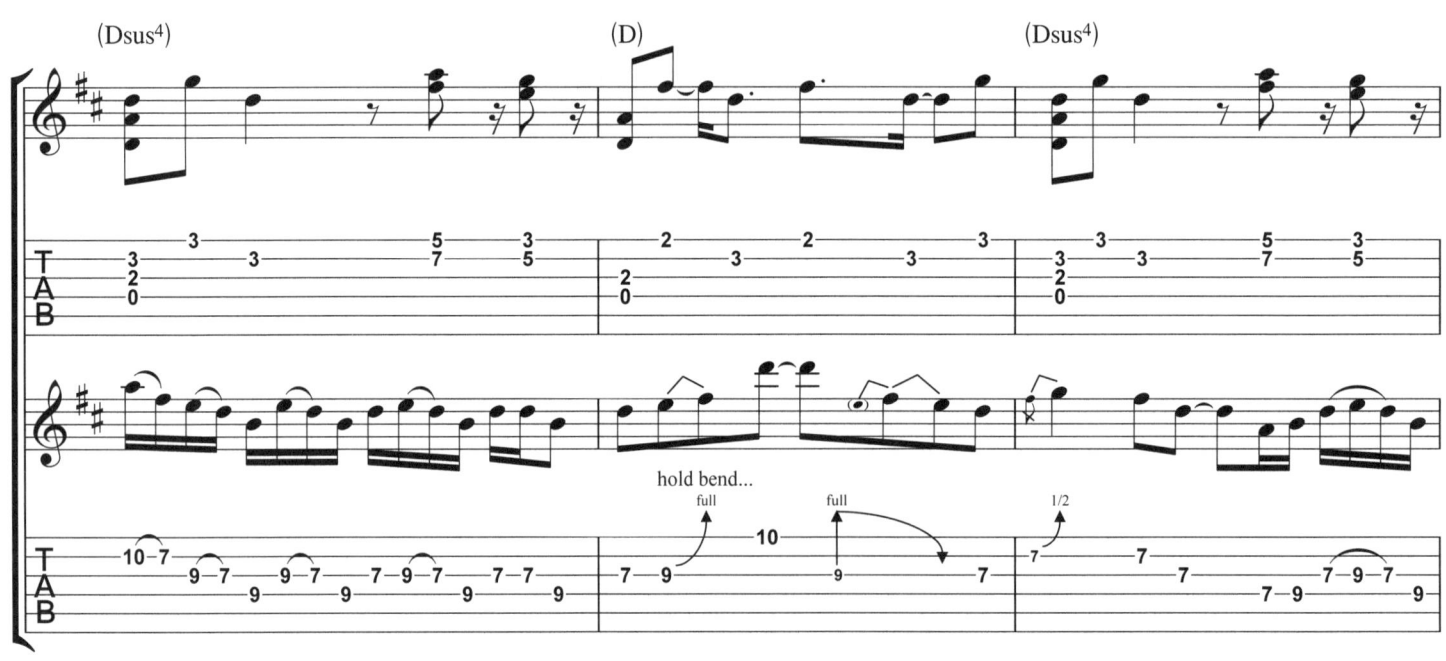

134

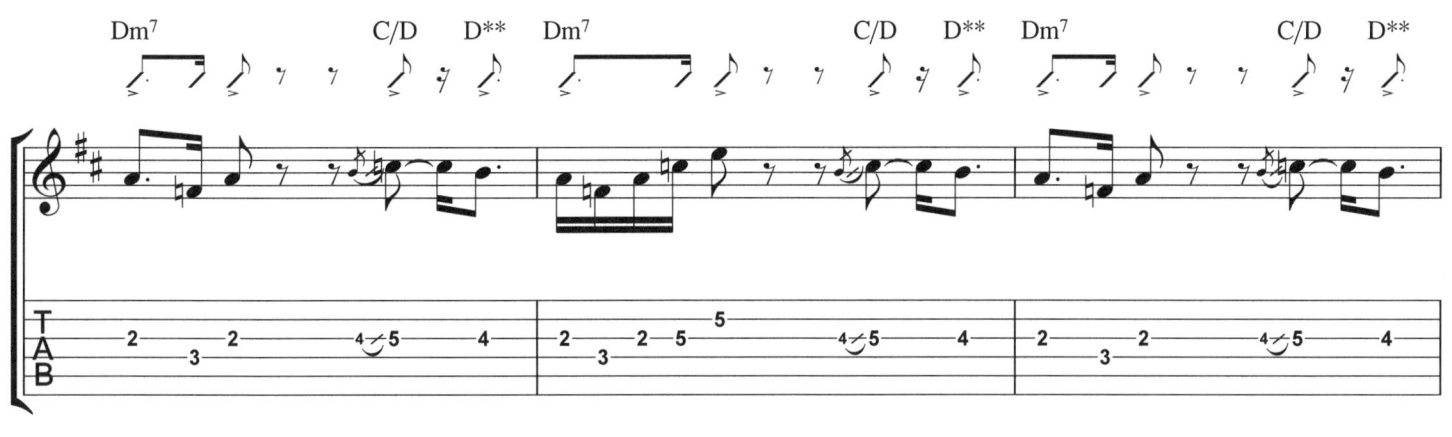
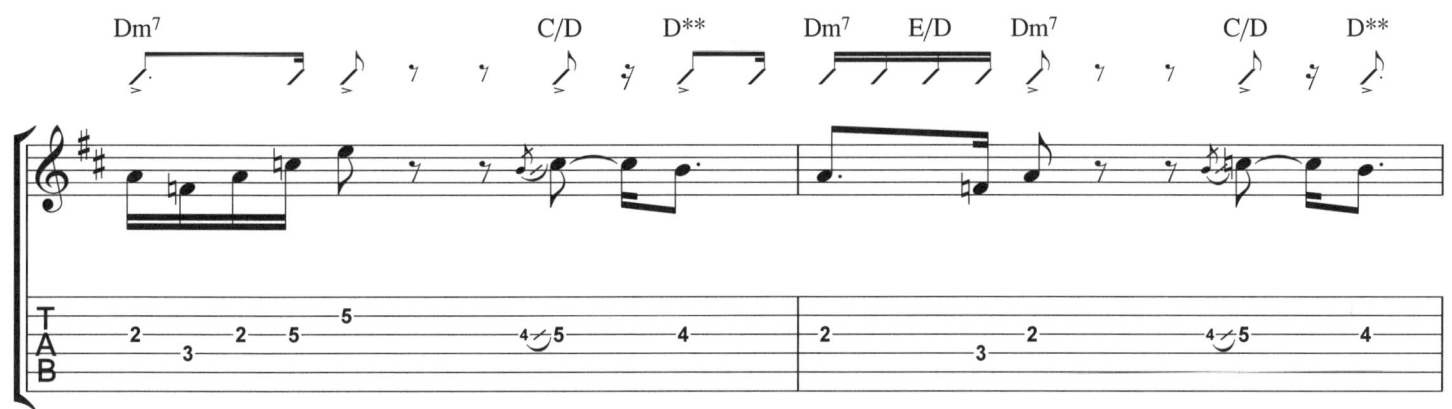
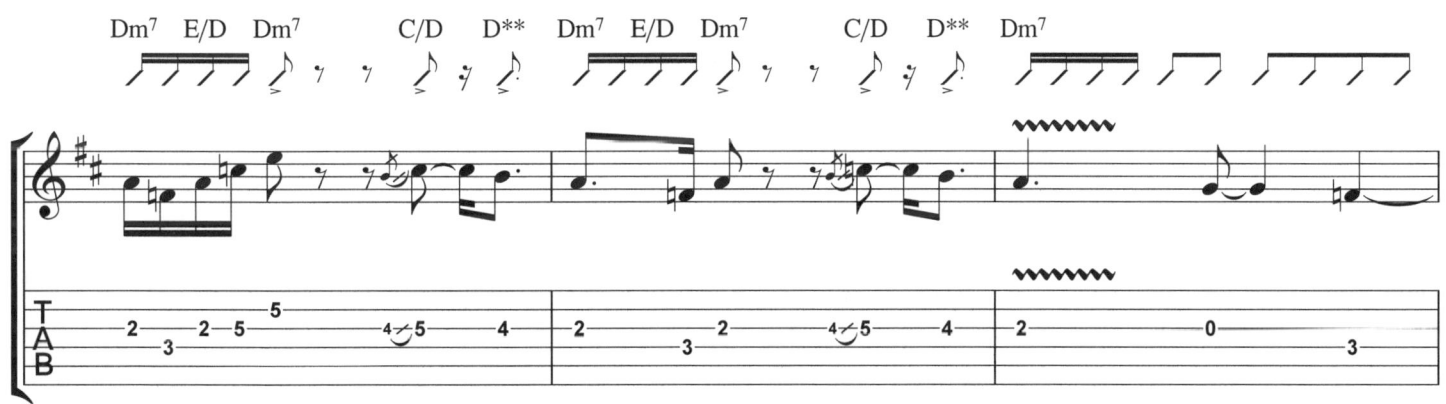

135

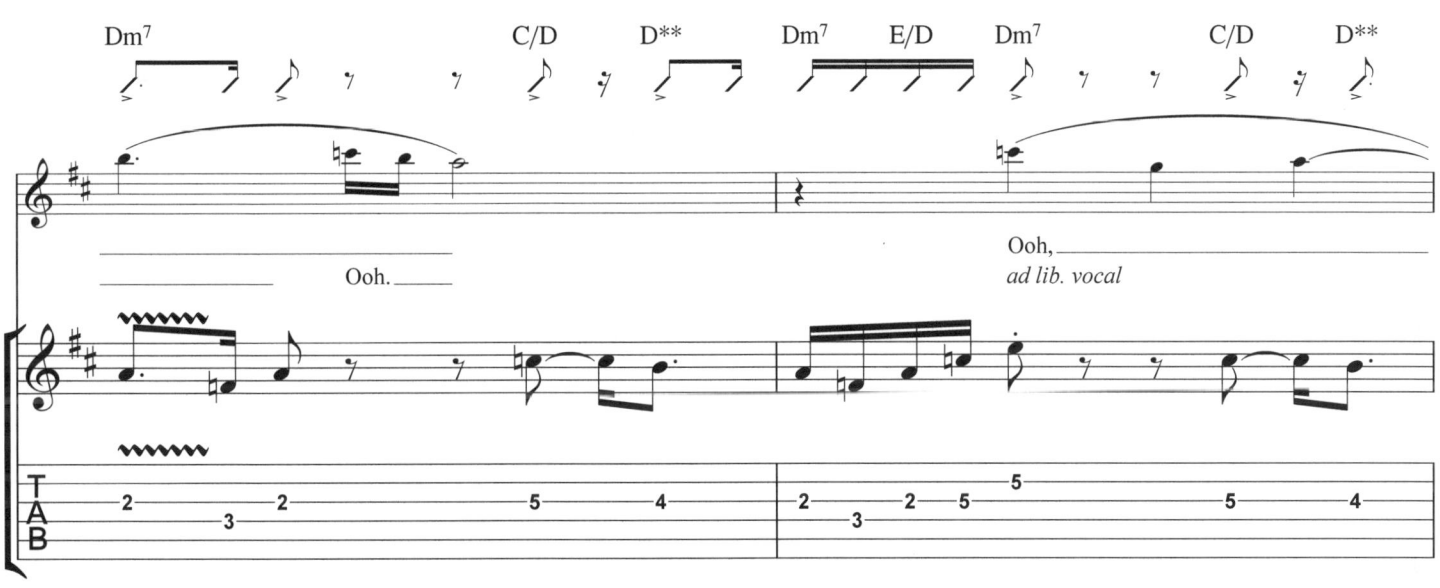
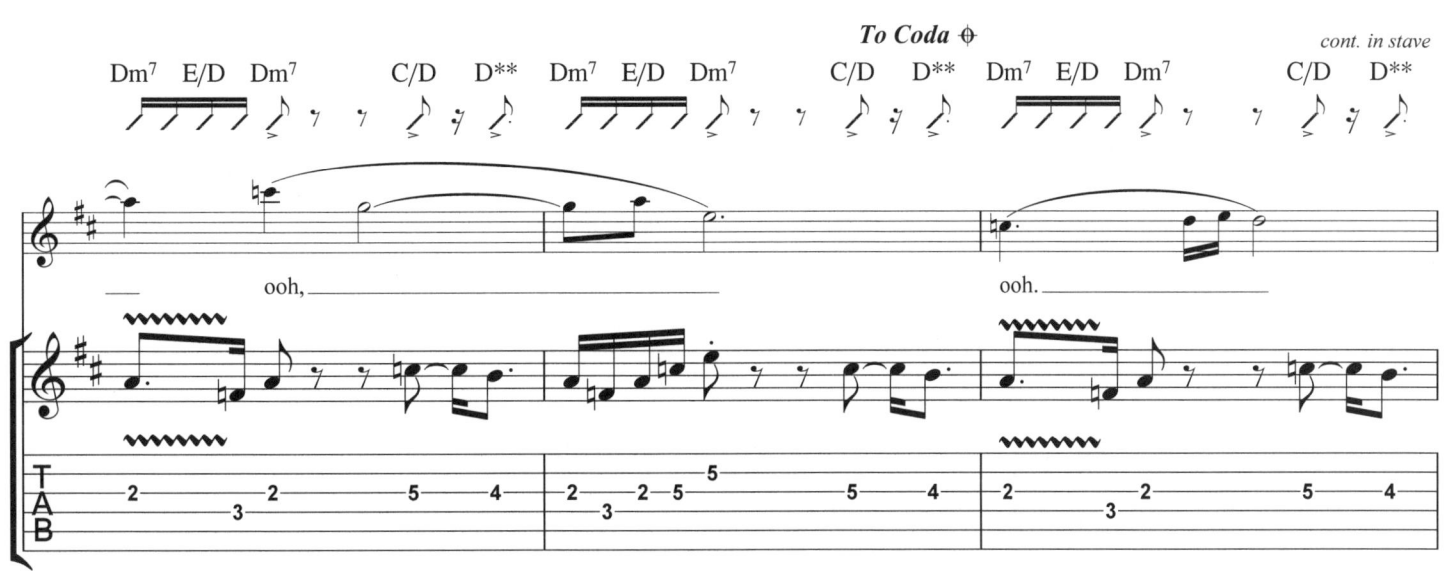

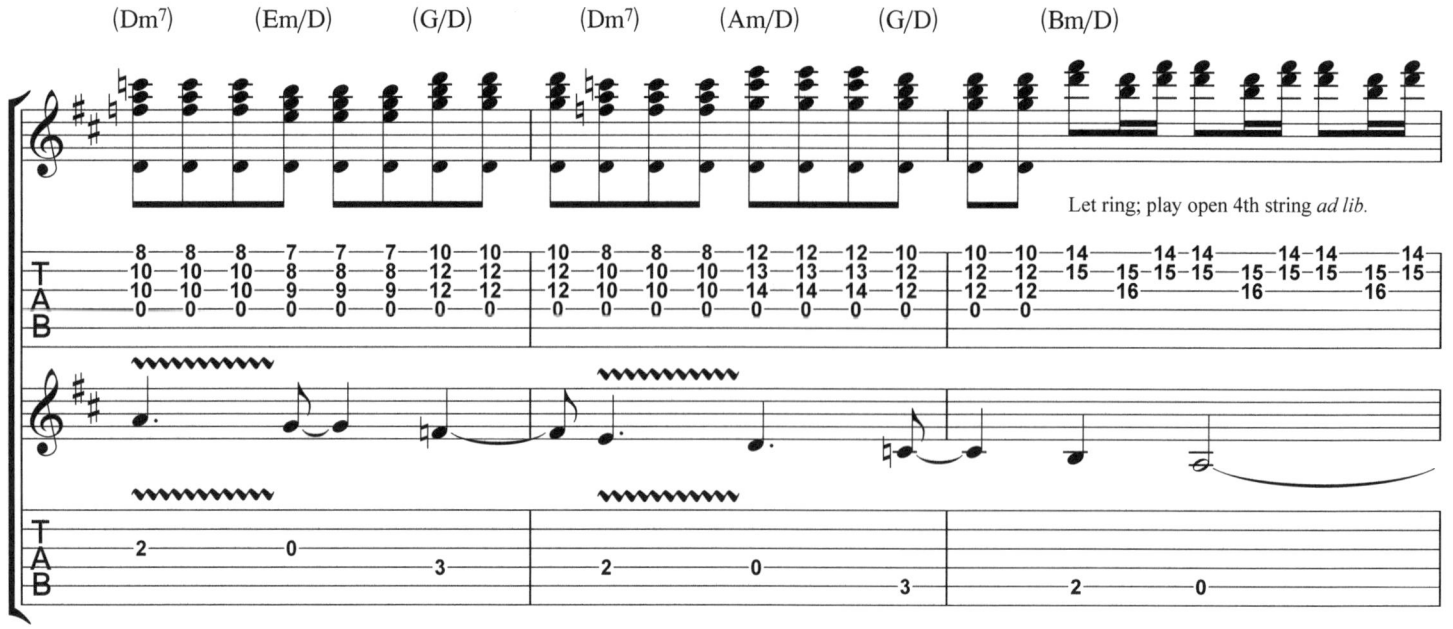
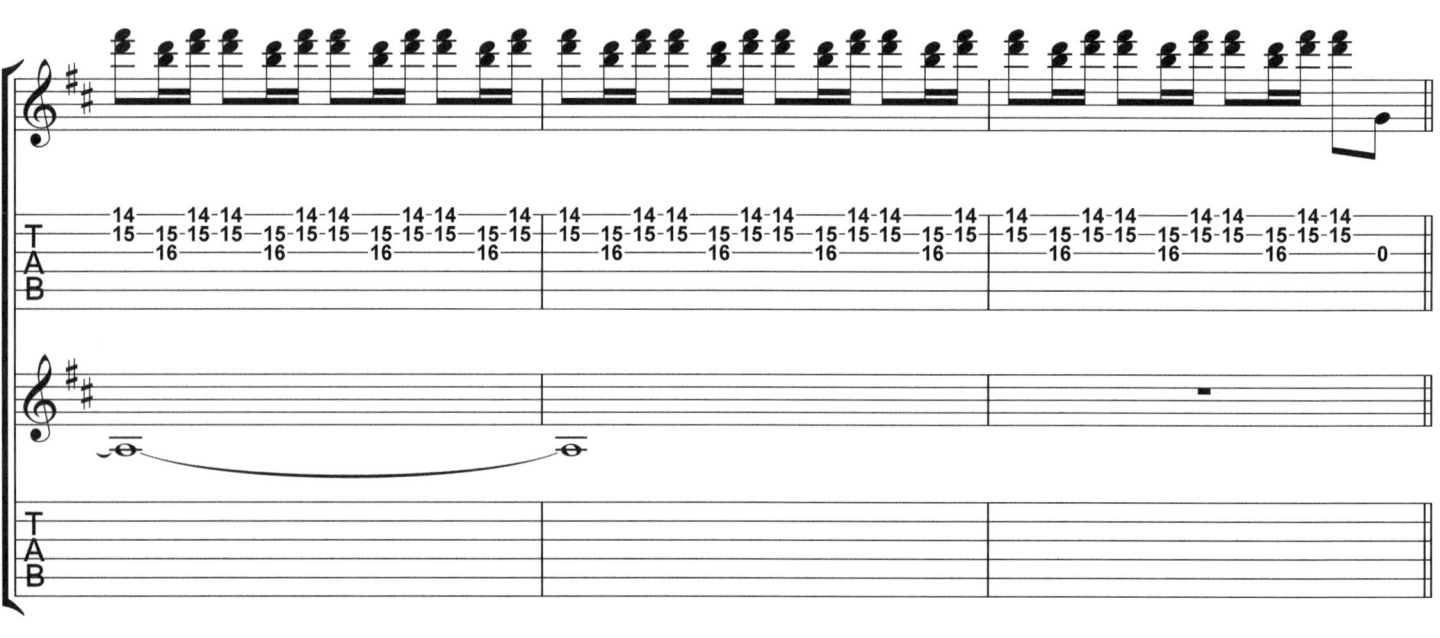
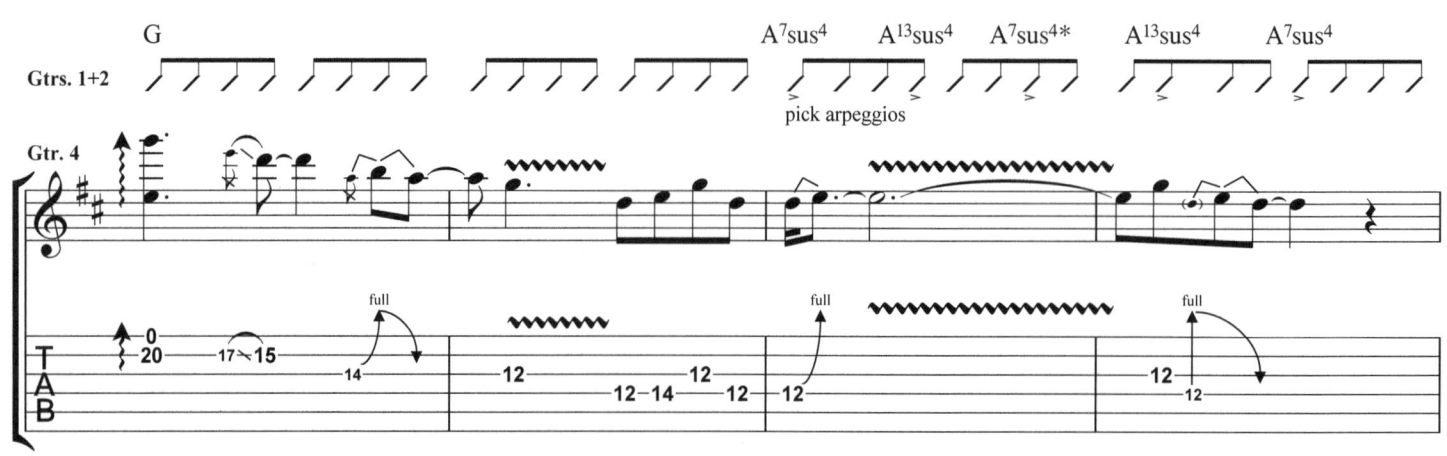

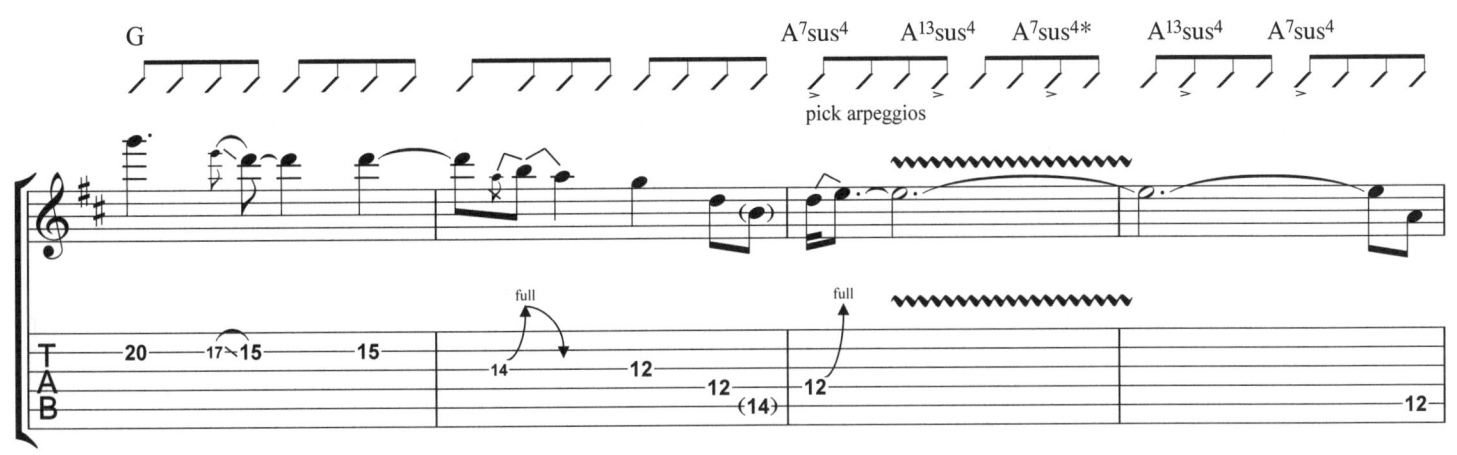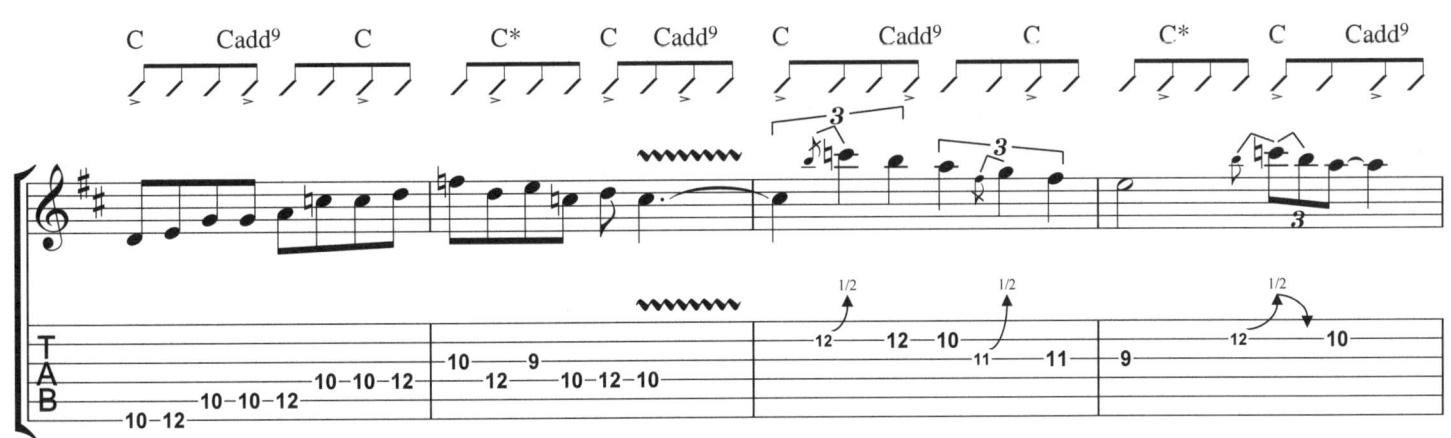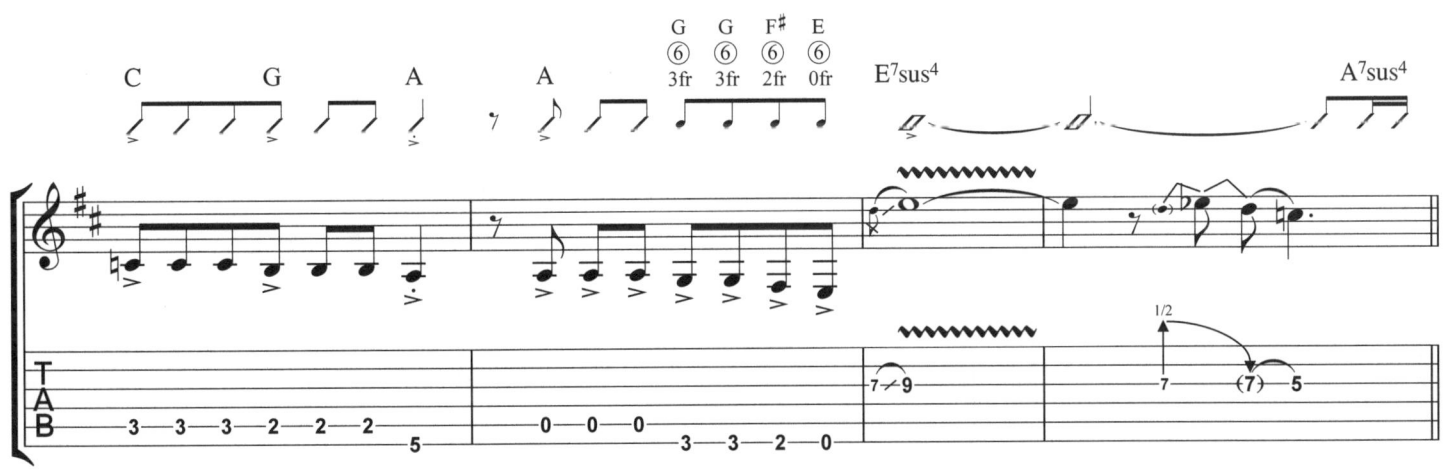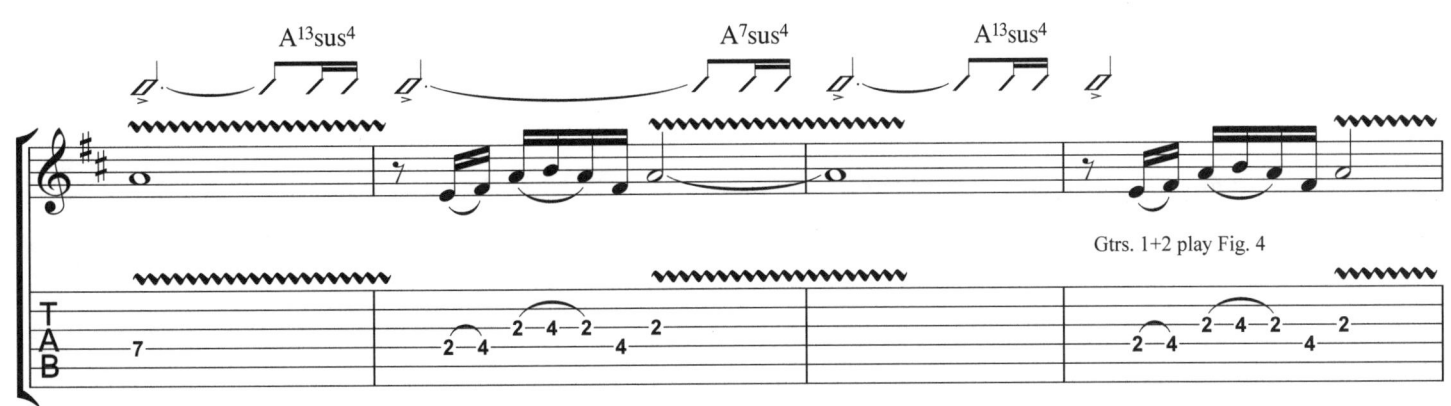

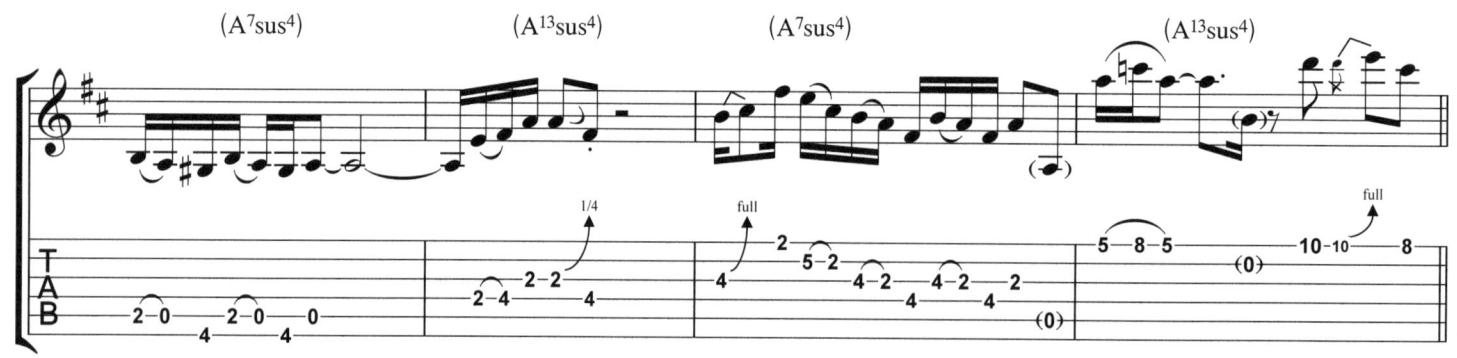
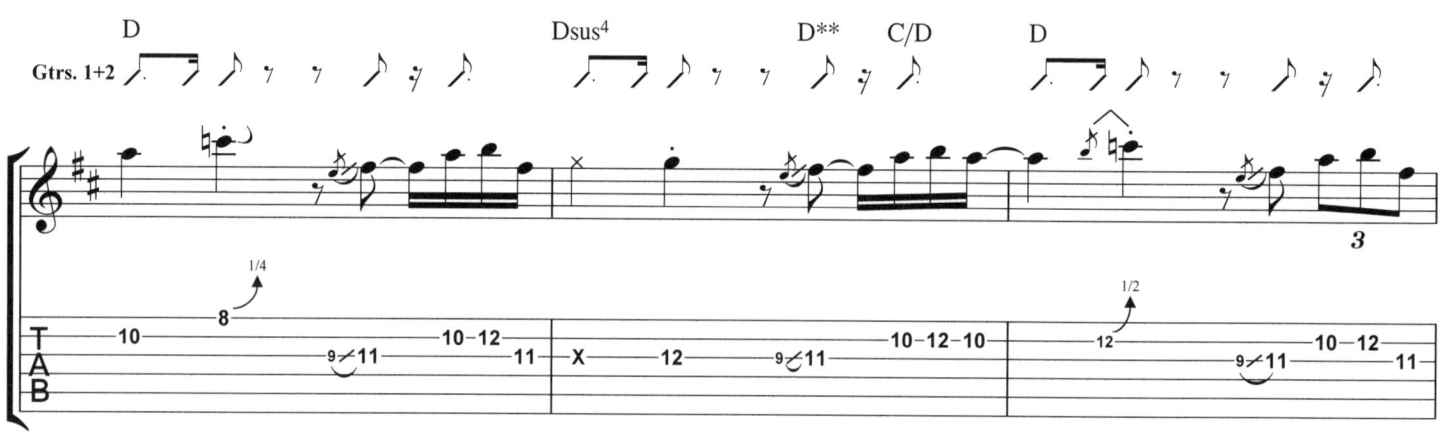

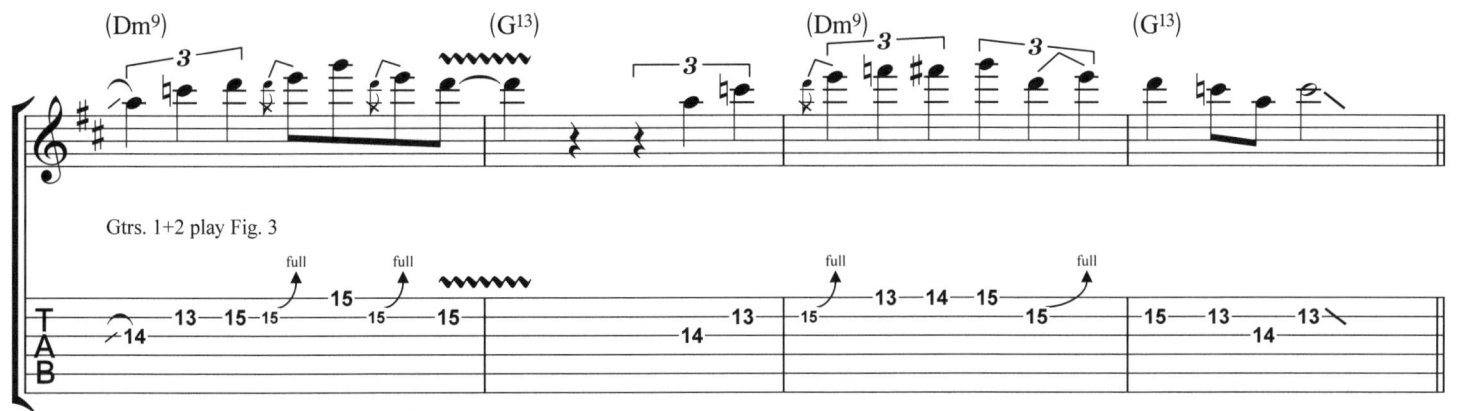
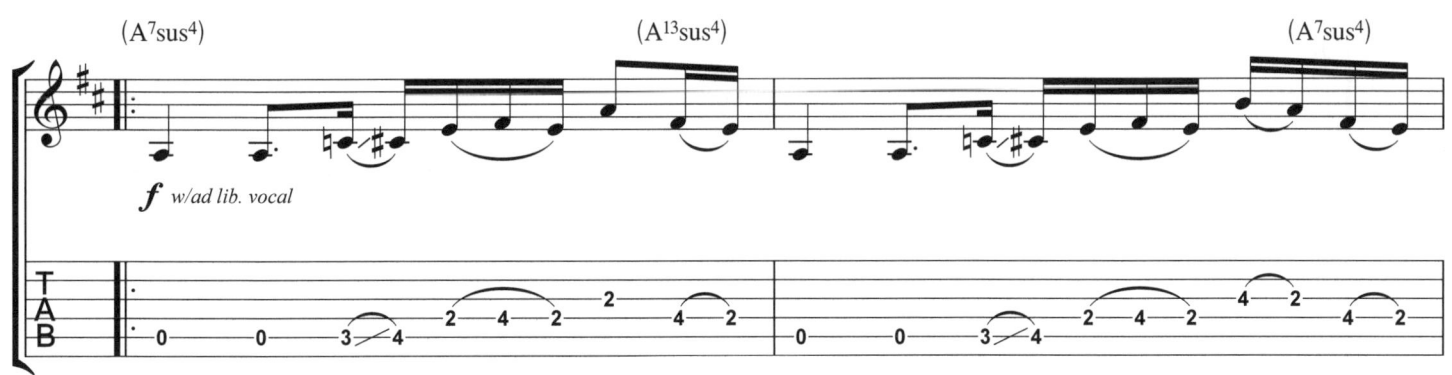

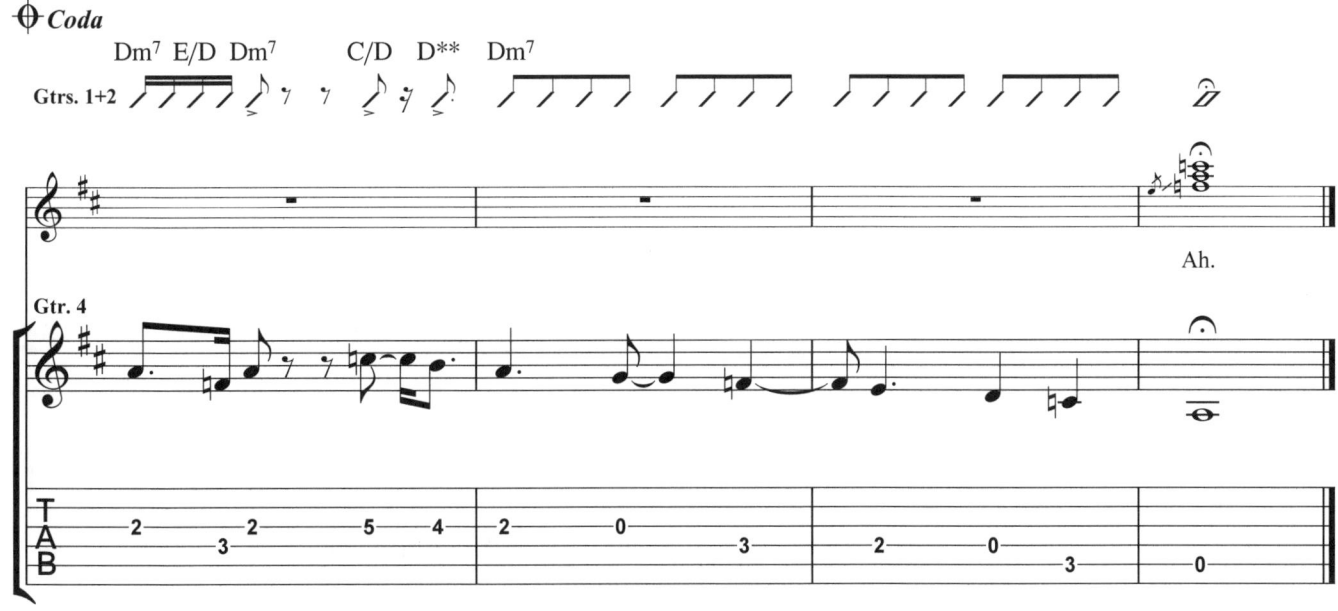

145

MISTY MOUNTAIN HOP
Words & Music by Jimmy Page, Robert Plant & John Paul Jones

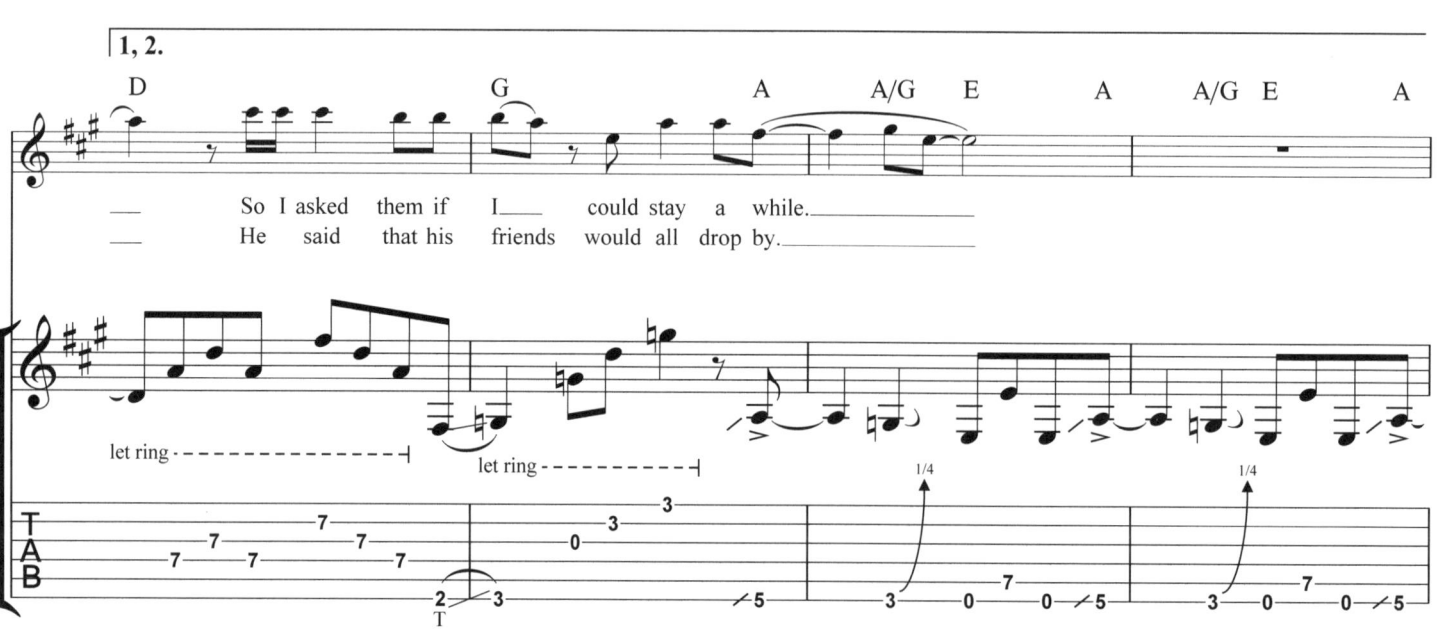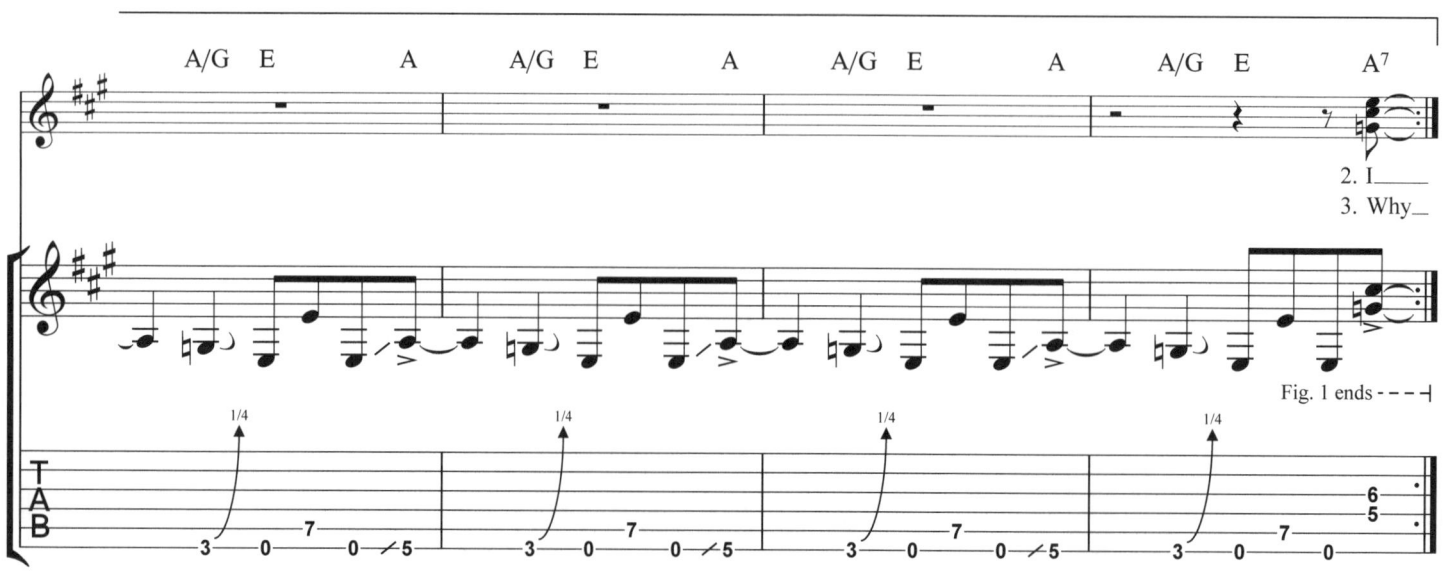

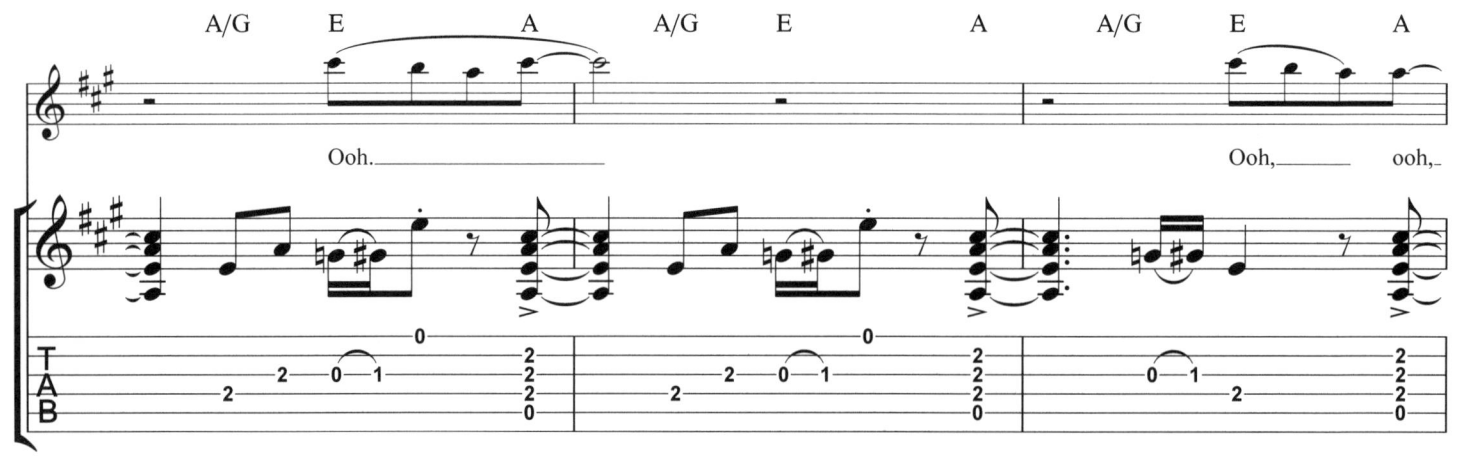
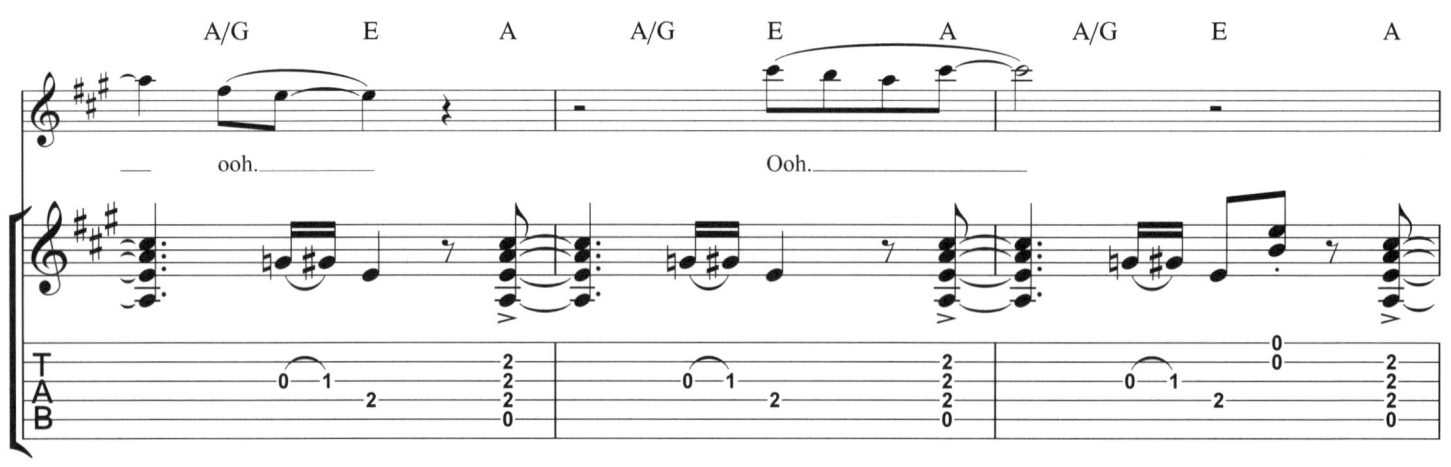
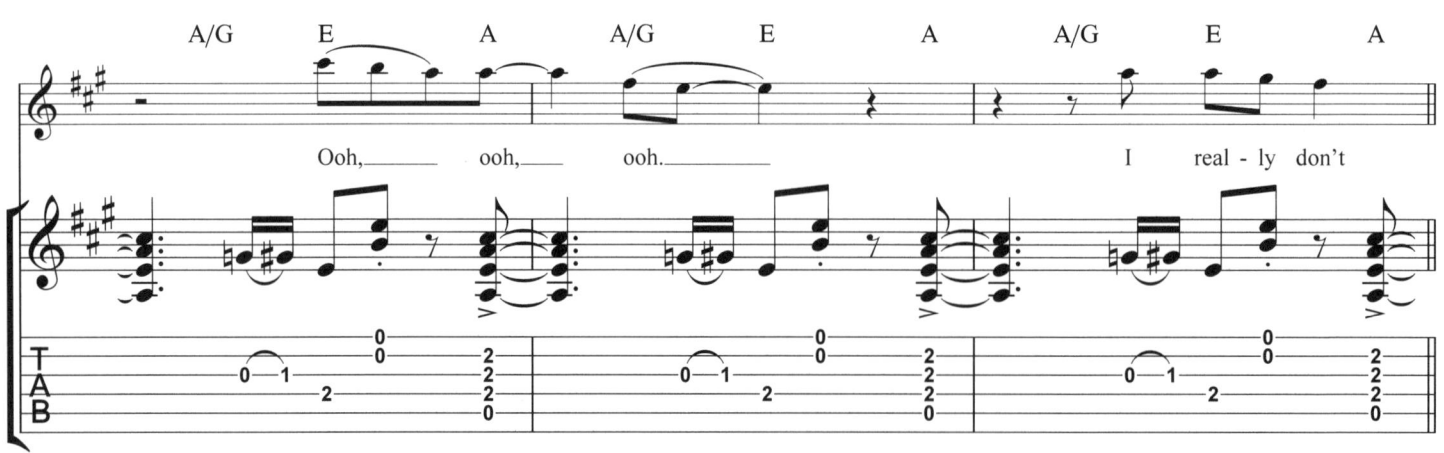
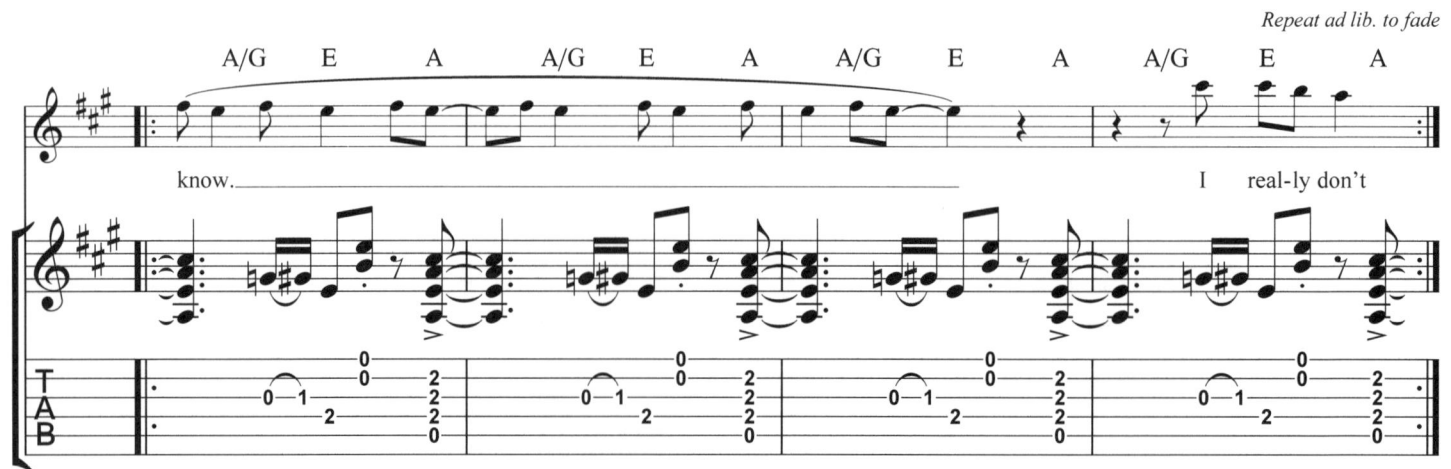

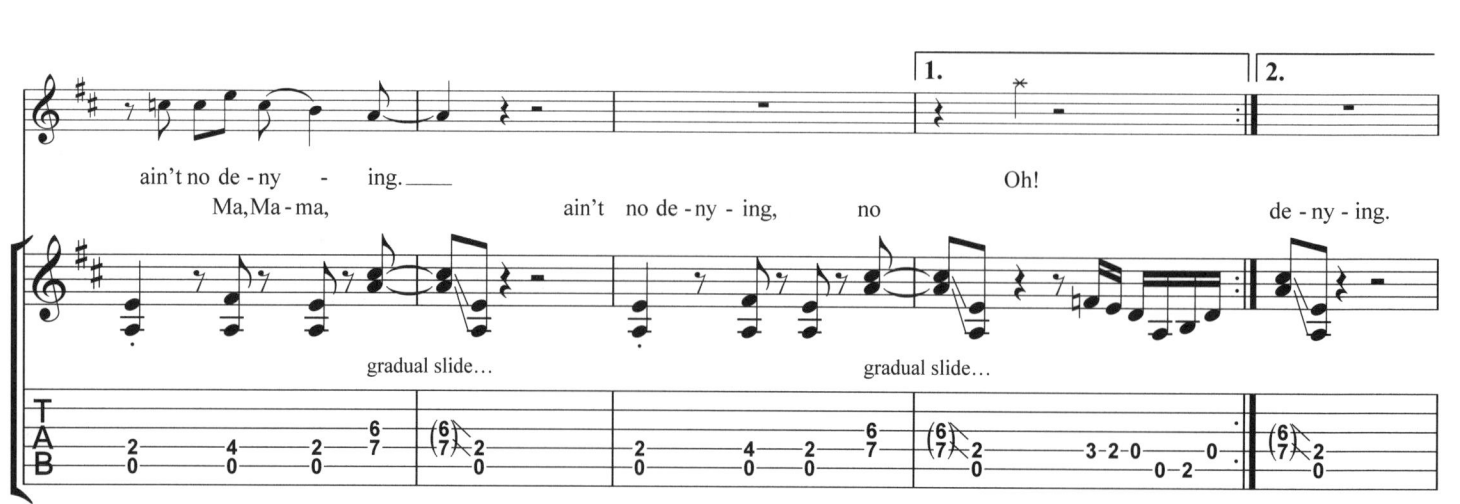

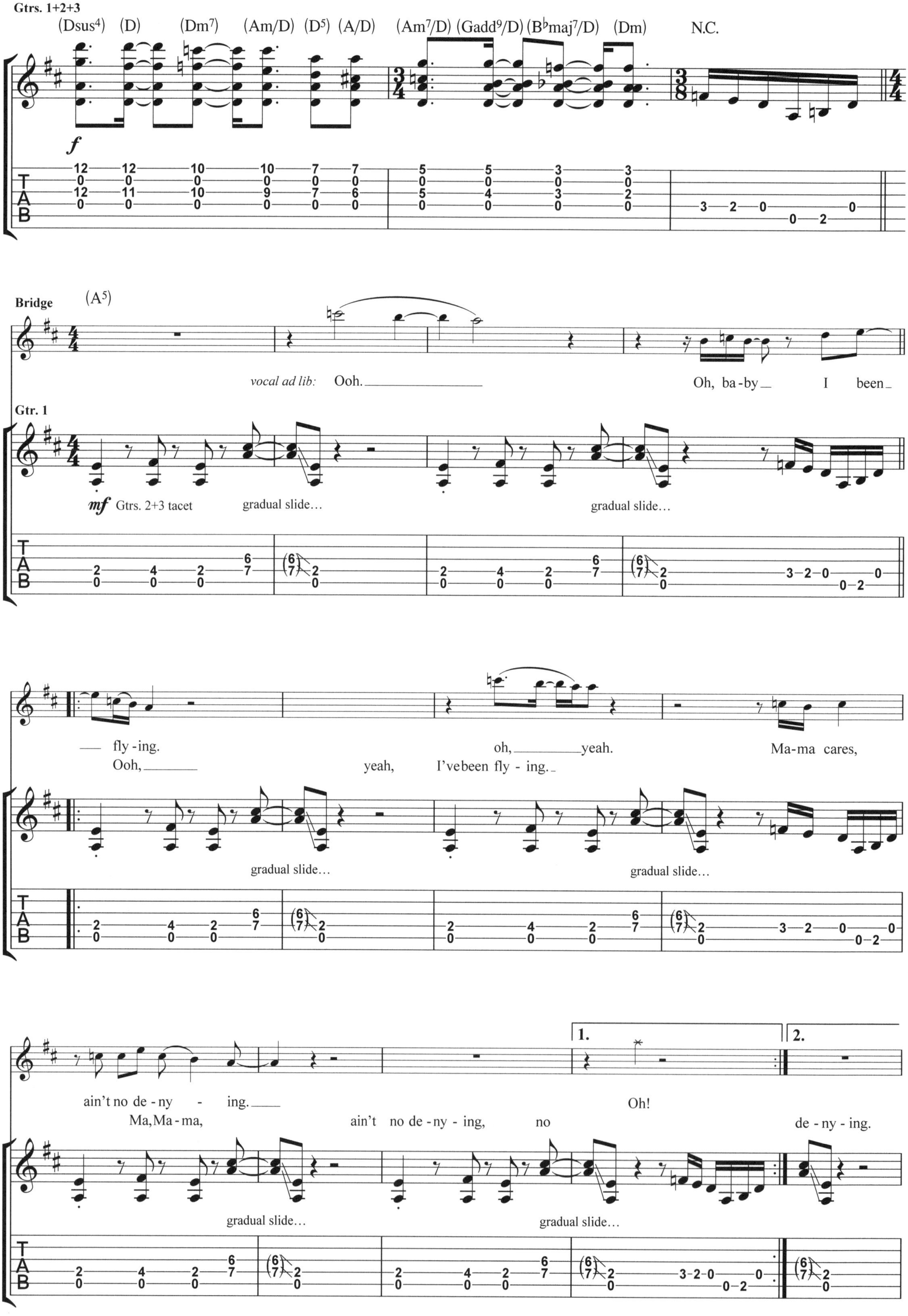
Gtrs. 1+2+3
(Dsus4) (D) (Dm7) (Am/D) (D5) (A/D) (Am7/D) (Gadd9/D) (B♭maj7/D) (Dm) N.C.
f
Bridge
(A5)
vocal ad lib: Ooh.
Oh, ba-by I been
Gtr. 1
mf Gtrs. 2+3 tacet
gradual slide…
fly-ing.
Ooh,
oh, yeah.
yeah, I've been fly-ing.
Ma-ma cares,
ain't no de-ny - ing.
Ma, Ma-ma,
ain't no de-ny-ing, no
Oh!
de-ny-ing.
1.
2.

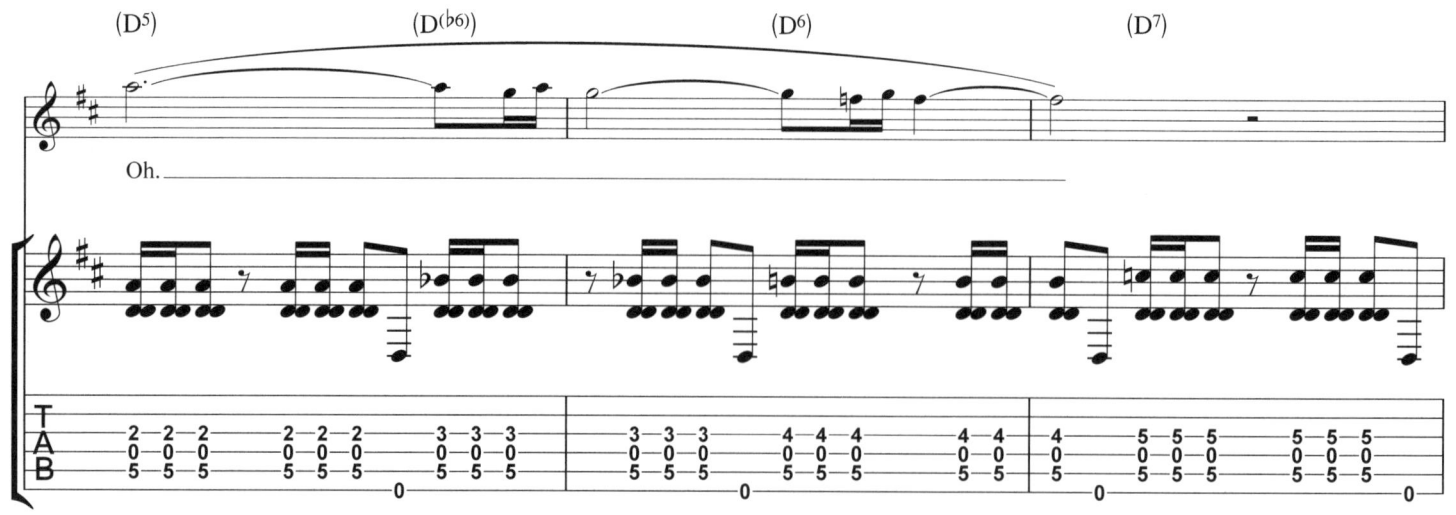

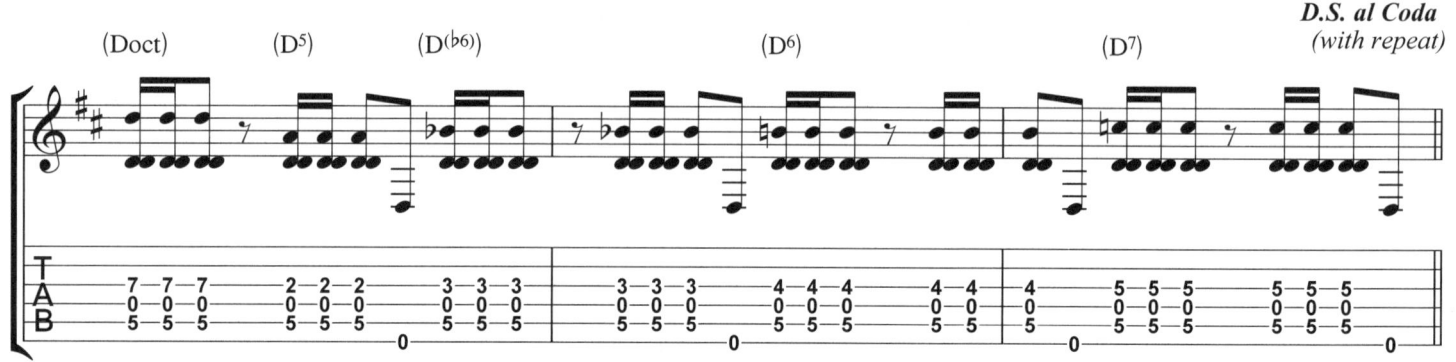

Coda

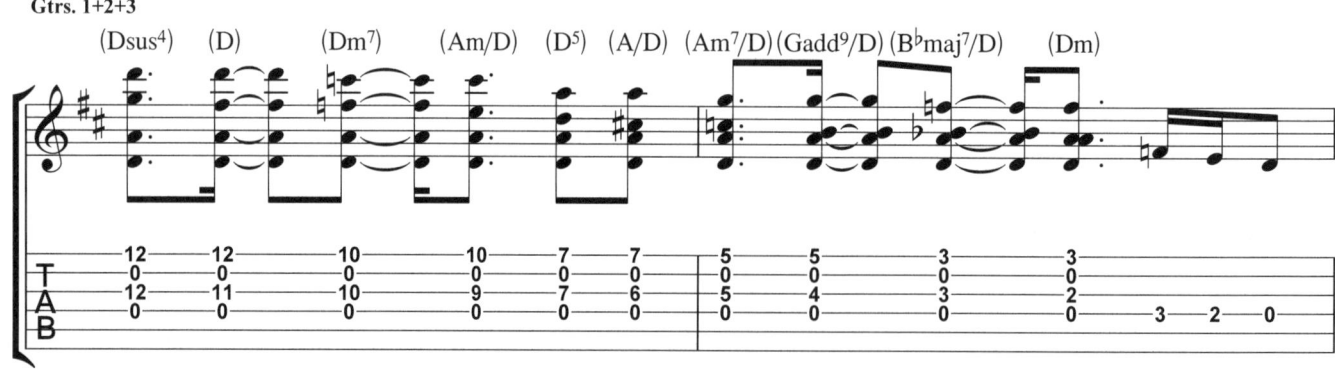

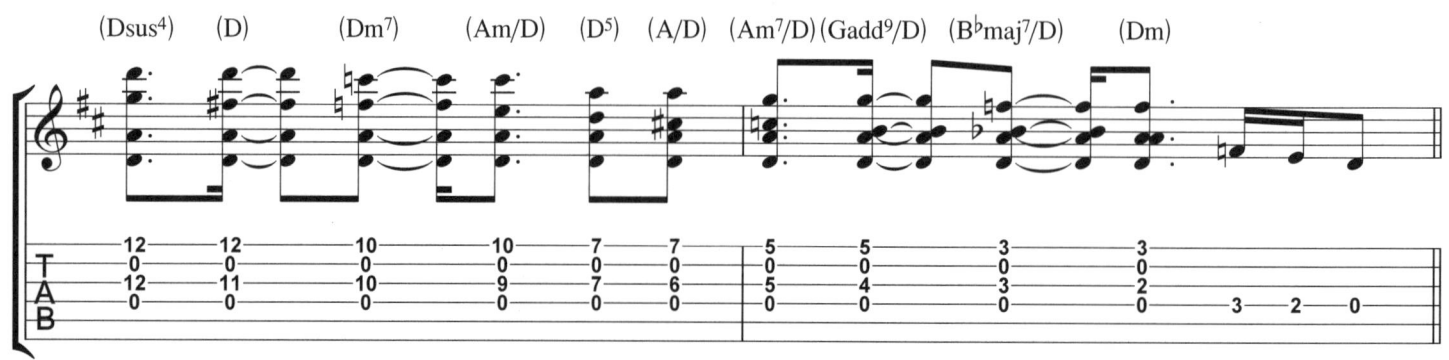

WHOLE LOTTA LOVE

Words & Music by Jimmy Page, Robert Plant, John Paul Jones, John Bonham & Willie Dixon

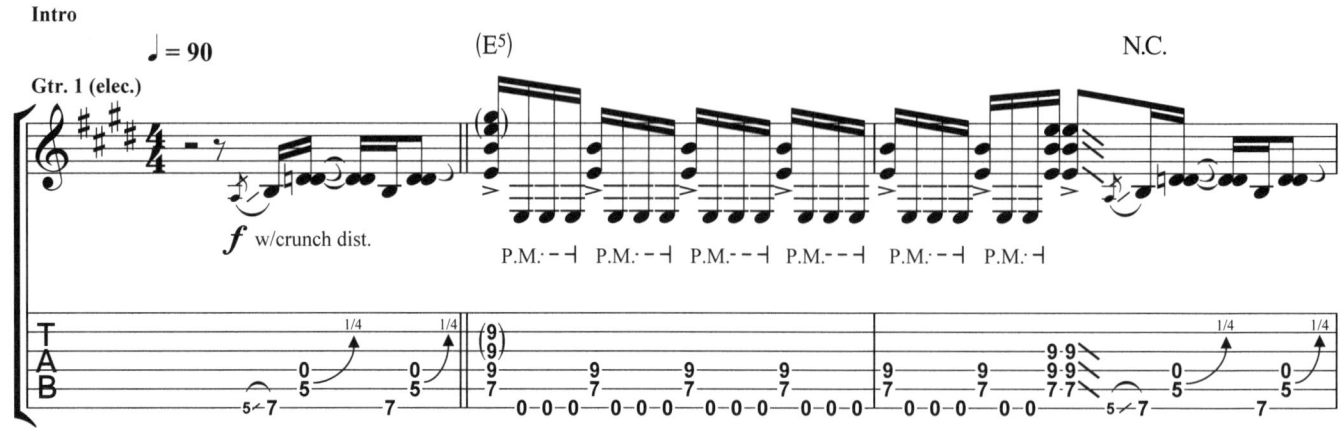

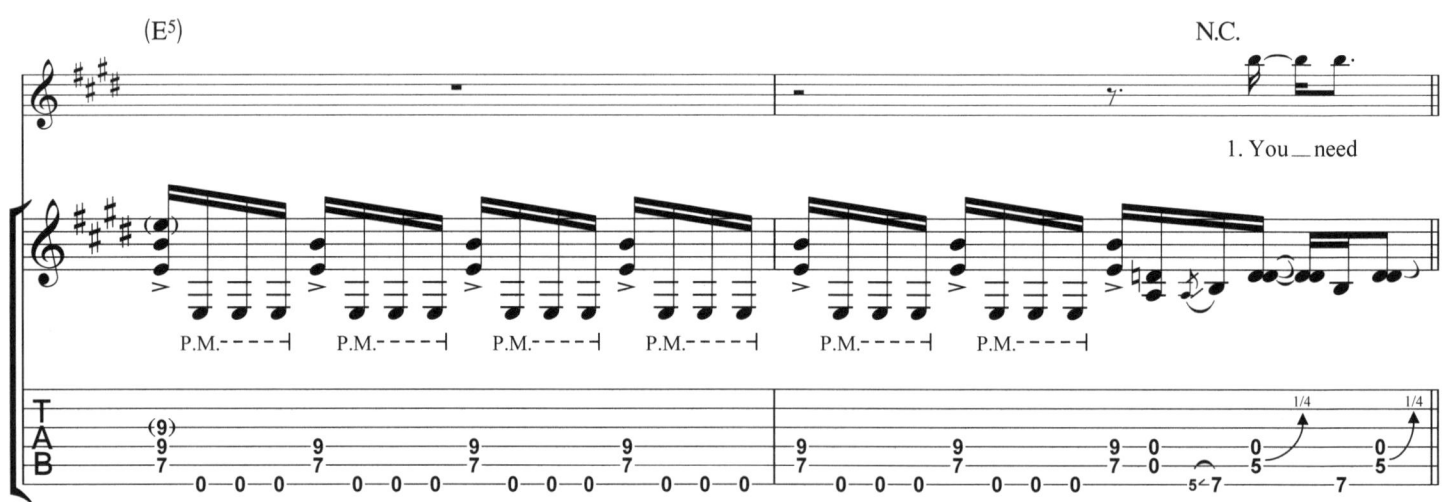

© Copyright 1969 Succubus Music Limited/Sons Of Einion Limited/Cap Three Limited/Estate of J. Bonham.
Print Rights Administered by Music Sales Limited.
All Rights Reserved. International Copyright Secured.

8va
(hold)
full
2 1/2

D.S. al Coda
3. You been
8va
full
1 1/2
1/4

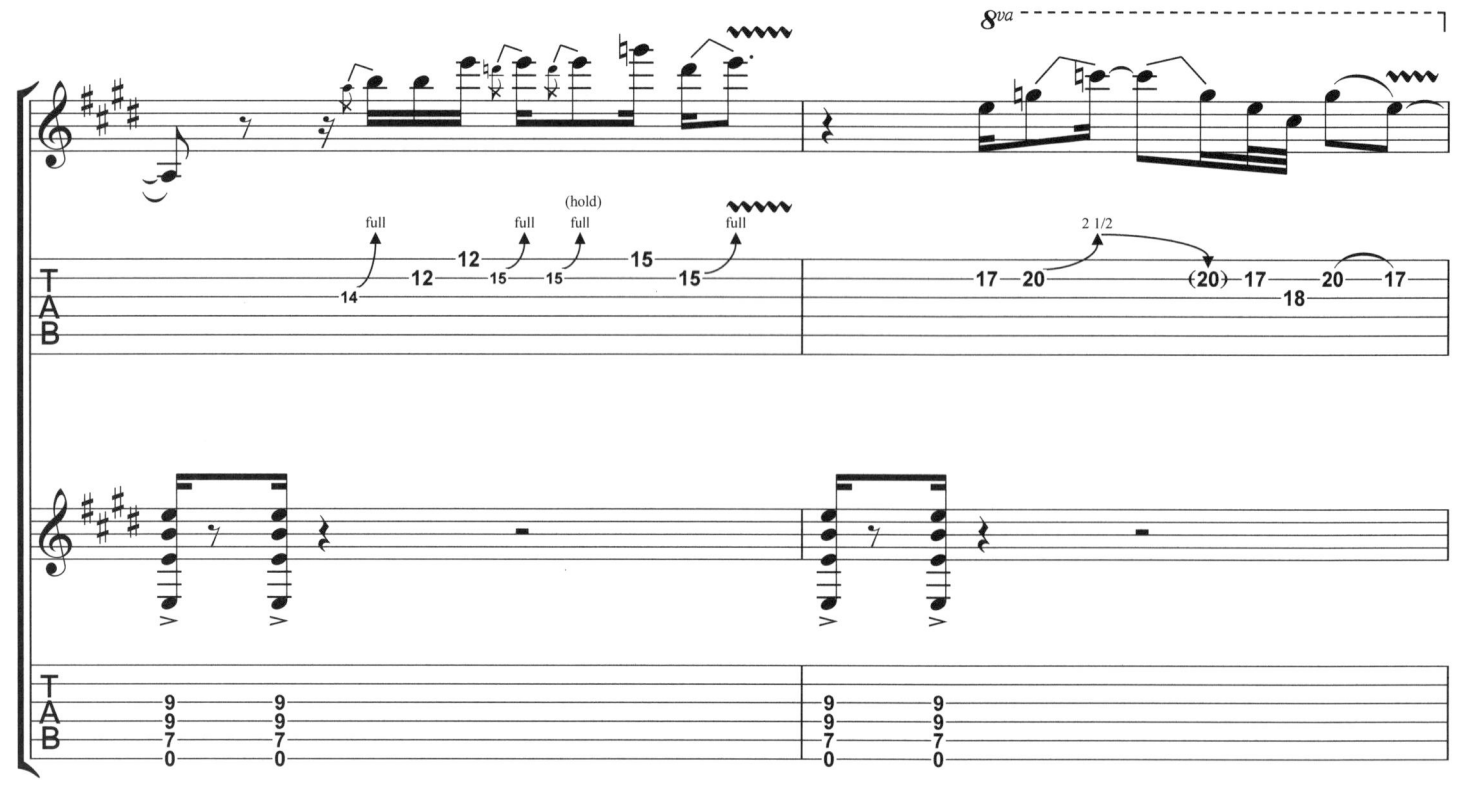

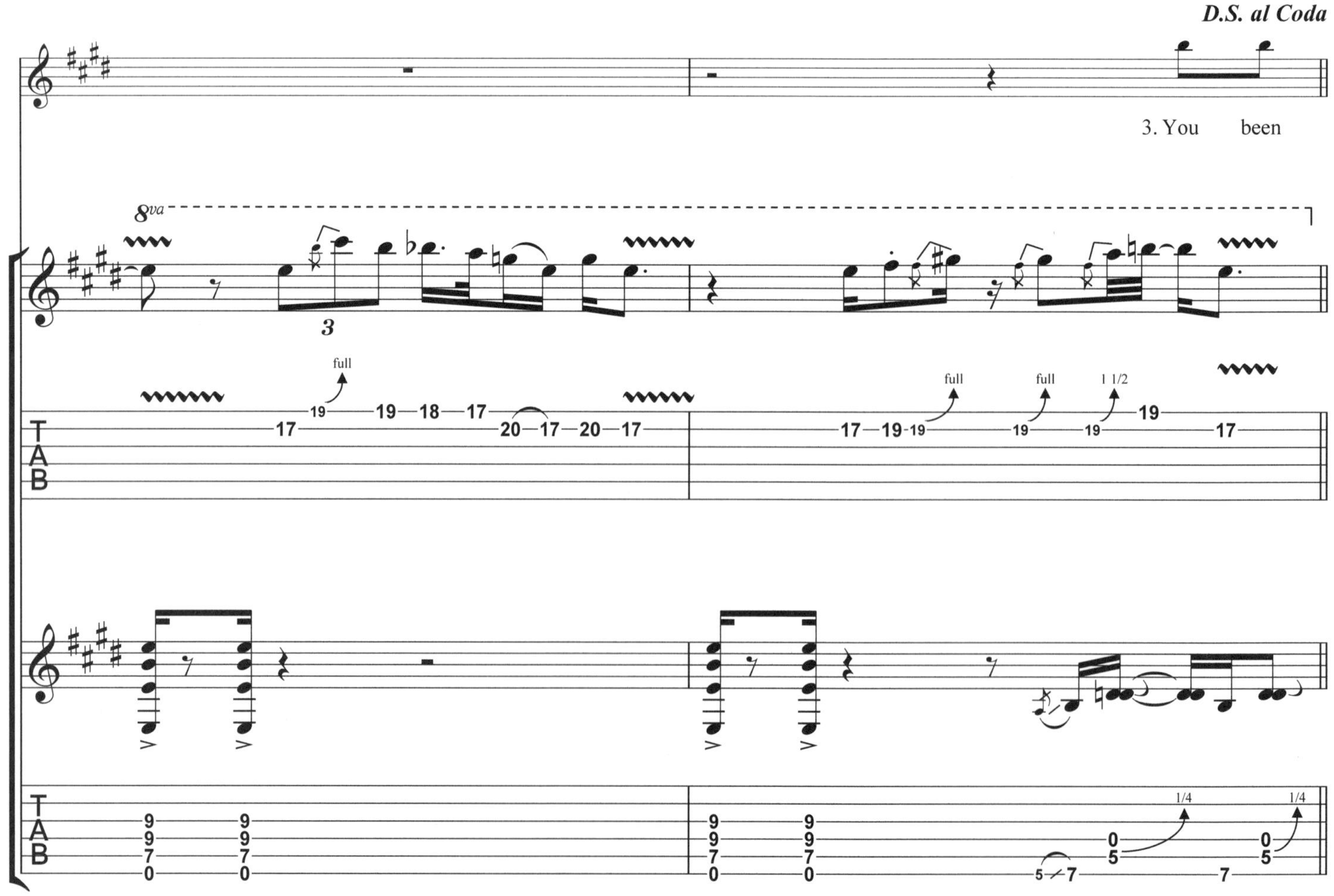

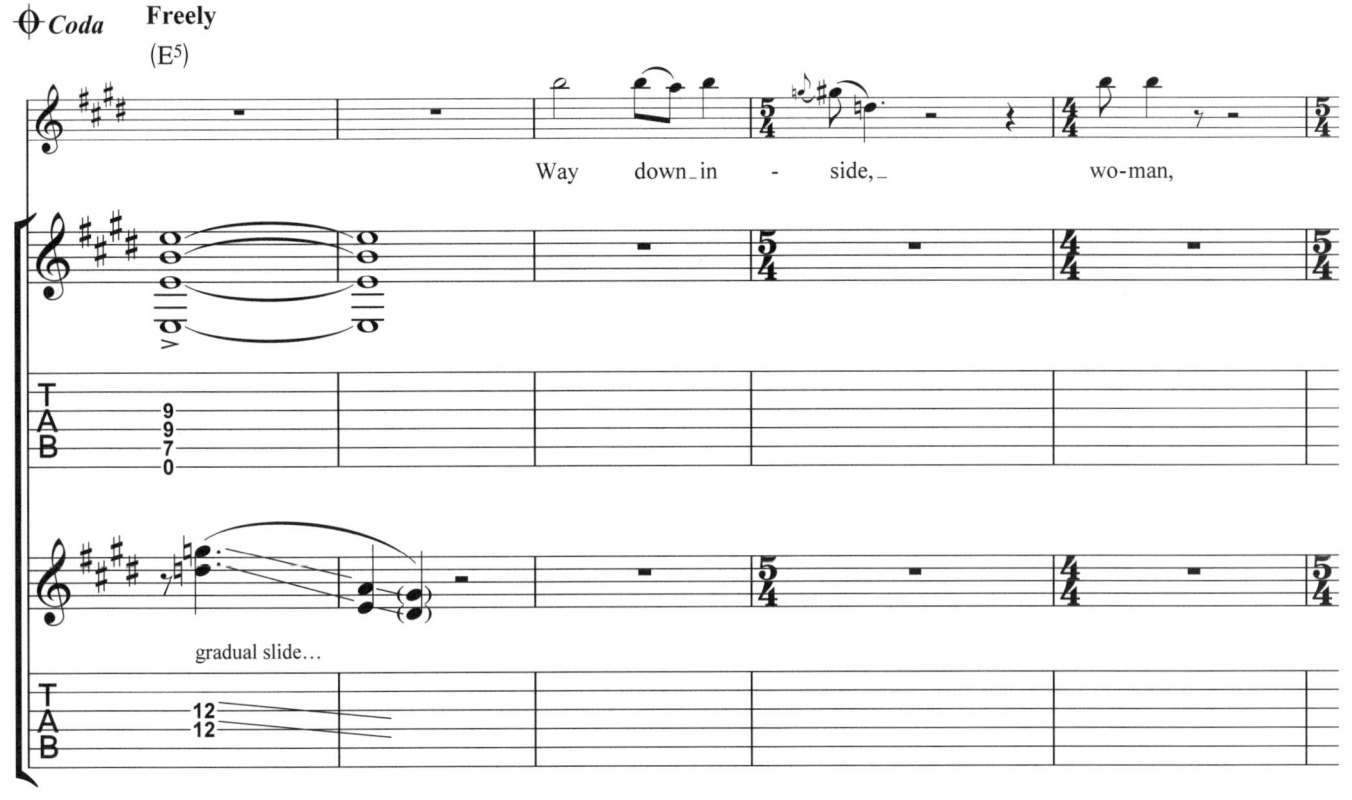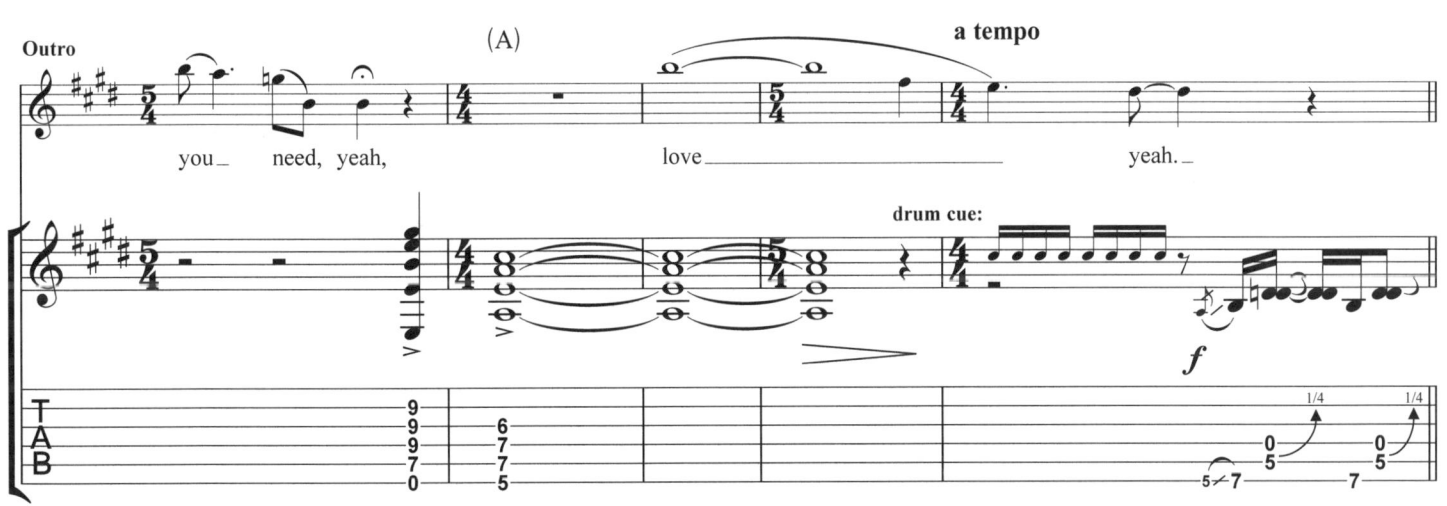

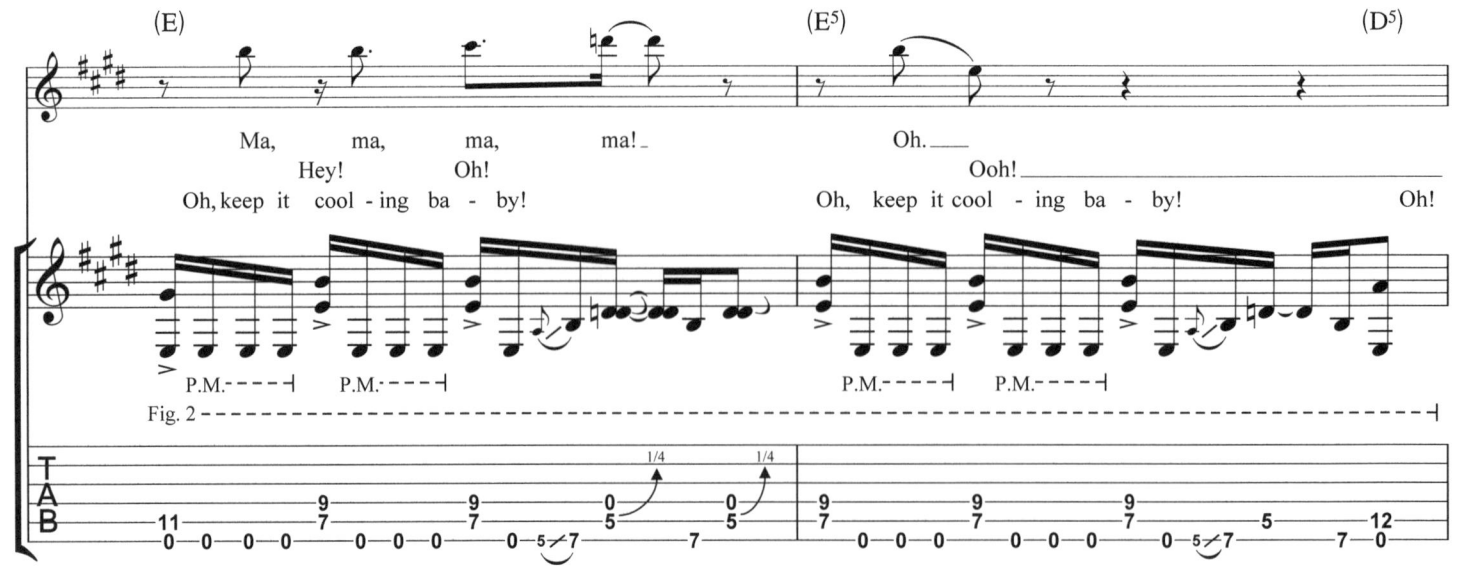
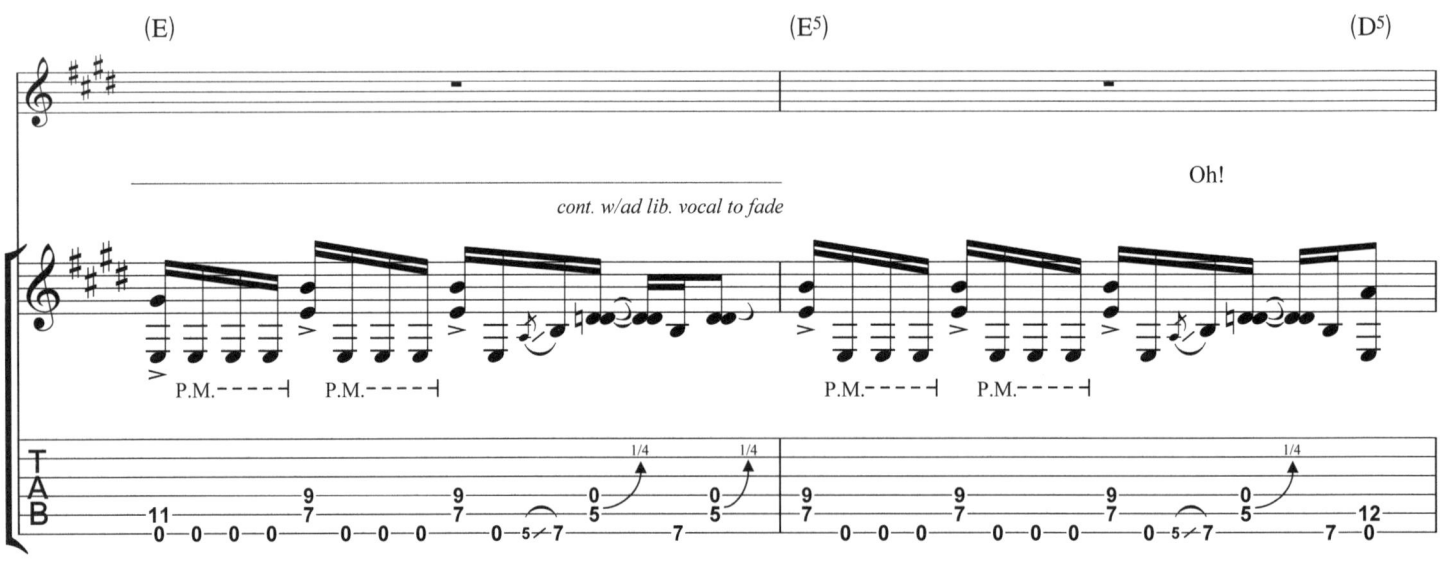
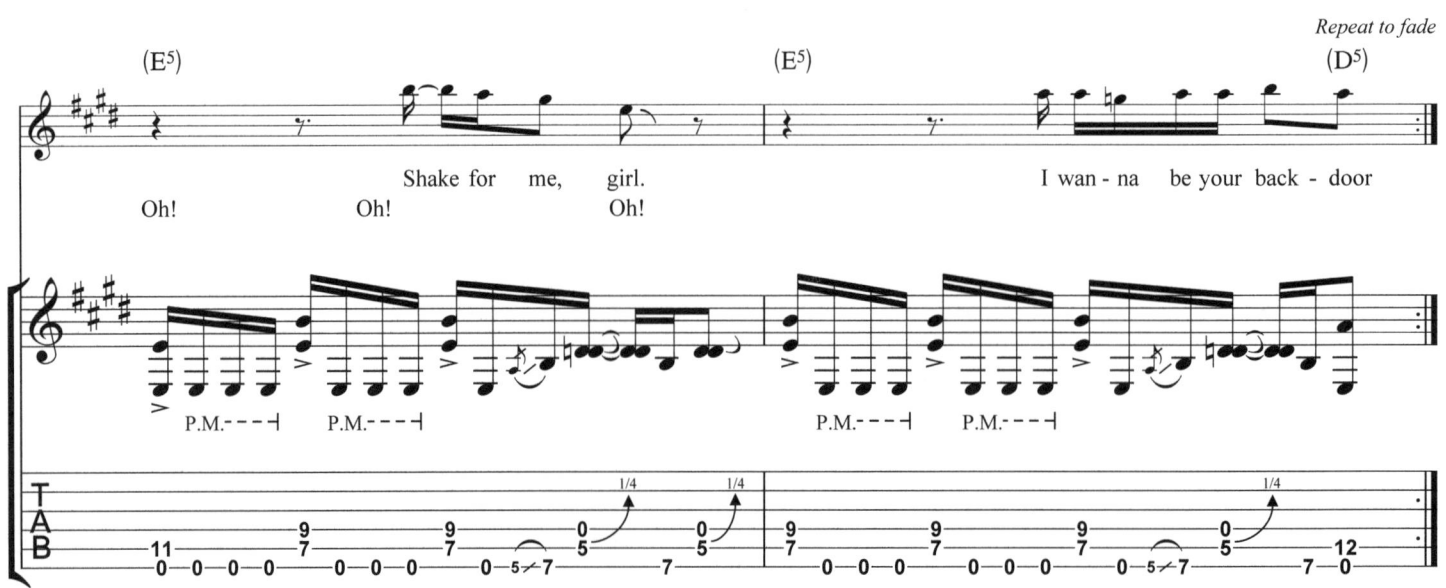

ROCK AND ROLL

Words & Music by Jimmy Page, Robert Plant, John Paul Jones & John Bonham

© Copyright 1972 Succubus Music Limited/Sons Of Einion Limited/Cap Three Limited/Estate of J. Bonham.
Print Rights Administered by Music Sales Limited.
All Rights Reserved. International Copyright Secured.

(A5)
1. It's
...Fig. 1 ends
1/4

Verse
(A5)
been a long time since I rock and rolled.
(2.) been a long time since the book of love.
(3.) seems so long since we walked in the moon - light.
It's
(I)
sim.
Fig. 2...
1/4

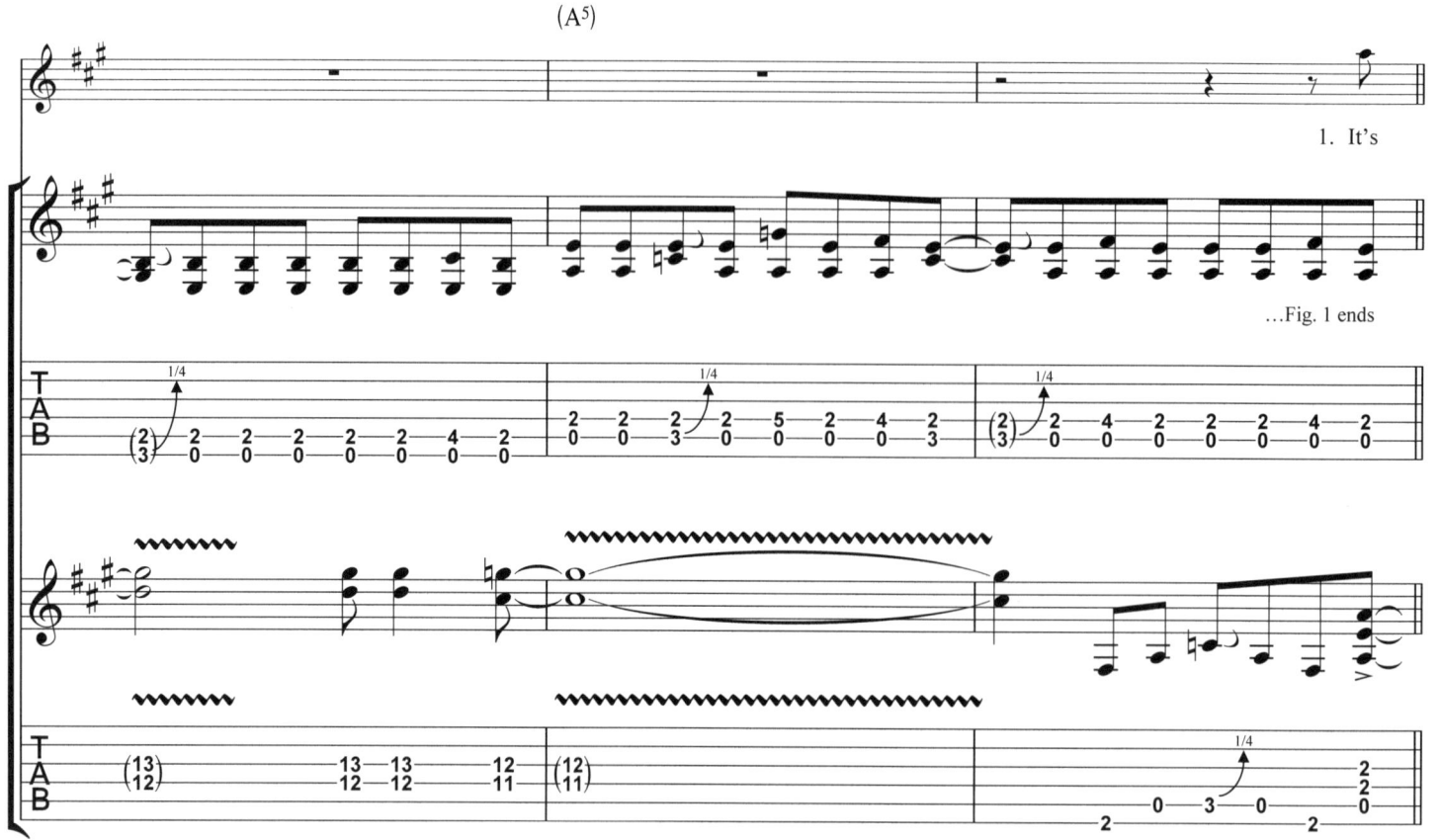

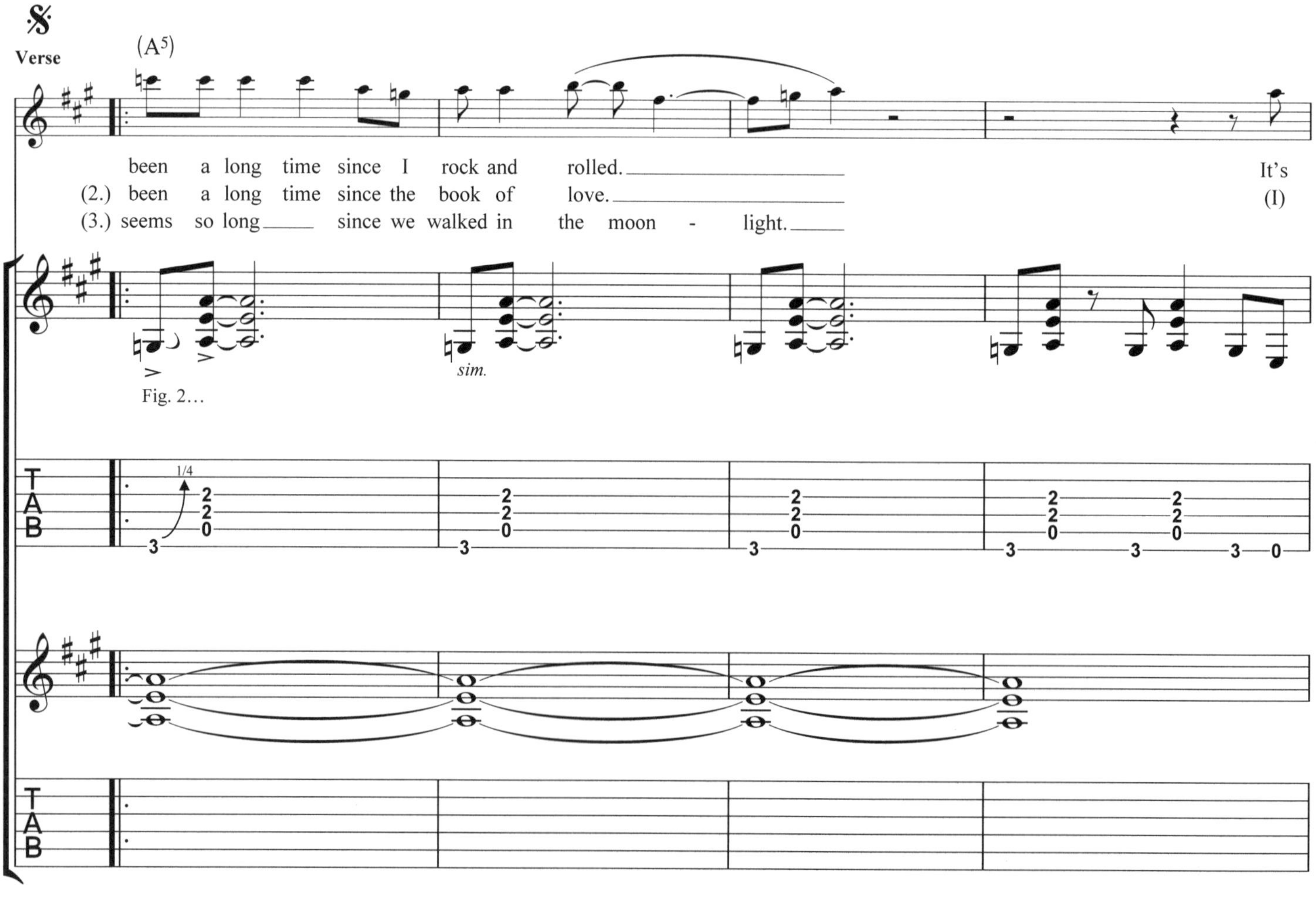

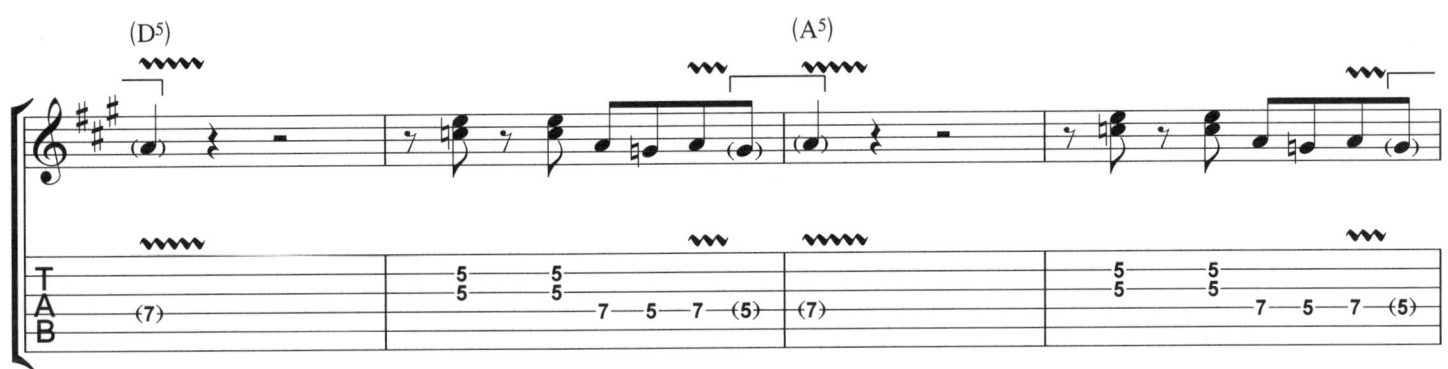
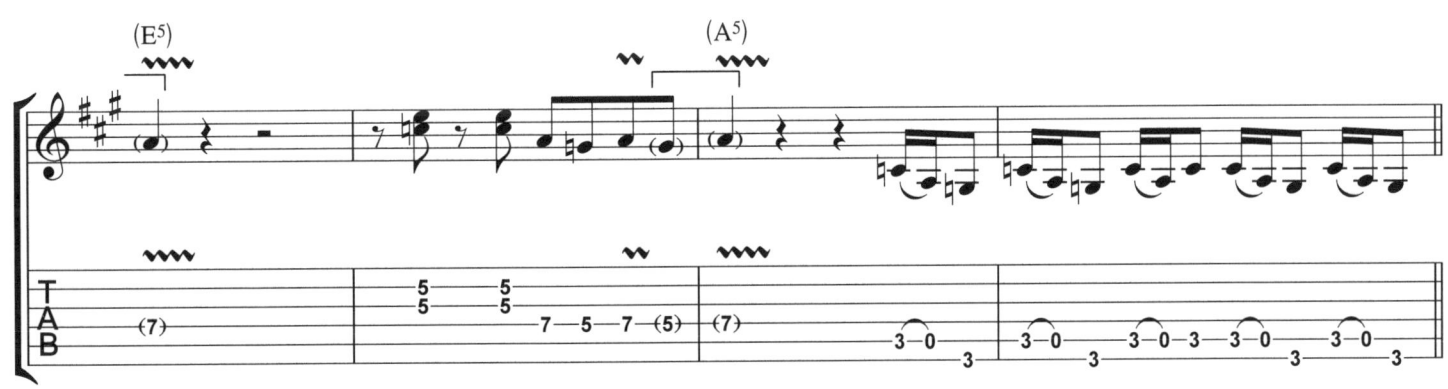

171

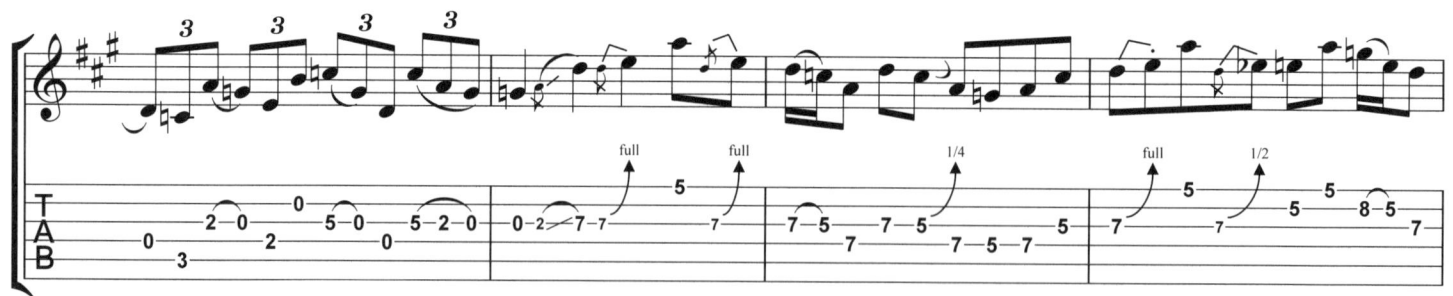
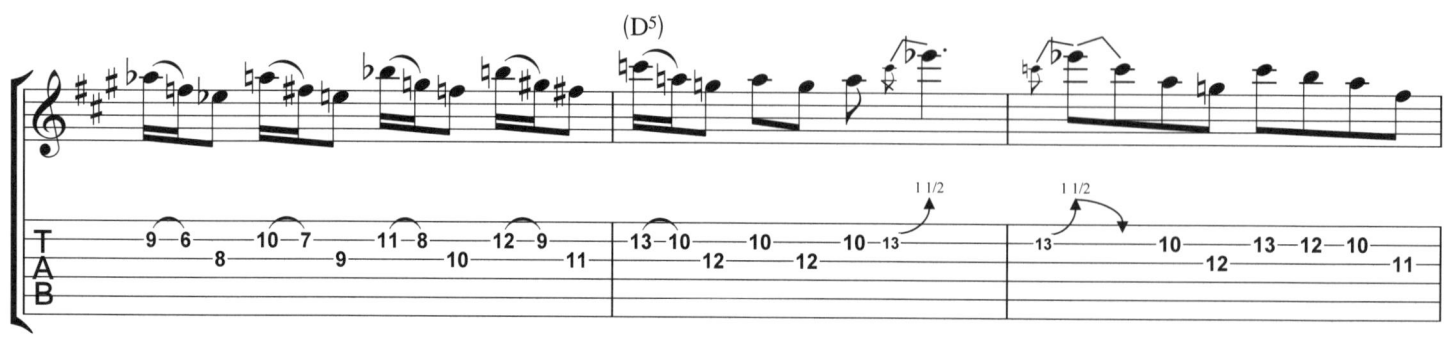
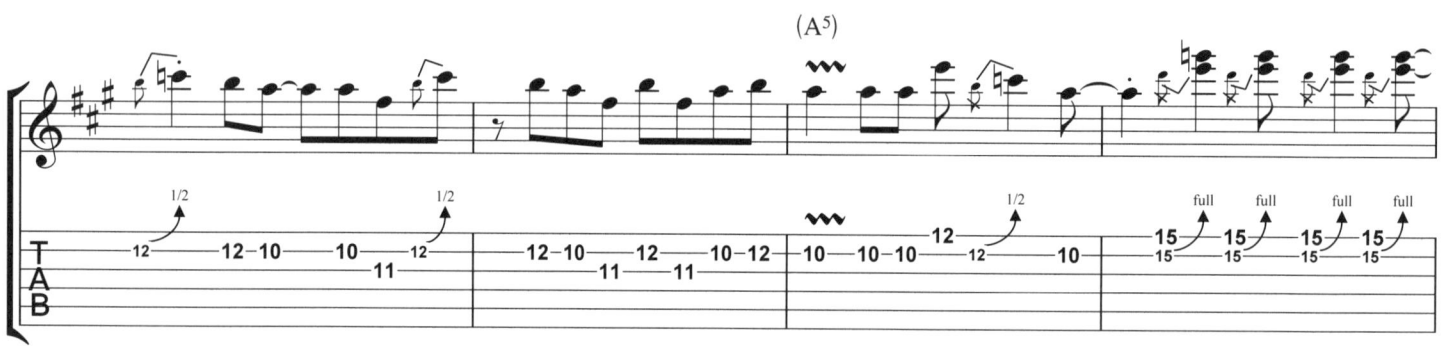
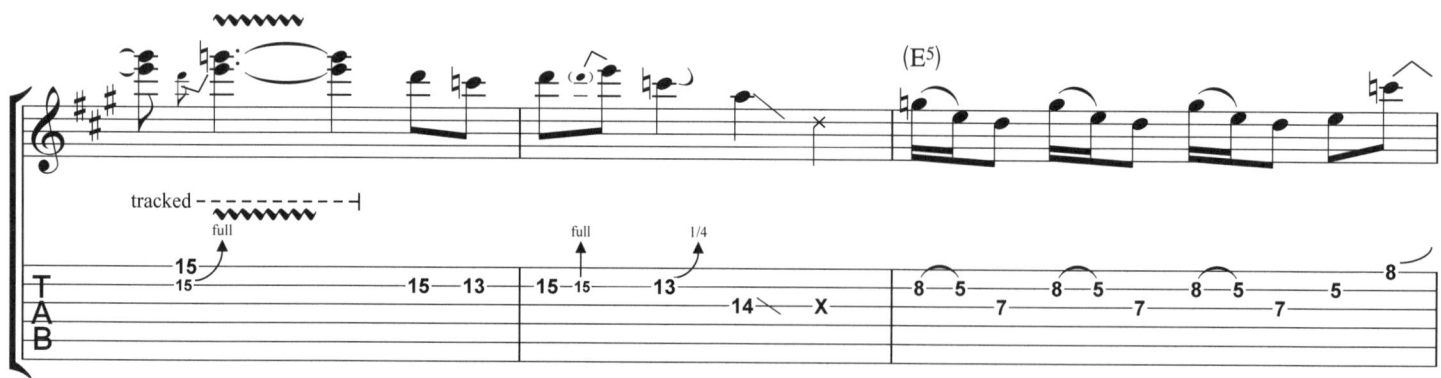
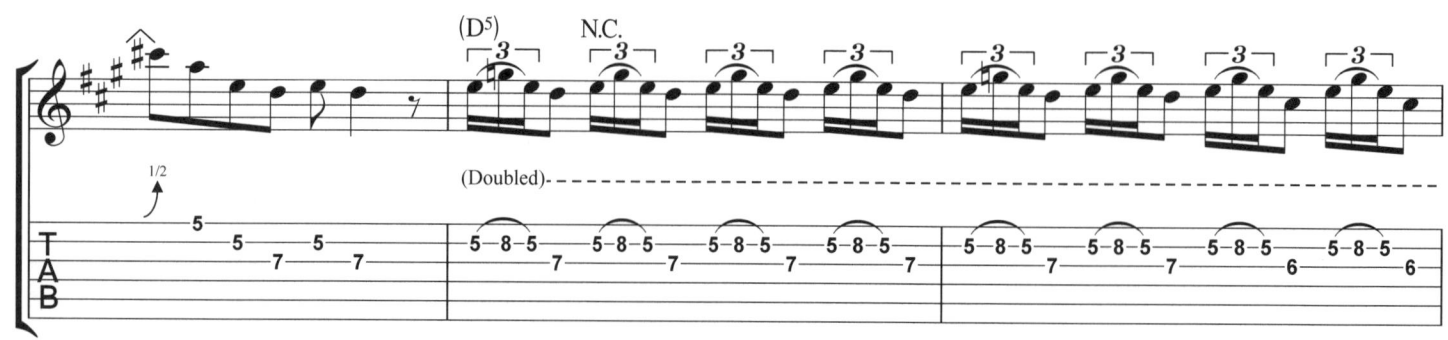

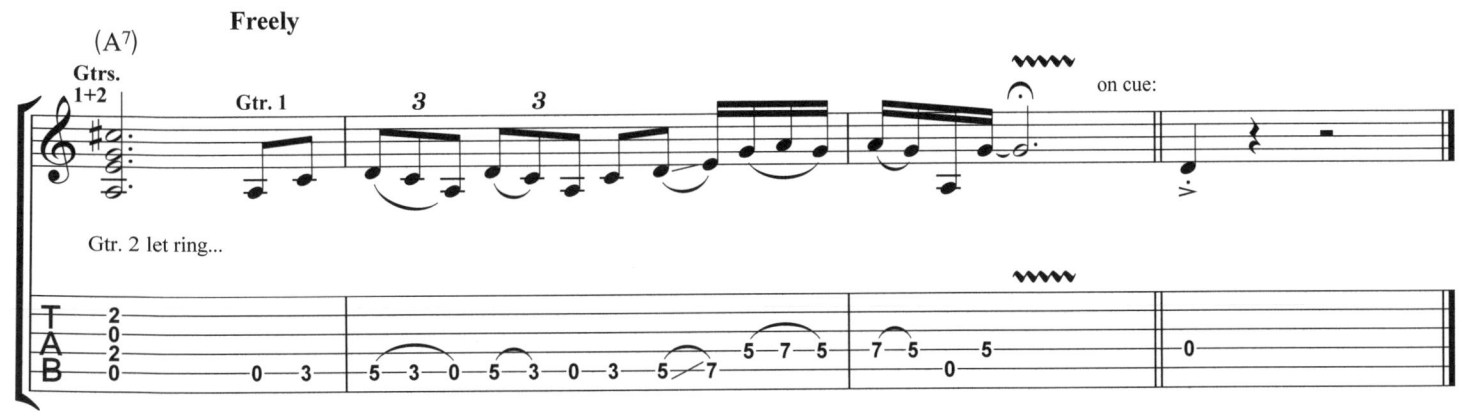

LED-ZEPPELIN · CELEBRATION DAY